L★E★F★T★Y
G★R★O★V★E
AMERICAN ORIGINAL

LEFTY GROVE

AMERICAN ORIGINAL

JIM KAPLAN

CONTENTS

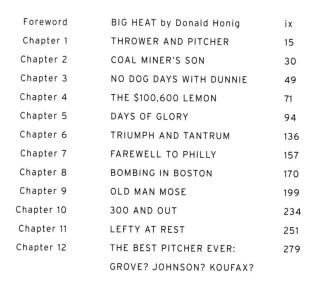

FOREWORD: BIG HEAT

By Donald Honig

The last time I saw Lefty Grove was in the summer of 1974, less than a year before his death. It was, appropriately enough, at Cooperstown, New York, where Grove was attending the annual Hall of Fame induction ceremonies. Silver-haired now, more ample around the middle than in his heyday years, the old fireballer was sitting in a rocking chair on the otherwise empty back porch of the Otesaga Hotel, watching a beautiful sunset upon the tinted waters of Lake Otsego. Sitting absolutely still, he was a portrait of serenity, an image far from that of the dour, irascible, flame-tempered fastballer who was probably the greatest lefthander in baseball history.

I had called Grove at his Norwalk, Ohio, home a few

weeks before, asking if I might meet up with him at Cooperstown to chat with him about a book of baseball nostalgia I was planning. "Sure," he shouted into the phone. "I'll see you there." Then he hung up. He hadn't sounded interested or uninterested, friendly or unfriendly. He had just sounded like Lefty Grove.

He didn't stir at all when I sat down next to him, but when I recalled our phone conversation, he nodded. "I remember," he said.

The conversation quickly segued from the tranquil beauty of the lake to the vanished years and the titans who had populated them. What to me were Cooperstown plaques and astonishing record book statistics, were to Lefty living memories. Ty Cobb, Babe Ruth, Lou Gehrig, Walter Johnson (Grove's idol), Harry Heilmann, and Grove's teammates from the illustrious 1929-31 pennant-winning Philadelphia Athletics: Al Simmons, Jimmie Foxx, and Mickey Cochrane. How did Lefty feel about pitching to Ruth?

"I wasn't afraid of Ruth," he said simply.

What about Cobb?

He shook his head. "I wasn't afraid of Cobb."

It brought to mind what Bob Feller said when I asked him if he had been nervous in his first big-league game.

"I was never nervous on a pitching mound," Feller said.

They are a species apart, these royal fireballers—and we are talking here of the nine-inning variety, not ninety-eight-mile-per-hour closers who muscle up for an inning or two and then are nurtured for a few days. Johnson, Feller, Sandy Koufax, Nolan Ryan—the few names come quickly to mind—went the full nine, more if necessary, and the heat at the end was as incandescent as at the beginning.

Grove stands among this elite, as tall as any. Arriving in the American League with Connie Mack's Athletics as a twenty-five-year-old rookie in 1925, Lefty led the league in strikeouts his first seven years. While his strikeout totals were not as thunderous as some of the aforementioned whizzers, 209 being his high, it must be remembered that batters did not strike out as frequently then as now. Jimmie Foxx led batters in whiffing with totals of 70 in 1929, 66 a year later. But, according to teammate Doc Cramer, "Lefty could strike you out any time he wanted. With a man on third in a close game, forget it. He just took you out. He'd just rare back and give you that fastball with a little extra."

That fastball. One believes in its high-octane speed because, like Johnson, Lefty seldom threw a curve, not until an arm injury in his mid-thirties turned him into a practitioner of guile and craft, good enough to win the last four of his all-time record nine ERA titles. But in his heyday, it was one thunderbolt after another. "Everybody knew what was coming," said Yankees third baseman Joe Dugan. "But so what?"

Lefty Grove on the mound was a sculpture of tenacious determination. "You never talked to him on the mound," A's teammate Jimmy Dykes said. "No matter if he was ahead by ten runs or behind by one, he was just plain fierce during a game. Not even Mr. Mack would go near him. If he lost a close game, he'd come in and tear the clubhouse apart. I mean literally—stools and equipment would be flying and lockers kicked in."

In spite of the tempests that blew through him, Lefty's teammates found him, as Dykes said, "a lovable character. He was basically a very shy man, uneasy with strangers and uncomfortable in big cities. The day the season ended, he was gone, back to Maryland, where he loved to sit alone and fish."

In repose, with his memory being gently jogged, Grove was soft-spoken, nostalgic, and charming, and under it all and quite evident was the pride of the old fastballer who had not been afraid of the Babe.

I asked which game he remembered most fondly. The answer was very quick to come. "My three-hundredth win," he said. "I was going to hang 'em up in 1940, but I was seven short and I decided to come back and get them. And I did"— he was shaking his head now—"but it wasn't easy."

His final big-league start came on September 28, 1941, the last day of the season, in the second game of a double-header. "Everybody remembers that game," he said, and showed a faint smile, "but not because of me. That was the game where Teddy Williams hoisted his average up to .406."

Lefty Grove pitched to Ty Cobb, who came to the big leagues in 1905, and he was a teammate of Ted Williams, who played until 1960. In all that time, and in time since, no one has seen a lefthander to match him. At his best, no one burned brighter. Between 1928 and 1933, his record was 152-41.

At the end of the conversation, the gracious Mr. Grove offered a friendly handshake. It was his right hand. Delighted though I was, I would have much preferred the left, the one that held the baseball and delivered it with a heat that still blisters the air, somewhere.

Donald Honig is a novelist and the author of many baseball books, including Baseball When the Grass Was Real.

THROWER AND PITCHER

thrower *(n.)* A pitcher without finesse; one who relies on speed and power as opposed to deceptive pitching.

pitcher *(n.)* A term of distinction for a pitcher with great control.

—The Dickson Baseball Dictionary

"What can you tell me about Lefty Grove?" I asked a friend who writes and edits baseball books.

"Well, I think he played in the 1930's and was very good—Hall of Fame, maybe. I can't remember who he played for, though."

Many close followers of baseball only dimly remember Grove, who is often mistaken for the Yankees' colorful Lefty Gomez. Their confusion is understandable. It's easy to forget the greatest pitcher of baseball's greatest *hitting* era. Bear with me through a brief statistical rundown. The only 300-game winner between the wars, Grove led the American League in strikeouts seven years running, won 20 or more games seven straight times, and ran up a 16-game winning streak to tie the league record. In his seventeen-year (1925-41) career with the Philadelphia A's and Boston Red Sox, he had the league's best earned-run average nine times and the top winning percentage five times, both baseball records by substantial margins. He was the most dominant pitcher in any era and unquestionably the finest lefthander of all time. Some historians consider him the greatest pitcher ever.

He was certainly one of the most unforgettable. You can look right through Randy Johnson, modern baseball's leanest lefthander, and see Lefty Grove. They're one and the same: a couple of Ichabod Cranes towering over the mound and throwing lightning from the sky. In an age when most players stand between 5-foot-10 and 6-foot-2, the 6-foot-10 Johnson, chinless, pinheaded, with that scraggly hair flowing out of his cap, pitches so blindingly fast he seems to hand the ball to his catcher. In an age when most players stood between 5-foot-8 and 6 feet, Grove, who was variously listed as 6-foot-2, 6-foot-2-1/2 and 6-foot-3, looked just as weird and pitched just as fast. With his wide, big-lipped mouth; his small teeth and prominent gums; his creased cheeks; his slitty, squinty eyes; and his prematurely graying hair that rose almost as high off his scalp as did Seinfeld's strange neighbor Kramer's, Grove's noggin resembled a cross between a pumpkin and a potato. Proportionately, though, his head was too small for his body, which itself almost disappeared in his billowing flannel uniform. Grove weighed between 170 and 190 pounds during most of his career. In the words of Westbrook Pegler, he was "a straight line with ears on it." Another famous writer, John Lardner, saw more meat on Grove. He described "a small, narrow head on top of vast sloping shoulders." Grove had average-sized hands and feet, but long arms and legs.

Scary enough to look at, Grove was even more frightening to hit against. After throwing his arms over his head—often two or three times—Grove would kick his right leg high, distracting the batter, reach back so far that the knuckles of his left hand nearly touched the mound, then throw with a huge stride, a vicious jerk of the wrist, and a sweeping follow-through. Batters were confronted with a cross between a dipping oil derrick and a gyrating windmill. Rarely had they seen anyone go so low. Rarely had they seen anyone go so high even when he threw his customary three-quarters delivery. Rarely had they seen anyone throw so fast, or so effortlessly. Even when Grove was in his late thirties, his motion impressed Hank Greenberg with its "ease," and Ted Williams with its beauty.

Grove was frequently asked to account for his speed. "They look at me and my skinny arms and think maybe I'm some kind of magician," he said. "I don't know any more about it than they do. The other guy hasn't got it. I have. That's all there is to it."

Not until late in his career did Lefty come clean. "I throw from my spine," he said, "not from my elbow." Grove improved his arm strength by throwing rocks "at anything"; his leg strength by biking and walking long distances. He was as supple as he was strong. Years after he retired, he could kick a leg over his head ballet-style and touch the string from an overhead light fixture eight to ten feet above the ground.

Grove's pitching career can be broken down into two general titles: thrower and pitcher. Within those general stages are four specific ones: undisciplined fireballer, single-pitch fireballer, thrower turned pitcher, twice-reconstructed wreck.

When he reported to the A's as a twenty-five-year-old rookie in 1925, Grove was too wild to be effective. So were the young Walter Johnson and Sandy Koufax. A winning fastballer differs from a run-of-the-mill fastballer in one respect: control. Johnson didn't start winning big until he discovered the strike zone. Nor did Koufax, whose unparalleled curve was actually his best pitch. Catcher Norm Sherry convinced him he didn't have to blow the house down with every fastball. Nor did Grove. Each of them took time to learn the most basic command in pitching: throw strikes.

Most pitchers yield about a hit an inning. If that's all they allow, they should be big winners. Alas, pitchers also give up walks. An awful pitcher will average a walk—hence, a second baserunner—an inning. A good pitcher—a control pitcher, a real "pitcher"—should average no worse than a walk every three innings.

The young fastballers, still "throwers," weren't close. Their problem went deeper than allowing four or five walks per game; the pitches they threw over the plate were often meatballs. Constantly behind on the count, they had no choice but to groove one or give up a walk. A batter takes advantage of these pitchers. Wild things make his heart sing.

Understand the pressure on a young hurler. It begins on the first pitch to any batter. Pitchers talk about an expanding and contracting strike zone. If the first pitch is a strike, the batter will likely chase a second pitch out of the zone because he doesn't want to fall behind 0-2. Instead of throwing to a standard seventeen-inch plate, the pitcher now imagines himself working to a twenty-inch plate.

When he misses on his first delivery, he can't go for the corners or he'll risk falling behind 2-0. Now he's working to a fourteen-inch plate; he almost has to throw one right over that vanishing dish. But because the hitter salivates over a meatball, the pitcher somehow has to perform the unlikely to be effective: throw both a strike and a tough-to-hit strike, or risk getting one lined past his ear.

If you throw a strike on the first pitch, you should retire the batter about eighty percent of the time. Leo Mazzone, pitching coach of the Atlanta Braves, baseball's dominant pitching staff of the 1990's, compiles first-pitch effectiveness. To take a mid-decade sample, in 1994 the Braves' Greg Maddux threw 524 first-pitch strikes and allowed only 31 hits on those at-bats. Tom Glavine was 415 and 35, Steve Avery 360 and 22, John Smoltz 339 and 21, and Kent Mercker 239 and 17. "People claim Maddux threw inside," Mazzone says. "That's nonsense. He put himself in position to pitch inside by getting ahead on the count. Once you're 0-1, you can expand your strike zone and change speeds."

On the other hand, some eighty percent of all walks occur after a ball on the first pitch. Makes you wonder why major leaguers throw strikes on only slightly more than fifty percent of their first pitches.

Young Lefty was anything but a control pitcher. His early numbers, to be sure, were deceiving. Starting his professional pitching career with the Martinsburg, West Virginia, team of the Blue Ridge League on May 21, 1920, Grove struck out 10 and allowed four hits while losing 4-1. After six decisions (3-3), he had fanned 60 batters and walked just 24 in fifty-nine innings. In all probability, though, the low-minor hitters he was facing swung at anything near the strike zone rather than pitches actually in it.

Advancing to the International League's legendary Baltimore Orioles, Grove went 108-36 in 4-1/2 seasons. The lineup was loaded with future major leaguers like Max Bishop and Joe Boley, the double-play combination on two championship Philadelphia Athletics teams, and George Earnshaw, a pitcher on three of them.

Was Grove, like them, a cinch to move up and star? Well,

yes and no. He gave up only seven hits per nine innings and led the league in strikeouts all four full seasons, but the "wild Oriole," as he was known, three times surrendered the most walks. For his first four seasons with Baltimore he was averaging an ungainly 5.6 free passes a game.

Not until 1924, when he went 26-6, with a 3.01 ERA and an improved 108 walks in 236 innings, about four per game, did Grove have scouts panting. An August exhibition game, in which he struck out 13 batters and allowed just two hits to the Philadelphia Athletics regular lineup, removed any doubts. Owner-manager Connie Mack bought Grove for an unprecedented $100,600.

Chosen to open the 1925 season against the Red Sox, Grove learned immediately that major leaguers, unlike the bushers he'd thrown to, didn't swing at bad pitches. Disappointing a crowd of twenty-two thousand at Shibe Park in Philadelphia, he walked four batters, hit one, gave up five runs on six hits, and left the game in the fourth inning.

For most of his rookie season, Grove was simply too pumped-up about pitching in the majors. "Get smart, Lefty," catcher Mickey Cochrane would plead to him. "Don't try to mow 'em down if you've got a big lead. Ease up with two out and nobody on base." Grove would listen, promise to mend his ways, and too often forget everything the moment he stepped on the mound. He rushed his pitches and missed the plate. If he led the league in strikeouts (116) for the first of seven straight seasons, he also had a league-leading and record setting 131 walks in 197 innings that first year. It was the only time a twentieth century pitcher allowed that many walks in fewer than 200 innings, and would remain so until 1941. At least Grove got his major-league lows out of the way: a 10-12 record for his only losing mark, and his only season in which his walks would top his strikeouts.

A 1-0, fifteen-inning loss to the Yanks' Herb Pennock taught Grove a lesson he could take home with him and think about all winter. "Pennock showed me what control meant," he said. "With half as much speed, he pitched a better game than I did."

Grove got plenty of well-meaning advice. To slow him down, backup catcher Cy Perkins induced him to slap the ball in his glove three times before each pitch. A coach, Ira Thomas, an old catcher himself, invented a system in which Grove counted to ten between pitches to slow himself down. Unfortunately, the fans and opponents got wind of it and counted with him. Picture the scene: the whole park counting to ten, then yelling "Throw!" while Grove fidgeted on the hill. He was not amused.

Pacing himself more in 1926, he improved significantly: a 13-13 record, with his strikeouts up to 194, while his walks dropped down to 101, and his ERA plummeted to a league-leading 2.51. Then he was off to the races: 20-13 in '27, 24-8 in '28, 20-6 in '29.

If Lefty's record was sensational, his style was baffling. Incredibly and almost uniquely, Grove was winning with one pitch. He threw nothing—at least, nothing effectively—but his fastball. "That's like saying that when Fred Astaire arrived in Hollywood, all he could do was dance," William Curran wrote in *Strikeout: A Celebration of the Art of Pitching*.

Nonetheless, it was just one pitch. Grove himself admitted that his curve didn't break until his fifth or sixth season. With the possible exception of a knuckleballer, virtually no one wins with a single pitch that a batter can anticipate in any clutch situation. Grove got some help from the hitters. Babe Ruth had introduced not only his home-run numbers but his home-run swing. Many batters followed his lead and held their bats at the end instead of choking up, and swung from the heels instead of taking a more controlled cut. It was hard enough for traditional choke-up hitters to make contact with Grove's lightning fastball, harder still for free swingers. "I used to love to see those guys come up to the plate who swung from the heels," Grove said. "I'd laugh to myself because I knew I had them."

Indeed, Grove yielded only nine homers in ten seasons pitching to Babe Ruth. His toughest outs were the rare contact hitters like the Indians' and Yankees' Joe Sewell, who almost never struck out.

Grove overmatched everyone else with his pure speed. Depending on who did the talking—Hall of Famers like Cochrane, Joe Cronin, Charlie Gehringer, and Casey Stengel were in his corner—he was either the fastest hurler since Walter Johnson or the fastest ever. "He was my idol," Wes Ferrell, another American League pitcher and for three seasons a teammate of Grove's, told author Donald Honig. "Lefty Grove, fastest pitcher I ever saw. He'd throw that ball in there, and you'd just wonder where it went to. It would just *zing!* and disappear. You can believe he was that fast, because that was all he threw."

Gehringer, the Tigers second baseman, echoed Ferrell. "Grove's fastball wasn't that alive," he said. "It carried a little but never did anything tricky. But it was so fast that by the time you'd made up your mind whether it would be a strike or a ball, it just wasn't there anymore. It's hard to believe that anyone could throw faster than Lefty Grove."

"You know, a lefthander's ball has a tendency to tail a little bit, but Grove threw it so hard it didn't tail—it didn't have time," Paul Richards, the White Sox and Orioles manager, once said. "It was on top of you before you knew it. Lefty had the type of fastball they tell me Satchel Paige had. You thought it was waist-high when you swung at it, but it was actually letter-high. It was four or five inches higher than you thought it was, which made the players think it was jumping, but it wasn't jumping. It came so fast it created an illusion."

At times, Grove's speed inspired lyrical praise and prose. "Grove could throw a lamb chop past a wolf," Westbrook Pegler wrote. Sewell, the Hall of Fame shortstop, was even more eloquent. "Sometimes when the sun was out, really bright, he would throw that baseball in there and it looked like a flash of white sewing thread coming at you .... Inning after inning, he never slowed up. He could stand out there for a week, and barrel it in at you."

Unfortunately, there were no reliable timing devices back then. We are left with many memories and one vivid illustration. In 1932, the Libbey Owens company unveiled a new product: "shatterproof and breakproof" glass. A company rep carried several sheets of the new glass to Shibe Park and asked Grove to throw at one. His first toss left a baseball-sized hole in the glass. The manufacturer then set up another and asked Grove to ease up a bit. His next pitch shattered the thing.

★　　　★　　　★　　　★

Grove threw uncompromisingly and in pain. He gripped the ball so hard with his index and middle fingers that he cracked the nails and drew blood blisters. When the blisters broke, pitches were said to be streaked with blood. Grove cut the nails, painted them with iodine, and never missed his turn to pitch. Asked to explain such a limited and painful pitch selection, Grove said simply, "If you don't throw that fastball when you have it, you can lose it."

When batters weren't intimidated by Grove's speed alone, he also practiced selective terrorism. His various traits—"6-

foot, 3-inch frame, scowl, stare and wildness," in the words of one writer—proved unnerving. Despite his improved control, Grove occasionally missed badly. That worked to his advantage, because hitters never knew when an occasional hummer might get away. So they tended to back off the plate. Grove made sure they stayed back by plunking hitters who dug in. "Never bothered me who was up there with the bat," he told Honig. "I'd hit 'em in the middle of the back or hit 'em in the foot"—he always aimed at a back pocket—"it didn't make any difference to me. But I'd never throw at a man's head. Never believed in it.

"I used to pitch batting practice," he went on. "Those guys, Doc Cramer and them, used to hit one back through the box, and they knew damn well when they did, they'd better get out of there, 'cause I'd be throwing at their pockets. They'd try to hit one through the box their last swing, those guys, just to rile me up. Yessir, boy, I was just as mean against them as I was against the others."

After five years with the Athletics, Grove had pretty mean credentials: 87 wins, a fearsome reputation, and that fastball. Before the 1929 World Series, manager Connie Mack, fearing that the Cubs' righthanded batters would rack his lefthanded pitchers, saved Grove for the bullpen. The Lonaconing Express—he was nicknamed after his hometown in Maryland—responded with 10 strikeouts and two saves in 6-1/3 innings of shutout relief. In Game Two he replaced Earnshaw after 4-2/3 innings and set down the Cubs on three hits, fanning six: A's 9, Cubs 3. Under the scoring rules of the time, the starter didn't have to finish the fifth to qualify for a win. Therefore, Grove merely contributed the greatest long-relief save in Series history. In Game Four he threw two innings of perfect relief, fanning four while preserving a 10-8 win that gave the A's an insurmountable three-games-to-one lead. "When danger beckoned thickest," Heywood Broun wrote, "it was always Grove who stood towering on the mound, whipping over strikes against the luckless Chicago batters."

Not that Grove was unbeatable in his first five seasons. The batters *did* know what to expect. He never *did* throw a no-hitter. And he *did* allow 1,191 hits in 1,254 innings, for a good but not great average of 8.5 per nine-inning game.

By then Grove had induced his curve to break a little and mixed in an occasional changeup. In 1930, he went 28-5, with a career-high 209 K's and a league-high nine saves, and was the only pitcher in the league with an ERA (2.54) under

Grove and his manager/protector Connie Mack pose in 1928. Mack was just the avuncular figure the hotheaded Grove needed. Mack knew when to tolerate Grove's excesses and when to ride him. Mack said he took more guff from Grove than from anyone else he managed.

3.00. Late in the season Grove won six games in nineteen days, then six games in fourteen days. Just for good measure, he beat the Cardinals 5-2 in the 1930 Series opener while pitching with a broken blister on the middle finger of his left hand, then won Game Five in relief. No wonder the A's went on to repeat as champs.

Encore, encore! Grove produced his otherworldly 31-4 MVP season in 1931—plus two wins in the Series loss to St. Louis—and a 25-10 mark in 1932. During the 1930-32 stretch, Lefty averaged only 8.16 hits and 2.08 walks per game. This was Grove at his absolute peak. A comment Reggie Jackson once made of his own batting prowess seems appropriate: "Everyone was helpless and in awe."

It is possible to overstate the importance of his breaking pitches in the A's days. They were effective, but Grove would almost always throw his fastball in a pinch. What's more, he was hardly a master at mixing pitches. Even Connie Mack commented that Grove was a thrower his entire time in Philadelphia. In the words of one player, "All he used to have was a fastball and a mean disposition." Yet he was virtually untouchable. The years when a player is twenty-nine through thirty-one are often the peak ones for a pitcher. Grove was no exception.

There followed a mid-career crisis that would have finished off most pitchers. It may have had its roots in 1933. With the A's threatening to drop out of contention early in the season, Mack called on his ace time after time to get them back on track. Pitching relief in late May and early June, Grove worked eight times in ten games over an eleven-day period, winning four, saving four, and allowing only one run in 23-2/3 innings. Columnist Joe Williams asked other pitchers and some catchers if the strain would show. "Their theory is that it is more wearing on an arm to pitch two or three innings at frequent intervals than to pitch whole games at regularly spaced intervals," he wrote. "They insist that a pitcher's arm needs just as much rest after a short workout as after a routine game of ball. They argue that it takes the snap and elasticity out of the pitching muscles, thus deadening the arm."

More likely, the combination of regular starts and increased relief took a toll. Grove finished the season in fine statistical form once more—a 24-8 record, a 3.20 ERA—but his strikeouts dropped from 188 to 114 in 275 innings. "Toward the end of the season he couldn't even straighten his arm out," a teammate told Williams the next season. "I don't care how many ballgames he won. I tell you he had definitely begun to slip last year and that he wasn't within thirty percent of the Grove of the year before."

That winter Mack decided to unload some heavy contracts to pay off Depression-era losses. Grove was sold to the Red Sox for $125,000. Next spring, he developed his first sore arm. No reason has ever been given, but the 1933 season surely factored in.

In 1934, Grove struggled to an 8-8 record, placing sixty-third out of sixty-five league starters with a 6.50 earned-run average and never fully recovering from his sore arm. He was called the "$125,000 lemon."

"Without Connie Mack to lean on he got panicky," said former A's teammate Eddie Collins, later general manager of the Red Sox during Grove's tenure. The Red Sox tried everything possible to right him, including the removal of his impacted teeth and tonsils. Nothing helped.

But Grove, as ever, was a quick study. Late in the 1934 season, he realized that curves were hurting his arm less than fastballs and started throwing more of them. By the spring of 1935 his arm had improved, and so had his pitch selection. "Curve and control," he called his new repertoire.

In the words of the astute catcher and author Moe Berg, then a Sox benchwarmer, Grove "improved the good curve he had to the point where it was almost a great curve." Adding a fast-dropping forkball, Grove won 20 games in 1935 and led the league with a 2.70 ERA. He once beat the Yankees while throwing only three fastballs. It was probably the most impressive comeback season by any pitcher in baseball history.

"I've got a lot of things now that I didn't have when I broke in," Grove told reporters. "Maybe I was faster then, but I didn't know the hitters. I didn't know when to let up and when to bear down. Right now my arm feels fine. By using it right, by not trying to strike out every one of these fellas as they come along, I can win plenty of games."

He won 17 games apiece in 1936 and 1937, and then he was really through. Had to be. At least he was assumed to be finished, because in 1938 his sore arm became a dead arm. Literally. Cruising to another great season with a 13-3 record, Grove fielded a swinging bunt by Charlie Gehringer, made an off-balance throw to first and not long afterward couldn't feel a thing in his left arm. "It's dead, Tom, like a piece of fish," he told owner Tom Yawkey.

Specialists couldn't find a pulse in the arm. They hospitalized Grove, called the circulatory ailment "intermittent claudification" and encased the wing in a strange glass sleeve, with rubber attachments moving it up and down six hours a day. The pulse returned completely, but the season was as good as over. He finished it with a 14-4 record and again led the league in ERA (3.02).

In 1939, critics proclaimed Grove "washed up and hung on the line," according to a 1942 *Saturday Evening Post* article by the legendary Boston sports columnist Harold Kaese. Yet Grove adjusted again by restricting himself to one outing per week. Bingo! Good health. Fifteen wins. His ninth league-leading ERA. At age thirty-nine. The awed Red Sox reverently called Robert Moses Grove "Old Man Mose." He had become the quintessential "crafty lefthander." He had become a pitcher.

Age finally caught up to him in 1940 and 1941, his final seasons. On July 25, 1941, Old Man Mose—now really old at forty-one—beat the Indians, 10-6, for his 300th and last win, and his 298th and last complete game. He was knocked out in his last five starts and retired after the season.

"The wonderful thing was that he refused to quit, but changed himself over as a pitcher, and went on to enjoy some of his best years in Boston," Collins said.

Grove had only one regret about his pitching: that he did not report to the majors soon enough to win 400 games. Well, he actually won 411—three for Martinsburg, 108 for Baltimore in minors so high they were almost majors, 195 for the A's, and 105 for the Red Sox.

There are two particular images of Grove worth framing. One 1969 afternoon at the Hall of Fame, reporter Maury Allen was asking Grove about the hitters he'd faced when Grove suddenly tired of the past tense. "Damn it," he bellowed, "there isn't a man playing the game I can't strike out!"

At the time Lefty Grove was sixty-nine years old.

Even better, just picture Grove pitching in the championship seasons of 1929-31. As Donald Honig commented, it was the only time in baseball history that baseball's best pitcher threw to baseball's best catcher while getting the best possible run support. "It was not a question of, 'Well, imagine what Walter Johnson could have done with a better team,' " says Honig. "Here was a perfect matchup. Lefty Grove was Babe Ruth on the mound: a force of nature with the wind at his back."

COAL MINER'S SON

★　　★　　★　　★

"Taken as a whole, this is a community of the
best-dressed miners I have ever seen."

–W.M. Wardjon, organizer
United Mine Worker's Journal
May 15, 1905

Lonaconing, Maryland, the birthplace of Robert Moses "Lefty" Grove, is an old mining town in the state's western panhandle. A fireplace clings to the outside wall of the former company store, testimony to improvements that weren't made after gas and oil began displacing the region's soft semibituminous coal in the 1920's. Empty storefronts tell what soon followed: some mines shutting down, the Depression closing in, people and businesses taking off like deer fleeing a forest fire. A hole carved in the top of Dan's Mountain fairly screams of the strip mining that followed. The ruins above George's Creek are the old bowling alley/pool hall Lefty owned, which washed into the "crick" during the 1996 flood.

There is also some good news in Lonaconing. A ten-year fundraising effort has borne fruit, and ground has been broken for a new library. Lefty's Most Valuable Player Award from the 1931 season, long held in a bank for fear of theft, is expected to reside in the library. Old, dilapidated houses are finally being torn down, having long since outlived their historical value. Main Street, a bottleneck of cars, trucks, and pedestrians, has been straightened, with new sidewalks and blacktop added, although it still needs a bypass. And now, as ever, the area's twenty-five-hundred-odd citizens, many of them seniors with good memories, are justly proud of Lonaconing's rich history.

We are all both "nature" and "nurture," limited by our inherent capabilities and shaped by our experiences. In order to understand Lefty Grove, we must consider his roots in a hardscrabble mining town inhabited by unusually upbeat and achievement-oriented citizens. Pronounced Loan-a-CONE-ing and usually shortened to Coney by natives, it means "where there is a beautiful summit," according to Hamill Kenny, author of *The Origin and Meaning of the Indian Place Names of Maryland*. It could also derive from the Shawnee chief Lonacona, whose name means "where many waters meet." Or so says *History of Western Maryland* by J. Scharf and A.M. Thomas. The waters are streams running into George's Creek (named after an adopted Indian boy, not, as rumored, George Washington), which bisects the town.

Whether or not Lonaconing means "where many waters meet," it certainly is where mountains greet. To the west sits Big Savage Mountain, to the east Dan's Mountain, both members of the Allegheny Mountains in Allegany County (both words are spelled correctly). Even the valley between them rises and falls. Just try to find a flat street in town.

The region has American history written all over it. Allegany County, one of America's first frontiers, opened for safe settlement after the French and Indian War ended in 1763. It quickly filled up with trappers, traders, speculators, surveyors, engineers, and travellers. The National Road ran through Frostburg, eight miles to the north.

Young George Washington discovered a regional wonderland: high-ridged mountains, dense forests filled with pine and oak trees, winding rivers, deep valleys, mild climate, hilly meadows, vast plains, fertile soil, mineral wealth, abundant animals, berries and nuts. "This wonderful country impresses me more and more each time I go through it," Washington wrote to the colonial governor of Maryland in 1755. "I am sure, Hon'd Sir, that it is destined to out-rival some day and outgrow His Most Christ'n Majesty's home country—England. These mighty forests of soft and hard woods will furnish the ships of the world, and with the native stones build the residences of future generations.

"… what is beneath the soil? There may be stored mineral wealth which will astonish the Countries of the Old World, while the fuel of the future may also be found therein."

Washington's forecast was eerily prescient. The region would furnish ships, but not so much with wood as with coal coming from the famous "Big Vein" descending fourteen feet into the earth. To exploit the region, a London and Baltimore syndicate created the George's Creek Coal and Iron Company in 1837. Owners John Alexander and Philip Tyson bought land along the George's Creek to build a town, later called Lonaconing, for the workers, and a furnace to turn iron ore into pig iron.

The village quickly numbered seven hundred, with neither "drunkard nor beggar," according the the 1839 company report. Plainly, the the two hundred and twenty employees of the iron works were too busy digging ore and erecting the impressive Big Vein Furnace in just two years (1837-39). The furnace stretched along the side of a hill: a gigantic, truncated pyramid standing fifty feet square at the base, twenty-five feet square on top, fifty feet high—fully twenty feet more than its predecessors—and made of stones weighing up to thirty-six tons. Seeing it for the first time, a visitor feels like Patricia Neal gazing at the huge alien robot in "The Day the Earth Stood Still."

The first American furnace fueled by coal and coke instead of charcoal, Big Vein operated from 1839 to 1855 and eventually employed two hundred and sixty workers to churn out sixty tons of pig iron a week. That was more than enough for the local towns. Shipping the ore elsewhere was a major challenge. Neither the C & O Canal nor the B & O Railroad extended to Lonaconing. Painfully and expensively, ore was sent fifteen miles by horse-powered tram and wagon to foundries in Cumberland, then another seventy-odd miles to Williamsport, where it was put on eighty-foot-long, thirteen-foot-wide, three-foot-deep flatboats holding fifty or sixty tons, and run down a dangerous stretch of the Potomac to markets like Harper's Ferry, West Virginia, and Georgetown, Maryland. The river trade all but ended when B & O tracks reached Cumberland in 1842.

But getting the coal to Cumberland was still a problem. Everyone in Lonaconing viewed the planned extension of the B & O tracks as the answer to their transportation woes. Unfortunately, by the time a company railroad from Lonaconing met a recently completed B & O railroad at the Potomac port of Piedmont, West Virginia, in 1853, railroad shipping costs had become prohibitive, Congress had lifted the embargo on Welsh iron, and the furnace had lost market access to its competitors. As a result, the furnace was abandoned in 1855 and is preserved today only as a landmark.

Furnace or no, when iron smelting left coal companies poured in. In 1853, the Lonaconing Ocean Coal Mining and Transportation Company was incorporated by the likes of steamship magnate Edward Cunard and New York financier August Belmont. The soft semibituminous coal was just too rich to resist. Called "supercoal," it could generate more steam than equal amounts of coal from the country's other mines. Converting from water power to steam, New England mills had plenty of use for Maryland coal. So did steamships. If you were to ride Cunard's British West India and New York-to-Liverpool ships in the last half of the century, or if you were heading into battle against the Spanish fleet in Santiago or Manila, you may have been steaming along on western Maryland coal.

Lonaconing, a quintessential company town, grew quickly. St. Peter's Episcopal Church and school were built, the latter in a company house with a company clergyman named Huntington as teacher. The company also opened a library and ordered these "reviews": "Westminster, Edinburg [sic], Quarterly, British foreign, Washington National Intelligencer, Phil Sat.y Evening Post." That same year the supervisors escorted miners to the polls under instructions to "control the vote of the Lonaconing voters in obedience to the Co. interests" regarding taxation.

The company erected a depot, a post office, a jailhouse, a feed mill, brickyards, and an Odd Fellows Club. The Lonaconing City Band, Maryland's first, was formed in 1857. When the Civil War temporarily disrupted development, Lonaconing soldiers were 100 percent pro-Union. After the Great Fire of September 7, 1881, destroyed fifty-three buildings, a fire company was organized. By 1887-88, according to Boyd's Directory, there were already quite a few hotels: McKinley's Hotel, the Commercial Hotel, the Merchant's Hotel, and the Brady House. Five years after an 1884 flood carried many houses and fences down the creek, the Lonaconing Electric Light and Power Company built a generating plant and the Lonaconing Savings Bank opened. In 1890 the town was incorporated, and eight years later, the county's third largest community, it claimed seven thousand residents. A silk mill, using material imported from Japan, sprang up in 1907, with local women working the looms. The Lonaconing Glass Company opened in 1914. There were two newspapers, three drug stores, two banks, and several hotels. Eventually, Jewish families owned many downtown stores—clothing, shoes, grocery, and general. The town was virtually self-sufficient.

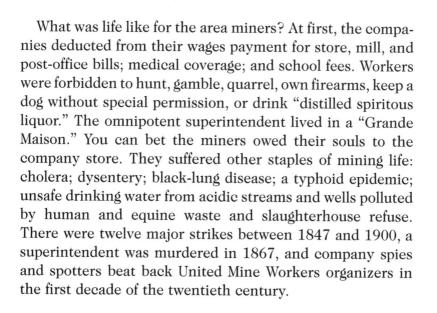

What was life like for the area miners? At first, the companies deducted from their wages payment for store, mill, and post-office bills; medical coverage; and school fees. Workers were forbidden to hunt, gamble, quarrel, own firearms, keep a dog without special permission, or drink "distilled spiritous liquor." The omnipotent superintendent lived in a "Grande Maison." You can bet the miners owed their souls to the company store. They suffered other staples of mining life: cholera; dysentery; black-lung disease; a typhoid epidemic; unsafe drinking water from acidic streams and wells polluted by human and equine waste and slaughterhouse refuse. There were twelve major strikes between 1847 and 1900, a superintendent was murdered in 1867, and company spies and spotters beat back United Mine Workers organizers in the first decade of the twentieth century.

Nonetheless, it was an "unorthodox" mining region. Or so says *The Best-Dressed Miners: Life and Labor in the Maryland Coal Region 1835-1910* by Katherine A. Harvey. "There are no dreary rows of tumble-down houses set in a gray landscape. There are no hard-core unemployed, no hordes of ragged, hungry children facing a life without a future."

According to an editorial in the November 9, 1899, edition of the United Mine Workers' Journal, the miners, skilled and unthreatening "old" immigrants, were "permanent fixtures": able, fearless, industrious, thrifty men with no axe to grind and little interest in leaving. First came German stonemasons and English furnace builders and superintendents. Then the Irish, Welsh, and Scots arrived. The Scots most influenced local customs. They contributed, among other things, scones, shortbread, and "first footin'," a rite in which celebrants went from house to house on New Year's Eve, knocking back a drink at each one. In another favored custom, "bull banding," kids would march to the home of a newly married couple and bang on pots and pans and buckets until the groom appeared to sprinkle coins among them. The good people of Lonaconing also adopted a common European custom, "chivaree," by kidnapping the poor fellow. It is said that the English dominated the population, in part because the Brits were so ornery no one else wanted to live with them. Actually, the Scots predominated.

Arriving with their families, the miners merged quietly and inconspicuously with the farmers and tradespeople of Maryland's two western counties. As late as 1910, miners constituted just seven percent of the agrarian frontier community. They lived far more comfortably than miners in other regions, in part because company stores were eventually outlawed, and miners were allowed to own land and build or buy their own homes. The local companies, though far from generous, were less repressive than those in West Virginia and Pennsylvania.

In Lonaconing, miners were spoken of as "all uncles and cousins." Even company agents liked them. One told the pro-company, antiunion Baltimore *American* that the George's Creek miners were "personally all that could be desired" and "the best men in the world." And they never left, as long as there was work. Even in the event of a strike, they wouldn't set off. No, they would stay home and mind their vegetable gardens.

Themselves miners, the Groves are the subject of much speculation and only slightly less interesting reality. Lefty was supposedly a descendant of Betsy Ross, though Grove family historians roundly dispute that claim. He was, however, related to patriots on both sides of his family.

Lefty's paternal ancestors, all of whom used the last name Groves, immigrated to Virginia from Wales circa 1726. His great-great-grandfather, William Groves, enlisted as a private in the Continental Army on August 1, 1780, marched to South Carolina and fought in the battles of Cowpens and Guilford Courthouse, where he was wounded by a cutlass swipe to the head. He later suffered a leg wound at the Battle of Eutaw Springs, and remained in the service until mustering out on November 15, 1783.

After the war William Groves lived in Prince William County, Virginia, and around 1812 moved to Allegany County, Maryland. Hence, the family mining history. Groves was given a pension at age sixty-three on October 15, 1818, and died at age ninety-four in 1849. He and his wife Mary left two of their four children: sons Jesse and Lefty's great-grandfather Dennis, who begat Robert, who begat Lefty's father John, a career miner born in 1865. This straight line of ancestry is taken from *Genealogy of the Grove and*

Top: Grove standing at his birthplace in the Charlestown section of Lonaconing. Below: Lonaconing's other landmark, the Big Vein Furnace, now a town park.

Groves Families by George N. Groves.

On March 6, 1900, Robert Moses Groves (official baseball publications didn't shorten the name until his fourth year in the majors[1]) was born the seventh of eight children to the issue of two mining families, John Groves and the former Emma Beeman. Lefty's mother was the great granddaughter of Moses Beeman, a Pennsylvanian who served in four periods of the Revolutionary War, three times as a substitute and once as an enlisted man, survived an Indian ambush that decimated his regiment, and was mustered out at war's end[2]. At five feet or so, Emma had petite features but an aura of authority. "I may have to look up at my sons," she said, "but I was the boss."

Emma kept potatoes, apples, jellies, pickles, and beets in the cellar. "A regular grocery store," says her granddaughter and Lefty's niece, Betty Holshey. Outside was a spring house, a kind of elementary icebox in which water from a spring circulated to keep perishables cool. Also separate from the main house was the most basic and critical utility of the day: the wash house. Water was heated in a copper pot on a stove, then clothes were scrubbed on a washboard, and churned dry by a hand crank on a three-legged dolly. Daily and quotidian: washing miners' clothes by hand.

John, a towering mountain man with a white brush mustache who stood about six-foot-five and spent fifty-four years digging coal without developing "the black lung," died suddenly and unexpectedly at ninety-two. "He was a splendid old fellow," says Jim Bready, a retired Baltimore sportswriter. "The stereotype—broke, bent, gasping for air—he wasn't like that at all. He had a sunny disposition, a nice outlook." On Sundays, blood relatives would walk a mile or more to

---

[1] "For simplicity's sake, he will be called Grove throughout this book.
[2] Research provided by Lefty Grove's niece, Mae Hacker Winne.

Grandma Emma and Grandpap John's for Sunday dinner, salivating at the vision of homemade breads and pies.

The Groves family lived in Coney's unincorporated Charlestown section, itself a kind of a company suburb filled with rudimentary six-room, one-and-a-half story white-washed wooden houses, part way up Dan's Mountain. Often constructed for two families, the buildings lacked plumbing or running water, but had fireplaces and stone foundations. They were nicely furnished, porched, and surrounded by flower and vegetable gardens. Some had pianos and carpets. There was always enough fuel from the nearby slate banks: monstrous piles of slate, rock, mud, and coal that the companies left behind. The miners themselves would haul it to your home in potato sacks for five cents a bag. "My two brothers and I always had a summer job: fill the coal house," says Holshey.

Lefty had four brothers and three sisters, two of whom died in childhood before he was born. William, whom the family never spoke of, lived from 1893 to 1894. Katie, remembered often and painfully, was born in 1892 and died in 1898 when she fell off a sled and was crushed by a horse.

Life centered on mining. Every morning when Lefty was finishing grade school, his father John and his older brothers Alfred James and Lee Dewey donned work clothes and boots, fixed brass carbide-fueled lamps on their caps, grabbed their large lunch pails, and walked or caught a wagon ride several miles through the dark to Midland, disappearing deep down a shaft of Waynesburg Mine in search of coal. It was a low mine, and the lanky Groves men often wielded their picks on their hands and knees. They made fifty cents a ton, loaded four tons a day, and returned, usually after dark, covered with coal dust.

"As they emerged from the darkness," William Cullen

Bryant wrote of Allegany County miners in 1860, "they looked like sooty demons of the mine with flaming horns coming from the womb of the mountain." Things were no different four decades later in the Groves family. Sitting in tin tubs, the family miners scrubbed the front of their bodies while Mrs. Groves and the daughters scrubbed their backs. Afterward, they changed clothes, enjoyed a hearty meal and smoke, then spent time with family members or neighbors before retiring early.

On Saturday nights the miners would don dark suits, white shirts, and ties—best-dressed, indeed—then proceed down the hill to a town that all week had been "quiet as if it had been policed night and day," according to the Baltimore *Sun*. So many men and horses milled around that people couldn't see the street.

Everyone headed for the town's twelve bars. Nonetheless, few miners got out-of-control drunk, the work being too hard for men to waste their bodies. There were also numerous Sunday pastimes, including footracing, curling, baseball, and "pic-nics." Admittedly, some miners engaged in what Bryant called "soul-debasing pleasure," including cockfighting and prizefighting. People still remember the cockfights at Shorty McKenzie's and Toad McNeil's "beer joints."

Pigeon shooting, a kind of poor man's skeet, was an especially popular activity. Jim Getty, a judge who was educated with Lefty's son Bobby, describes a typical competition. "They shot live pigeons at forty to fifty feet using a twelve-gauge shotgun, with a thirty-inch barrel and full choice number-six shot. The trapper stood beside the shooter, holding a string attached to the trap containing the pigeon. When the shooter said 'Pull,' an official yanked on the string to open the trap. You had to shoot the bird holding the stock of the gun below your elbow, and it had to fall within a radius marked on the ground. All of the pigeons shot during the match ended up in a large pigeon pot pie.

"You could buy pigeons for a dollar apiece and train them. You used cut-up flour sacks. If you pulled them across the head of a pigeon when it was released from a box, you could prevent them from flying straight up and get them flying low. All this was very public. Weeks before a match, the officials would tell you which pigeons to use. They would base their decisions on the weakness of the shooters."

In an 1859 match between two miners for a purse of $50, two men shot at twenty-one birds apiece. One hit seventeen, the other eighteen, probably the "most successful shooting ever done in the United States by laboring men," according to the Cumberland *Democratic Alleganian*. A good seventy-five years later, purses of $1,000 and crowds of twenty-five hundred people were routine.

Lefty Grove strode out of the Paul Simon song "My Little Town." He was nothing but his father's son, a tall, rawboned, quiet kid, friendly enough but with a smoldering temper, who raced his bike past the factories, walked around with a baseball glove hooked onto his belt, and built up his arm by throwing rocks at railroad tracks high above a runoff creek from the town reservoir.

Kids played on streets with names like Seldom Seen and Never Seen. According to childhood friend Ruth Bear Levy, who in 1987 and 1988 wrote a two-part article on Grove for *Maryland Historical Magazine*, Lefty and his friends played marbles on a lot or under a tree, ran around town and, of course, spoke the local dialect. A celebration was "a time" and "Shiverly" meant Chevrolet. All that was missing from

Levy's description was the ritual dipping of girls' pigtails into inkwells.

Lefty certainly wasn't a student, although later accounts of his illiteracy were nothing but big-city blooey based on his use of a rubber stamp, with a facsimile of his autograph. Charlestown School, a two-story wooden landmark, was right next door to his house. Lefty attended until the grades ran out at eight, then drifted into a series of jobs. When one of his brothers sprained an ankle in 1916, Robert replaced him in the mines for two weeks.

On his last day of work his father awakened him at 5:30. "Robert, it's time to go to work."

"Dad, I didn't put that coal in here, and I hope I don't have to take no more of her out," Lefty said.

Leaving the mines was not a revolutionary act. Though there was neither a G.I. Bill of Rights nor community colleges—in short, the opportunity for social mobility we know today—local miners' sons had become teachers, lawyers, doctors, ministers, bankers, and businessmen. An old friend of Lefty's, the late John Meyers, produced a brown pay envelope dated March 2, 1918, designating $11.30 for his week's work as a "bobbin boy" at the Klotz Silk Mill, where Lefty worked on large spinning spools to make silk thread.

Another receipt, for $31, rewarded Lefty for an unspecified amount of work amid belching furnaces as an apprentice glass blower at the J.M. Sloan & Son glass factory, where one of his future brothers-in-law, Ernest Peterson, was his boss. The receipt carried the words, "Include a sack of GOLDEN LINK FLOWER with your next order. You'll like it." When the factory burned down, Lefty spent a summer laying rails and driving spikes for the railroad. He later worked for the new glass factory as a needle etcher, making astonishingly big money for the time: $5.25 a day.

Meanwhile, the kid was playing baseball with homemade balls. "We'd get some old wool socks, unravel them and, using a cork stopper for a center, wind ourselves a ball," Grove told one interviewer. Sometimes a twenty-five cent Rocket was used, and rewrapped with black tape when the cover tore off. If a bat wasn't available, a fence picket was used.

There was no Little League and precious few school teams at the time, except in colleges. Once you taught yourself some skills, you advanced to town and industrial competition, which offered relief and escape from mines, mills, and factories; community pride; and, occasionally, access to professional ball. "[The town team] evolved into an American institution meriting a place alongside other symbols of America's past as the little red schoolhouse, the fervid revival meeting, and the old-fashioned Fourth of July celebration," Harold Seymour wrote in *Baseball: The People's Game*.

First Field, carved out of pasture hidden by trees in back of Big Vein mine, became a popular meeting place when a seventeen-year-old[3] Lefty began playing real baseball. He began as a first baseman but was soon and pitching Sunday games against teams from nearby Detmold and Midland. Ruth Bear Levy asked an old friend, Bertha Hutton, about those games. "She recalled the weekly family custom of Sunday church and dinner. Her brothers and her fathers always ate in a hurry, while her mother and sisters took their time. One Sunday Bertha decided to get to the bottom of this situation. 'You are always in such a hurry to finish Sunday dinner. Why?' she asked her brother. Karl answered, 'So we can go to the First Field' ....

"Bertha pressed on with her questions, 'Why do you all

---

[3] "I know of only one player who ever reached the majors who didn't play the game until he was seventeen," said former infielder Lew Fonseca. "That was Bob Grove."

want to go up there?' 'Well,' continued Karl, 'do you know Lefty Grove?' [He undoubtedly said "Groves," and Levy forgot the family name later.] 'Yes,' Bertha replied. 'But what does that Lefty Grove have to do with it?' 'Even though it's a Sunday, there's a ball game going on up there, and Lefty Grove is pitching. Everybody comes to see Lefty pitch.' "

Imagine the scene: hundreds of Lonaconing residents gathering at the field, hard by forest and mountains, enjoying their lone day off. Burly miners arrived, still clean and fresh from their Saturday night off. Their wives came too, aprons off, picnic lunch in hand. Children were everywhere, romping around the outskirts of the field playing games. All brought together by the lanky lad right out of a John R. Tunis novel: Call it *The Kid from Lonaconing*. How perfectly wonderful, this Sunday scene straight from the palette of a Rockwell or Wood. A regular American pastoral.

In 1919 Richard J. (Dick) Stakem, proprietor of a general store in Midland, started Grove pitching real baseballs. Lefty played twice a week for the town team on a field sandwiched between a forest and train tracks. Grove and his teammates charged twenty-five cents for admission to their fenced-in park and divided the income, which typically amounted to $20 apiece, at season's end.

He may or may not have had dreams of pitching professionally. He did take the hundred-and-fifty-mile round trip train ride some Sundays from Cumberland to Washington, D.C., to see his idol Walter Johnson pitch, and marveled at the Big Train's sidearm deliveries.

Grove himself was quickly mowing 'em down with his aspirin-tablet fastball. "Bobby never pitched a game [for Midland] until Memorial Day, 1919," Stakem told the Philadelphia *Evening Bulletin*'s John J. Nolan. "He pitched a seven-inning game which was ended by rain. He fanned fifteen batters, walked two men, hit two, and made a wild pitch.

"Here's the score book to prove it.

"Bob's best game was a postseason series against [the Baltimore & Ohio railroad team in] Cumberland, the big team around here ....We went down there with Bobby and he held them hitless, fanned eighteen batters, and the only man to reach first eventually got around to third. The reason he got there was because Bobby told me he let him steal second and third as he was sure he could fan the next batters and the runner wouldn't steal home. The score was 1 to 0, the other pitcher allowing just one hit."

The B & O manager supposedly said, "I'll get him a job and we'll have him on our team next year." Sure enough, in his last prebaseball job, Grove was an apprentice mechanic cleaning the heads of cylinders on steam engines at the B & O yard in Cumberland. From coal dust to train oil, as a Grove historian put it.

In May, 1920, a local garage owner named Bill Louden, manager of the Martinsburg, West Virginia, team in the Class C Blue Ridge League, asked Grove to play for him and offered a salary of $125 a month, a good $75 more than his father and brothers were making. His parents gave him their blessing. Still working for the B & O at the time, Lefty signed on May 5, got a thirty-day leave and a round-trip rail pass from his master mechanic, but was taken to Martinsburg in a large car provided by the Midland team.

Contrary to legend, he didn't walk or bike across the mountains. He spent one game at first base, then moved to the mound when Johnny Neun (who later played first base for the Tigers and Braves, managed the Yankees and Reds, and scouted for several teams) reported to Martinsburg. Grove's first pitching start, on May 21, was prophetic. He lost to Hagerstown, 4-1, but struck out 10 batters and yielded only six singles and four walks. In short order he was 3-3, with 60 strikeouts in fifty-nine innings (and a tidy .200 batting average). In his last start, on June 25, he shut out Hagerstown, 5-0, on two hits.

History is not always exact; sometimes it is little more than conjecture. How Grove came to the attention of the Double-A (there was no Triple-A until 1946) minor-league Baltimore Orioles is unclear. There were no scouting combines or computer reports. Nothing but hearsay and word-of-mouth. By one account, a Hagerstown pitcher who had twice been shut out by Grove decided to run him out of the league. The pitcher supposedly wrote Walter Fewster, the Orioles' trainer, and told him Grove was sure to be picked up soon if the Orioles didn't act quickly. The problem with this story was that Grove had already been purchased when he shut out Hagerstown for the last time.

According to another story, told by Lefty's Orioles teammate Tommy Thomas when the two men were sitting in a hotel lobby at the 1972 World Series, an old Baltimore pitcher who summered in the Blue Ridge League was so impressed with Lefty that he wrote Baltimore owner Jack Dunn directly. Both accounts agree on what happened next. Dunn, who always built his teams around pitching and was about to suspend the misbehaving Rube Parnham, sent his son Jack, Jr. to scout Grove. Dunn Jr. saw a blindingly fast stringbean whose hair had prematurely grayed after a struggle with flu during the worldwide epidemic in 1918.

Louden was reluctant to part with Grove, but the club needed money. Martinsburg had started on the road and stayed on the road until local businessmen bought a plot of land and laid out a field and a small grandstand. All that was lacking was a fence. Louden sold Grove to the Orioles for the building price and may have added something for himself.

Accounts have pinpointed the total at $3,000, $3,200, and $3,500. There was also a pitcher named Bahr who went from Baltimore to Martinsburg. One newspaper account had the Giants wiring a $5,000 offer two hours later. According to Joe Ward, a newspaperman who managed the Martinsburg team the year after Grove played for it, Brooklyn wired an offer for the same amount four hours after Baltimore closed the deal; a Detroit scout arrived later, and a Pittsburgh scout who lived nearby passed on Lefty.

Credit Baltimore not only for discovering Grove but signing him promptly. The Baltimore buyer arrived at noon, the deal was signed over lunch, and Grove pitched his last game with Martinsburg before joining the International League's defending champions. "I was the only player," Grove said later, "ever traded for a fence."

NO DOG DAYS WITH DUNNIE

★　　　★　　　★　　　★

"So I went in [to pitch batting practice] and after I lobbed a few over I cut loose my fast one. Lord was to bat and he ducked out of the way and then throwed his bat to the bench. Callahan says What's the matter Harry? Lord says I forgot to pay up my life insurance. He says I ain't ready for Walter Johnson's July stuff.

"Well Al I will make them think I am Walter Johnson before I get through with them."

–Jack Keefe, hero of the Ring Lardner's
You Know Me Al

In late June of 1920, Robert Moses Grove left the Cumberland, Maryland, station on a steam-powered train that stopped in Washington, D.C., before heading to Baltimore's Camden Station. He rode into his new town through an industrial area containing railroad yards and factories, and he probably smelled the redolent product emanating from McCormick Spices.

Baltimore, then as now, was a fascinating place. A bustling, industrial community especially strong in maritime activities, the Maryland city had many working-class, ethnically distinct neighborhoods. It wasn't a question of "This neighborhood is mostly Irish (Italian, German, Jewish, black)." It was, "This neighborhood is entirely Irish (Italian, German, Jewish, black)."

The streets were safe. Oh, there might be some trouble within the neighborhood, but no one expected masked marauders from outside. Local culture flourished, especially in the black neighborhoods. Along Pennsylvania Avenue, better known as "the Avenue," the spirit of the Harlem Renaissance surfaced in the Roaring Twenties. The Douglass Theater in the 1300 block, later renamed the Royal, eventually featured musicians like Eubie Blake, Count Basie, Cab Calloway, and Duke Ellington. In the neighborhood were clusters of clubs, a YMCA, and occasional black-owned businesses. You took whatever pleasure you could in a district otherwise ignored by the city government and white power structure and known for its "Lung Block," the locus of rampant tuberculosis. In the words of bluesman William (Smokey) Robinson, who later made some stops in Crabtown, "You gotta dance to keep from cryin'."

In truth, the early 1920's were tough in many parts of town. Jobs, union recognition, better salaries, and working conditions brought on by the war gave way to job scarcity, housing shortages, traffic congestion, visible slums, and bitter strikes in its wake. Establishment leaders preyed on fears by blaming the workplace battles on Bolshevik Communism. A natural breeding ground for the Klan, Baltimore had many of that wretched organization's favorite enemies: blacks, Jews, Catholics, unionists, immigrants. And the Klan thrived in town until revelations of scandals and an antimasking ordinance led to its decline.

There were spin doctors then as now, and it was possible to put a positive glow on things. The city annexed 46.5 square miles of Baltimore County, and 5.4 square miles of Anne Arundel County to accommodate the flow of citizens on the move. New industries like Glenn L. Martin Aircraft, American Sugar, Western Electric, and Bethlehem Steel built factories and plants. The city's volume of foreign trade rose from seventh to third in the country from 1920 to 1925. The Democratic Party, at least its southern wing, took over city politics. Swimming pools were built—segregated, of course—and a museum of art sprang up near the Johns Hopkins campus. In response to the endlessly upbeat projections by what local hero H.L. Mencken called "the boosters, boomers, go-getters and other such ballyhoo men," the famous wit asked who exactly was benefiting. A good question.

More upbeat as the decade turned prosperous, Baltimoreans ate their celebrated crab cakes, went swimming and boating in the bay, reveled in the Roaring Twenties. Jazz was hot, and so were theatrical presentations with themes of realism and tawdry sex at night clubs and burlesque houses patronized by seamen on shore leave. Prohibition enforcement lapsed, speakeasies proliferated. Indeed, the city's forty-two-mile shoreline fairly cried out for importation of Cuban and Canadian liquor. Citizens loved rebels like Mencken, even when they left town.

Grove couldn't have cared less about all of this. The cities he played in meant little to him. He would have perked up had someone told him the amazing story of Baltimore baseball. Baltimore teams have played in the National Association, the American Association, the Atlantic Association, the Union Association, the Eastern League, the National League, the American League, the Federal League, and the International League. The best player and manager in baseball history, and two of the best teams—the major league behemoths of the nineteenthth century and the minor-league giants of the twentieth—sported Baltimore uniforms.

In the beginning, as almost everywhere, Baltimore baseball was a novelty played by young men of the business class, who took Saturday afternoon off for athletic activity. The first recorded games were in 1859, and there were at least twenty amateur teams at the end of the Civil War. When the 1869 Cincinnati Red Stockings brought their epic tour to town, they played the "Marylands," supposedly champions of the South, and won, 47-7, in an "exciting game of baseball," as a Baltimore *Sun* reporter

*Grove tossing batting practice with the Orioles,
showing his long stride and erect carriage.*

wrote. Professional baseball was on the way.

In 1872-4, the Lord Baltimores of the National Association played well for two of their three seasons. They were called the Mosquitoes on the road. The name Orioles grew out of the 1881 Oriole Festival, honoring both "our bird" and the harnessing of water from the Gunpowder River. A Union Association team finished fourth in 1884. In 1882-89 the Orioles played in the American Association. Their dismal records—last, last, sixth, last, last, third, fifth, fifth—were at least highlighted by Matt Kilroy's 46 wins in 1887. When players on many teams broke loose and founded their own league in 1890, the majors briefly numbered three leagues: the National League, the American Association, and the Players League. Baltimore accounted for only 38 games, having replaced the failed Brooklyn team in the American Association.

The next season the Orioles finished third. In 1892, Ned Hanlon, a former outfielder, began managing the team in the expanded (twelve-team) National League. Like an eagle sighting fish, Hanlon could spot talent where no one else saw it. While the team struggled to a last-place finish, he traded a .300-hitting veteran to Pittsburgh for twenty-year-old Joe Kelley, who was batting .239. Kelley turned out to be perhaps the greatest Old Oriole, averaging .360 in the 1894-98 glory years, fielding and slugging superbly, and missing only seven games in one four-year stretch.

After the Orioles arrived in Louisville for a series in 1893, Hanlon traded Voiceless Tim O'Rourke (in counterpoint to the famous Orator Jim O'Rourke), hitting .363, in exchange for shortstop Hughie Jennings, who was hitting .136. Over the next five full seasons, Jennings hit .335, .386, .401, .355, and .328. Voiceless Tim's average immediately dropped, and by 1895 he was "batless" Tim: out of baseball.

Early in 1894, Hanlon pulled off his greatest coup. He traded two .260 hitters to Brooklyn for first baseman Dan Brouthers, who appeared to be over the hill at thirty-six, and Willie Keeler, a frail twenty-one-year-old outfielder. Brouthers still had one more big year left in him, while Keeler averaged nearly 220 hits and 50 stolen bases for six consecutive seasons. A big thing in a little package, he was immortalized for having perhaps the most endearing nickname and quote in baseball history. Said Wee Willie Keeler, who once batted safely in 44 consecutive games, "I hit 'em where they ain't."

With this lineup in place, Hanlon won games by any means possible. The Orioles would scuff up balls or rub tobacco into them, cut behind the sole umpire's back to bypass second base when en route from first to third, grab a runner's belt or step on his feet as he rounded third, hide extra baseballs in the outfield, tap endless foul balls to wear down the pitcher, throw masks in a runner's way as he tried to score—all of which made them perhaps the most unpopular team in the game and assuredly the most successful. "The Old Orioles were mean and vicious, ready at any time to maim a rival player or an umpire," said John Heydler, an 1890's ump who later was National League president. "The club was never a constructive force in the game. The worst of it was that they got by with their browbeating and hooliganism."

Perhaps the worst miscreant was third baseman John McGraw, who later became arguably baseball's best manager ever with the New York Giants. He loved the role. "We were in the field and the other team had a runner on first who started to steal second, but first of all he spiked our first baseman on the foot," he recalled. "Our man retaliated by trying to trip him. He got away, but at second Heinie Reitz tried to block him off while Hughie … covered the bag to take the throw and tag him. The runner evaded Reitz and jumped feet first at Jennings to drive him away from the bag. Jennings dodged the flying spikes and threw himself bodily at the runner, knocking him flat. In the meantime the batter hit our catcher over the hands with his bat so he couldn't throw, and our catcher trod on the umpire's feet with his spikes and shoved his mitt in his big face so he couldn't see the play."

But say this for the Old Orioles: they were absolutely fearless. "We'd spit tobacco juice on a spike wound, rub dirt in it, and get out and play," said McGraw, though he wasn't exactly an Iron Man himself. And they could win legitimately, too. When the distance from the mound to the plate was increased from fifty feet to sixty feet, six inches in 1893, Hanlon began seeking pure hitters. A generally small but nimble team, the Orioles perfected Inside Baseball: the hit-and-run, the sacrifice, the squeeze, tilting the basepaths to keep bunts in play, the Baltimore Chop (of course), and other run-creating plays we take for granted today. They could score a run with a walk, a sacrifice bunt, a stolen base, and a sacrifice fly, but mostly they just plain hit. In 1894, every regular in the lineup batted .335 or better, the Orioles won the National

League pennant, Baltimore's first ever, and twenty thousand Baltimoreans snake-danced through the streets. "I'm going to run for mayor," said Hanlon.

The Orioles went on to play in the first of four straight Temple Cups—the NL's postseason series during much of the 1890s—but were too tired and hung over to compete seriously. The New York Giants beat them, four games to none. Nonetheless, they won two of the four available Temple Cups, and in 1894-98 had a .662 winning percentage that would prorate to 107 wins a year today. What a team. What a city.

"Individually, you haven't lost much in having missed the Old Orioles," a reader wrote New York *World-Telegram* columnist Joe Williams. "But collectively, my dear scribbler, could you have seen them, your whole life might have been different."

And, then, all too soon, it was over. Hanlon and fellow Orioles owner Harry Von der Horst entered into a syndicate agreement with the Brooklyn owners and merged the Orioles and Dodgers into essentially one operation running two teams. Hanlon managed Brooklyn in 1899 and took Kelley, Keeler, and Jennings with him. The McGraw-managed Orioles played surprisingly well, finishing fourth among twelve teams and discovering a major talent in pitcher Iron Man McGinnity. When the National League was reduced to eight teams in 1900, the Orioles were gone. They resurfaced in the American League the next two seasons, before McGraw left to manage the Giants in midseason 1902. In 1903 the franchise was moved to New York, where it became the Highlanders and later the Yankees. (Stump your friends with this trivia question: Where did the Yankees play before New York?) Baltimore wouldn't have another American League team until 1954.

Baltimore wasn't through influencing the national pastime. The Orioles drifted back to minor-league obscurity for a few years. When Jack Dunn, a former Oriole, by then a "thin, bald, reedy-faced old pro," whose Providence Clamdiggers had nosed out the

Orioles in the 1905 race, came to town two years later, he created a minor-league dynasty.

A native Pennsylvanian whose first trade was barrelmaking, Dunn played ball from 1897-1904 for Brooklyn, Philadelphia, Baltimore, and the Giants, winning 23 games as a pitcher in 1899 and batting .309 as an infielder in 1904. Counting his years as player-manager for Providence, he served for three major-league and two minor-league pennant-winners. But the best was still ahead of him: a twenty-one-year reign at the helm of the Orioles.

Baltimore immediately won the 1908 International League pennant, with Dunn himself at second base. The next year he bought the franchise from Hanlon for $70,000. It was an open question whether he was more impressive as a manager or a breeder of talent. The 1914 World Series was a showcase of Dunn's former Orioles, with outfielders Jimmy Walsh and Eddie Murphy and pitcher Bob Shawkey playing for the A's, and first baseman Butch Schmidt for Boston's Miracle Braves.

In 1914, Dunn discovered a juvenile delinquent named George Herman Ruth at the St. Mary's Industrial School for Boys. Dunn had heard of his prodigious pitching and batting, but St. Mary's superintendent Brother Paul was his legal guardian until age twenty-one. The brothers finally "paroled" Ruth to Dunn, who informally "adopted" him. Dunn gave Ruth a $600 contract for the season and put him on a train to spring training in Fayetteville, North Carolina, where his older teammates began calling him "Babe," a common name at the time. He was also known as "Dunn's babe." When Ruth struck out stars like Home Run Baker, the Giants' McGraw came a-calling. A meal ticket in hand, Dunn refused McGraw's offer.

Nonetheless, the Orioles struggled to stay alive. The new Federal League placed a major-league team called the Terrapins, or Terps, in Terrapin Park, right across the street from the less imposing Oriole Park. With $160,000 in backing from six hundred

Lefty Grove, second from right on back row, as a Baltimore Oriole.
In his early days with the team, he felt ostracized.

Baltimoreans eager for major-league status again, the Terps finished third with a colorful team including Frank "Piano Mover" Smith and Kaiser Wilhelm.

Virtually unnoticed, the Orioles were staging a much more interesting show across the street, where young Ruth, all of nineteen, won 14 games by July 6. In his autobiography, Ruth claimed that the Terrapins tried to woo him with a $10,000 signing bonus and an equally unlikely $10,000 first-year salary. He declined, evidently fearing he'd be banned from the American and National leagues. In any case, Dunn doubled Ruth's salary to $1,200 and hung onto him. Alas, attendance sank, because Baltimoreans, especially the newspaper opinion makers, wanted to be, watch, and think major league. Dunn had to peddle Birdie Cree, his leading hitter, to the Yankees for $2,500, and Ruth, catcher Ben Egan, and pitcher

Ernie Shore to the Red Sox for $8,500, the steal of the century.

Dunn moved his club to Richmond, Virginia, for one unhappy year, then sold it and relocated the Jersey City franchise to Baltimore. Meanwhile, the Federal League was having its own financial problems. The league directors sued Organized Baseball on January 5, 1915, charging it with violating the Federal antitrust laws. But as 1915 ended, the Federal League's owners decided to give up and go out of business. Kenesaw Mountain Landis, then a federal judge, helped cut a deal in which the majors bought a few Federal League ballparks and took back players who had jumped to the Federal League. Only the Terrapins, last-place finishers in 1915, were not taken care of in the peace agreement. So the club sued in U.S. District Court. On appeal, in 1922, the U.S. Supreme Court decided the suit in favor of the defendants. In one of his lesser opinions, Oliver Wendell Holmes Jr. for a 9-0 court ruled that baseball is a sport, not a business, and as such is exempt from the antitrust laws. The decision legalized the reserve clause, which bound players to their teams until they were released.

Back in a one-team, minor-league city, Dunn in 1916 set about convincing Baltimoreans to settle for his new Orioles. It was an uphill climb in a city that still considered itself major league. Indeed, the column-one and column-eight stories on the sports pages covered the majors, with the Orioles stuck somewhere in the middle . Dunn did get a break when the disbanded Terrapins sold him their real estate, which Dunn renamed Oriole Park.

During World War I there was a movement afoot to curtail all pastimes. The majors eventually shortened their schedule, and only nine minor league teams were able to open the 1918 season. It was the last straw for the beleaguered minors, who under the National Agreement had to lose any player drafted by a major-league team willing to pay $7,500. In 1919 the National Association that ran the minors, feeling more than a little rebellious, withdrew from the National Agreement, voiding the draft rule. Dunn, who was especially hostile to the compact—the International League didn't reinstate it until after his death—elected to keep his players until their price was driven up.

In the process he established the greatest dynasty in the history of the high minors. The 1919 Orioles won 100 games and their first of seven consecutive International League pennants. In 1919-25, they went 779-354 for a .688 winning percentage. Five times they won 113 or more, as the schedule was lengthened, ultimately to 168 games, and they never won fewer than 100.

Old-timers can still cite the sweet-named players: Merwin (Jake) Jacobson, a centerfielder as graceful as a glider, who hit .404 in 1920; the euphonious Joe Boley and Max Bishop double-play combination; cat-quick infielder Fritz Maisel and pitcher Harry (Socks) Seibold; catcher Lena Styles, who sometimes came to the plate strumming his bat like a guitar. They kept coming, with jaw-slackening achievements. Jack Bentley was 41-5 in 1920-22. Just for good measure he hit .412 and won 10 games in relief in '21. Rube Parnham won 33 in '23. Jack Ogden simply won more often —213 times—than anyone to that point in minor-league history.

Robert Moses Grove, the only Hall of Famer from the 1919-25 Oriole teams, arrived as tremulously as a burglar crashing a police convention. "Kid, when I cuss you and bawl you out, don't pay no attention to me," Dunn told him. "I get steamed up sometimes, but don't mean anything by it."

Grove was less than relaxed around his teammates. "I was suspicious of everybody," he told Ed Rumill of the *Christian Science Monitor* many years later. "And, I guess, I was scared of big cities. My attitude was the best defense I could think of. I figured that if I scared people away, they wouldn't steal my money and my watch."

Actually, Grove had reason to be suspicious. Rube Parnham, whom sportswriter and baseball historian Fred Lieb described as an Oriole Dizzy Dean, would take him out, then stick him with the check. There was razzing, Grove said, and, most of all, there was silence. Well, maybe. In a July 1, 1920[1] debut stopped after seven innings, Grove gave up a triple on the first pitch he threw, followed by a single, but beat Jersey City, 9-3, on five hits, three walks, and four strikeouts. Dunn immediately announced he wouldn't sell Grove for $10,000—he was paying him $175 a month—and the writers said Grove was just the infusion of pitching talent the O's needed. The next day he was rewarded. "Dunn, Jack Bentley, Merwin Jacobson, Lefty Groves and Fritz Maisel spent yesterday at William Ashton's place down on the Magothy," the Baltimore *American* reported. "They spent the day shooting at targets, fishing and swimming. Groves proved the champion swimmer, and swam across the river a couple of times. His cleverness in the water made the party ready to back him against all comers."

Lefty won his next two starts on complete games, and only then, he insisted later, did the veterans deign to speak to him. It's possible. Behind Lefty's open-faced-sandwich appearance lay an equally guileless interior. He had an uncanny if unconscious knack for making enemies and influencing people the wrong way. A batting-practice pitcher is supposed to throw easy-to-hit deliveries over the plate. Grove couldn't groove. He threw so hard and so wildly that no one wanted to hit off him.

His wildness carried over into games. "Young Jack Dunn [the son, though both the owner's son and grandson answered to that label] caught Lefty when he first came up from Martinsburg," Jacobson wrote years later. "The first ball he caught bounced off his glove. And about three or four times he couldn't hold the ball it was so fast. We were all watching to see what he was like. I guess they finally put Ben Egan in to catch him. He made Lefty a good pitcher. But he'd walk fourteen and strike out sixteen. He didn't have that groove yet. And he didn't have a curve ball. Jack Dunn [presumably Sr.] said, 'All you've got to do is throw that damn fast ball and throw it!' That's all. No matter where it went."

1 The same day Walter Johnson threw his only no-hitter, against the Red Sox.

"Who taught you to pitch?" Dunn asked Lefty after a few wins. "Nobody," said Grove. "Learned myself."

"Well, learn the rest yourself," said Dunn.

It was not the last instruction he gave Grove. "Give him a high fast one, but put something on it," Dunn would yell during a close game. It was not only a perfect command for an Oriole, but for a future American Leaguer. For years, the league's umpires stood behind a bulky chest protector. Unable to bend low, they tended to call balls on pitches low in the strike zone and strikes on high pitches, even if they were out of the zone.

Lefty could have used more instruction. He evidently thought the stretch was something one did upon rising. When he lost his fourth start, 5-0, to Buffalo, seven Bisons stole eight bases. If he could throw the ball, he couldn't field it very well. "Lefty Groves, Baltimore's new pitcher, may have curves [!] and speed, but he is being described as being mighty awkward in a fielding way and batters get his goat when they bunt his way," *The Sporting News* reported on July 29.

Lefty's place of business, Oriole Park, at 29th Street and Greenmount Avenue, was a wooden bandbox with a brick-tough infield. (It burned down in a July 4, 1944, fire probably caused by somebody's discarded cigarette.) Neutral about catching and fielding, Dunn loved pitching above all else and already had the recruits—big guys who could throw hard and high, as per his instructions—to show for it. Harry Frank, Jack Ogden, and Bentley, who won 25, 27, and 16 games, respectively, were staff enough. Jacobson, who cracked .400 for the first time in a quarter-century, and the .371-hitting, two-way threat Bentley led a .318-hitting team. Even so, Lefty made a mark. He one-hit Syracuse, 8-0, on September 2 and finished 12-2 with a 3.81 ERA, wowing the league with 88 strikeouts in 123 innings. So what if his 71 walks had people calling him "the wild Oriole"? He was on his way.

Like all the Orioles, he was delighted to play for Jack Dunn.

"We were good because Jack Dunn just let us play baseball," said Tommy Thomas, an Orioles pitcher in the '20s. "He didn't pull pitchers. He stuck with them. We didn't even have signals. If you [as batter] had a three [ball] count, he'd tell you to use your own judgment and wing at the next one if it was good. If you thought you could steal, you stole. You didn't look for his decision. It was a team built on ballplayer instinct, and that helped us win."

Actually Dunn—Dunnie to the fans—was slightly more hands-on than that. Seated in the dugout, he used three prime signals: "Hit it" (nod of head), "Don't swing" (shakes head), and "Squeeze" (looks at diamond ring). "Jack Dunn was a very hard loser," Jacobson said. "He wanted to win every game, and eventually he instilled that same spirit in his ballplayers. If the ballplayer loafed in a game or two, the rest of the team took care of him. We wasted no time in getting rid of that kind of player."

"Dunnie told us … that he didn't care what we did on the outside, but once we walked on the ballfield he wanted us to give him everything we had," Grove told an interviewer. They gave him everything, and more. Joe Boley played a Little World Series with two broken fingers on his throwing hand.

Only Parnham, who took unauthorized vacations, gave Dunn trouble. "Don Riley, the veteran baseball scribe, tells about the night Parnham, slated to pitch the next day, dogged Dunn for a $10 loan," Baltimore newsman Ralph J. Sybert wrote. "Suspicious, Dunn refused. Parnham disappeared and soon a bellhop presented Dunn with a bill for two bottles of whiskey 'that tall gentleman, who said he is your secretary, bought for you downstairs.'

"Dunn exploded with roars that he would fire Parnham. Then he dissolved into laughter. Rube sampled the bottles liberally, but won the game the next day without trouble."

The players lived in homes or boarding houses near the park, at New York hotels for series at Newark or Jersey City. "See, we had an easy-going club. Real loose. No rules. No clubhouse meetings.

Grove on the road with the Orioles. Broadway Charlie Wagner, who later teamed with Grove on the Red Sox, watched him pitch in Reading and couldn't believe how wild he was. In fact, during his rookie season with the Orioles, he was known as the "wild Oriole."

It was a good life," Grove said.

"I've seen the ball club sitting up in the hotel playing cards all night ... no night games then, see ... and we'd have a Pierce Arrow limousine hired waiting for us at the hotel at a certain time, and around one or two in the afternoon we'd go downstairs and pile into that son-of-a-gun car and get to the ballpark just in time to start the game," Grove told Donald Honig. "No practice or nothing. Fifteen minutes after we got there the game would start."

With no sellout crowds, visitors from Lonaconing had little trouble alerting Grove to their presence. Presence begot presents. "To our delight, up from the dugout would come packages for us— souvenir baseball schedules, gift scorecards, pencils, and other knick knacks," Lefty's old neighbor, Ruth Bear Levy, wrote in the Summer 1987 issue of *Maryland Historical Magazine*.

When Dunn promised to try to arrange with the American Association for a postseason Junior World Series if they won the pennant (the event had been discontinued), the Orioles won a league-record 25 straight to nip fast-closing (24 of 26) Toronto and finish with a .719 percentage. And that didn't count the team's exhibition victory over the Yankees and their four ex-Orioles. Ruth, streaking to a 54-homer season, struck out twice, and the Orioles won, 1-0.

The previous season had actually ended on a sour note, when the Baltimore Dry Docks, an industrial league team with several major-leaguers, won four of seven in an intracity set-to. In 1920, the stakes were higher. The minor leagues' Junior, or Little, World Series, begun in 1904 but held only three times, resumed with the Orioles playing the St. Paul Saints, American Association winners by 26-1/2 games. Baltimore won five of six, but Lefty, a not-ready-for-prime time player, just relieved in the one loss. With a $1,861 Series share in his pocket, he rode proudly home to marry Ethel Gardner, a fellow resident of Lonaconing's Charlestown neighborhood and a silk-mill worker four years his senior. They tied the knot on January 30, 1921.

The 1921 Orioles kept winning and setting records: 27 straight victories in May, 119 in an expanded 168-game schedule. Indeed, it was Grove who beat Buffalo for the team's twenty-seventh straight win that not only set a minor-league record but topped a major-league record set by the Giants. Grove also struck out 13 Syracuse and 15 Newark batters. Again, Lefty, who became the father of a son, Robert Gardner Grove, that year, had accomplices. Ogden went 31-8. Jack Bentley—the noted pitcher, mind you— took his turn at first when his arm went bad and led the league in singles, doubles, homers, hits, and total bases while batting .412, the league's highest average of the century.

And again Lefty was the talk of the circuit. He went 25-10, his speed drawing comparisons with that of the old-time fireballing Philadelphia A's lefty of earlier years, Rube Waddell. If Grove walked 179 in 313 innings, he also struck out 254. Lieb felt Grove was ready for The Show.

On September 9, the Orioles played an exhibition game in Frostburg, just up the road from Lonaconing. Stores took a half-day holiday, and fans arrived on special trains from the George's Creek area and Cumberland. Naturally, Lefty pitched. Naturally he won, beating the Frostburg Demons, 10-3, before a crowd that may have measured several thousand.

Joe McCarthy's Louisville Colonels beat the Orioles, five games to three, in the Little World Series, with Grove losing three times In a pattern that would repeat itself from time to time, he was too nervous to pitch effectively and walked 15 batters in 13-1/3 innings. The following season the Orioles (119-47) won their fourth consecutive pennant, and beat St. Paul, five games to two, in the postseason. Though he missed a month with a broken finger, Grove was 18-8, with 205 strikeouts—and 152 walks—in 209 innings. It was not uncommon for major- and minor-league teams to play in-season exhibitions at the time, and Grove, growing

Lefty and his wife, the former Ethel Gardner.

more comfortable in the spotlight, struck out 12 New York Giants in one. While the Orioles were beating St. Paul five games to two in the Series, he lost a 2-1 thriller and allowed three runs over five innings in another start. Dunn, weakening in his resolve to keep the team together, sold Jack Bentley to the Giants for a figure variously reported as $65,000 and $72,500.

On March 18, 1923—the very day the fifteenth and last of his father's ghost-written series ran in the Baltimore *Sun*—Jack Dunn *fils*, who was expected to follow in his father's footsteps, died of pneumonia at age twenty-seven. Dunn *père*—himself to die of a heart attack five years later at fifty-six, falling from his horse while watching dog trials—was distraught in his grief. Whether he began losing interest in baseball is debatable. Grove thought so. Dave Howell, an International League historian, feels Dunn may have buried himself in the game as a form of therapy.

In any case, the team and the franchise player kept winning. Grove, who had a new daughter, Ethel Doris, went 27-10 in 1923 and set International League records with 330 strikeouts (including a personal-best 17 on April 19) and 186 bases on balls in 303 innings. He tried throwing a curve, but it barely broke. It was just one fastball after another, and that was all he needed.

Dunn refused offers for Grove from major-league clubs, saying "He's pitching for me." With the right offer, Dunn might have changed his mind.

He certainly didn't get it from the White Sox. On August 24, 1923, Harry Grabiner, the White Sox secretary, took in a Grove start in Buffalo. Grove breezed through the first four innings, entered the fifth with an 11-1 lead, then "lost his nerve, control, speed and everything else," according Ernest A. Bowersox (Is that a great baseball name, or what?) of the Baltimore *American*. After three walks, four hits, and six runs, Grove was lifted. "They knocked off the lefthander for my benefit," Grabiner later joked.

On September 28, however, Grove beat a former Oriole teammate, the Giants' Jack Bentley, 4-3, in a ten-inning exhibition. The Giants were amazed by his speed, although one account said "his sweeping curves had the Giants guessing throughout." This is hard to believe. Chances are he threw an occasional hook, but even Grove said it scarcely broke until well into his big-league career. In any case, the win vindicated not only Grove but Dunn, who, after calling Bentley his "second best" Orioles pitcher, had bet McGraw $1,000 and half the gate receipts on the game.

In the Little World Series, Baltimore lost to Kansas City, five games to four, with Grove (1-2, two no-decisions) blowing a five-run lead in one game, lasting just two-thirds of an inning and walking everything but the manager's dog in two others. Winning teams or not, some of Dunn's players were simply too good to keep. He peddled Max Bishop to the A's for $50,000. When the Giants offered $75,000 for Grove, Dunn wouldn't budge for anything less than $100,000. Grove was glad. He later said that he never wanted to play for the feisty John McGraw. Just imagine that clash of egos.

Much has been made of the fact that by this time Grove was making $750 per month, plus playoff and exhibition shares—all told, an decent big-league salary—and liked playing for the Orioles. But for years he had been taking the train ride from Cumberland to Washington and watching Walter Johnson. The laconic fellow from Lonaconing was given to neither expressiveness nor, as far as we know, self-analysis, but his steely will surely must have propelled him forward. As the song asked, "How ya gonna keep 'em down on the farm after they've seen Paree?" And how ya gonna keep 'em in a minor league city after they've the bright lights of the majors? Lefty's eyes were on bigger prizes. He could taste big-league cooking, savor big-league bucks.

In 1924, Grove pitched as if he were already in the big leagues, going 26-6, leading the league in wins despite six weeks off with a wrist injury, striking out 231 batters in 236 innings, and reducing his walks from 186 to 108 with help from Lew McCarty, a former Giants, Dodgers, and Cardinals catcher. Grove fanned 13 A's in an exhibition that he won, 5-0.[2] He may have even posed and postured like a major-leaguer. In an exhibition against the Yankees, a Grove fastball tipped Ruth's shirt. "Those dumb minor-leaguers,"

---

[2] According to a story by Rodger H. Pippen in the October 16, 1925 Baltimore *News*, Grove struck out between ten and fourteen batters in each of his exhibitions against major-league clubs. The figure is somewhat less impressive than it sounds, because major-leaguers were reluctant to dig in against a wild youngster. Ruth may have been especially nervous. It's more significant that Grove is believed to have lost only one exhibition, to the Senators. When they continued to beat him early in his major-league career, Washington owner Clark Griffith claimed he had a hex on Grove.

Ruth is alleged to have said on his way to first, "They don't know where they're throwing the ball."

"I'll know where I'm throwing the next one when you come up," Grove supposedly responded. "It will be right at you, Ruth. I'm not afraid of you." Grove struck out Ruth nine of the eleven times they met in exhibition games. Ruth, who hit nine homers off him in the majors—tying Hank Greenberg and Lou Gehrig for the most off of Lefty—eventually responded by omitting Grove from his traveling all-star team in 1931. Which was too bad, because Grove and Ruth had much in common, their talent and inability to remember names in particular. Grove referred to one player as the "big guy with the big feet" and another as "that lug with the ugly kisser."

The Yankees never forgot Lefty's disrespect. But so what? The "elongated fork-fister," in the words of Baltimore *American* writer Jean Rouchard, looked as if he could beat anyone. In 4-1/2 seasons with Baltimore, Grove won 108 games, lost 36, pitched .750 ball and struck out 1,108 batters, a minor-league record.

The Orioles prepared for the Junior World Series by losing three games to Waterbury, Connecticut, champions of the Eastern League. Bring on St. Paul. After winning twice in Baltimore, Grove lost two games in Minnesota, helping the Orioles blow a three-game lead and drop a ten-game postseason marathon, five games to four, with one tie. Though he had a 3-8 record, with nearly eight walks a game, in postseason play, Grove had won four consecutive strikeout titles and established himself as the best in the bushes. So the bidding began. According to a November 20, 1924, story in the Philadelphia *Evening Ledger*, both the Cubs and Dodgers offered $100,000. Dunn sold Grove to his old friend, Philadelphia Athletics manager Connie Mack, who had personally been scouting him on off days, for $100,600. The $100,000 was paid in ten annual installments. The extra $600, variously described as interest and carrying charges, made it at the time the most expensive minor-league purchase ever and technically $600 more than the sale price when Ruth went to the Yankees after the 1919 season (counting notes, interest on notes, and a $300,000 loan, New York actually spent more than $400,000). Hype wasn't born yesterday.

In a scene described by the Baltimore *Sun's* Don Riley, Grove was called into Dunn's office shortly after the Little World Series. "I've sold you to the Athletics, Lefty," Dunn told him.

"Anything you say goes with me," Grove replied.

Dunn proffered a $6,500 contract that Grove was happy to sign, the absence of a significant raise notwithstanding, and the new major leaguer thought the session had ended. "How many games did you win for me?" Dunn went on.

"I think it was 108."

"Well, I am not going to let you go without a remembrance." Dunn sent him on his way with an unspecified bonus estimated in excess of Mack's $600 bonus.

Grove wafted out of Dunn's office, and the hype built. "I think that one good pitcher will give the Athletics the necessary punch to make us a pennant contender," Mack said. "That man is Groves of the Orioles. He is the best pitcher I ever saw in the minors and I believe he will become a popular idol in Philadelphia."

The writers began favorably comparing Grove's speed to that of his idol. "Even if Walter Johnson retires from the Senators' staff, the American League will still be the smoke consumer of baseball," wrote a Baltimore columnist, "for Lefty's fast one won't make anyone feel lonesome for lack of speed."

THE $100,600 LEMON

★   ★   ★   ☆

"He had so much wiggige he was gigless."

–Jazz expression describing a musician
who is too pumped up to perform

The Philadelphia that Lefty Grove entered in 1925 had returned to normalcy. As the redoubtable city year-book boasted, the "ice-cream capital of the United States" was producing one-fourth of all American-made goods, leading all communities in leather and tanned goods, knit goods, hats, cigars and cigarettes, carpets and rugs, ships and boat building, saws and files. The Philadelphia mint produced two-thirds of all U.S. currency. The city's signature boulevard, Broad Street, was the longest (fourteen miles) urban thoroughfare in the country. Philadelphia had fifteen percent more skilled workers than the Empire City to the north, ten percent more than Broad Shoulders to the west.

Growing rapidly—a baby born every thirteen minutes, a new resident moving to town every twenty-six—Philadelphia was governed by the Vare Republican machine, itself dominated by wealthy patricians running city businesses and charities.

But not all was well. There were bank closings, strikes, unemployment. The sesquicentennial being planned for 1926 would lose $5 million. "Ostentatiously wet," Philadelphians ignored Prohibition to the distress of the public safety commissioner. The eighteenth amendment, passed in 1919 to punish immigrants as much as inebriates[1], produced not temperance but illegal distilleries, warehouses, speakeasies, and mob violence among rival bootleggers—the very birth, according to some historians, of organized crime in the United States. The population of 1,823,779, including 397,927 foreign-born, was already at war with itself, albeit in relatively subdued fashion. The fifty-five thousand Italians chafed under the Irish domination of the Roman Catholic Church. New Italians from south of Naples, mostly unskilled laborers, coexisted uneasily with skilled craftsmen from the north who had arrived in the previous century. Established and assimilated German Jews clashed with their later-arriving, more Orthodox, Eastern European cousins. Blacks, whose population would increase from 67,132 to more than 220,000 during the decade, were for the most part "Lincoln Republicans" easily exploited by the Vare machine. Indeed, African-Americans had only one ward leader in 1925.

Whatever differences they had, nearly everyone was captivated by stories about the excesses of the Jazz Age.

---

[1] "Impassioned about drink, moralistic, often rural Protestants wanted to protect the nation from the scourge of liquor. They linked it to urban districts populated by foreigners and their foul saloons." Bruce Kuklick, To Every Thing a Season: Shibe Park and Urban Philadelphia (Princeton University Press, 1991), p. 58. Reprinted with permission of the author.

Consider the front page of the Philadelphia *Inquirer* on April 14, 1925, the A's opening day. Among more than a dozen stories and boxes crowded into eight columns was a juicy account headlined "Student Suicide Bares Dizzy World of Love and Jazz." Robert Preston, a Northwestern student, had gotten into a boat, weighted his body, shot himself, and tumbled into the water after succumbing to depression over incurable diabetes. In his last days he'd fallen into "some drinking, some wild automobile rides and considerable 'petting,' " the story recounted in detail.

Closer to home, a child was killed by a runaway team of horses, and a State legislative committee, pressured by powerful utility interests, killed a bill that would have given the public service commission broader powers. Under "Editorial Comment," we find much provincialism. It was directed north: "Now that New York has refused to permit [Jack] Dempsey to fight there, everybody ought to be satisfied. Dempsey probably didn't want to fight there, anyway." And south: "Demotion for General [William] Mitchell didn't seem to satisfy the War department. They also sent him to Texas. Isn't this cruel and unusual?"

On other inside pages Mrs. Calvin Coolidge hostessed an Easter egg roll on the White House lawn, and the Women's Club announced it had spent $5,548 caring for crippled children. There was a "war" over the proposed eight-cent subway fare. Spring overcoats at Perry's were advertised for $23, spring suits at Geo. Kelly's for $17.50, apron dresses at Wanamaker's for $1.

Mark Twain, citing an old American joke, once wrote of Philadelphia, "In Boston they ask, How much does he know? In New York, How much is he worth? In Philadelphia, Who were his parents?" Details aside, what wafts through the newspapers and other contemporary documents most of all is the aura of a WASP, Episcopalian establishment led by men with two last names (say, Ashworth Pennypacker III). In this we-know-what's-right-for-you world, how did an Irishman gain such a prominent position? Well, Connie Mack was no threat to the established order. To Episcopalians, he was lace-curtain rather than shanty Irish, not some brawling barhopper, not some … some … some … Democrat!

The Tall Tactician sat upright in the dugout in a dark suit and straw or derby hat, directing the team with a rolled-up program. A perfect figure for the "City of Undertakers," he appeared stern and distant. Yet players from a great variety of backgrounds considered him kind and considerate: everyone's uncle.

In 1862, Mack was born Cornelius Alexander McGillicuddy in East Brookfield, Massachusetts, the son of Irish immigrants Mary McKillop and Michael McGillicuddy, a Civil War soldier who was a wheelwright. Following stints with four minor-league clubs, Mack joined the Washington Nationals and won the catcher's job. Mack's eleven-year big-league career with Washington, Buffalo (of the Players League), and Pittsburgh gets little notice because he hit only .245, but the catcher's job was not really to hit. There were few tools of ignorance, or even intelligence, at the time. There were no shin guards, and the meager mitt, mask, and chest protector offered little protection. With no men on base, the catcher stood several feet behind the batter. Once someone got aboard, he had to move forward and take his chances with foul tips, all the while chasing down bunts, directing the other infielders, and throwing out baserunners. It was a significant feat to catch 100 games a season.

Connie was nothing if not cunning. He was known for tricking hitters by talking to them, tipping their bats with his glove (immediately apologizing each time), calling for quick pitches while messing with his equipment, and freezing baseballs overnight to deaden them for his pitcher. Foul tips counted as outs, and Mack could imitate the sound of a tipped ball while catching a swinging strike.

A man this cagey was made to manage. As a player-manager in Pittsburgh (1894-96) of the National League and a manager in Milwaukee (1897-1900) of the Western League, Mack trained himself for the main event. In 1901, he began a fifty-year association with the Philadelphia Athletics as manager and twenty-five percent owner (he would subsequently become majority owner). Mack said pitching was seventy-five percent of baseball and developed it superbly. In 1902, the A's won their first pennant behind the pitching of Rube Waddell and Eddie Plank. Mack recruited both Plank and Chief Bender directly from college campuses—Plank pitched for Gettysburg College but never enrolled—and somehow turned them into instant winners.

He had an excellent public relations touch. When New York Giants manager John McGraw said a Philadelphia team would be a "white elephant," Mack put the creatures on the uniforms and presented a white-elephant statue to McGraw at the 1905 World Series. McGraw, delighted, bowed deeply to the crowd. Peerless teachers and evaluators—McGraw won ten pennants and three Series, Mack nine and five— they were pleased to face each other in that famous Series dominated by Christy Mathewson's three shutouts, then again in the 1911 and 1913 classics won by Philadelphia. At a banquet for his rival, Mack said, "There has been only one manager—and his name [is] McGraw." Later, on a visit to Napoleon's tomb, McGraw said, "I, too, met the Duke of Wellington, only his name was Connie Mack."

Mack managed both men and the media. A figure beyond

reproach for years, he handled college players like Eddie Collins with the same equanimity with which he tolerated the immature Waddell. The A's won four pennants and three World Series in 1910-14, while Mack's share of the club increased to fifty percent. The team was best known for the "$100,000 infield" of Stuffy McInnis, Jack Barry, Frank (Home Run) Baker, and Collins, and Hall-of-Fame pitchers Waddell, Plank, and Bender, and 1910-11 ace, Jack Coombs. Someone, somewhere was muttering "Break Up the A's."

And then, incredibly, Mack did. During the 1914 season Mack couldn't—or wouldn't—meet the $25,000 price tag that old friend Jack Dunn placed on a couple of young Orioles pitchers named Ruth and Shore. Immediately after the Series, in which the 99-game-winning A's were swept by the Miracle Braves, the newly established Federal League began enticing major-leaguers by offering high salaries. Claiming A's fans were bored with winning—attendance had dropped dramatically—Mack dismantled his pennant winners rather than pay to keep the team together. He sold Collins (.344 in 1914) to the White Sox for a bagful of Comiskey money, and refused a raise to Baker (.319 and a league-leading nine homers), who sat out the 1915 season. Plank (15-7, 2.87 ERA in '14) and Bender (17-3, 2.26) jumped to the Federal League.

The Athletics immediately bottomed out with the worst run of tail-enders in baseball history, finishing last in 1915 (43-109), 1916 (36-117), 1917 (55-98), 1918 (52-76), 1919 (36-104), 1920 (48-106) and 1921 (53-100). Anyone, it seemed, could play for Philadelphia. They didn't even have to exist. Tryout-seeking Danny O'Neill, a character in a James T. Farrell novel, purportedly wrote a letter to "Mr. Connie Mack, Shibe Park, The Philadelphia Athletics, Philadelphia, Pennsylvania." A real local boy, Jimmy Dykes, took several trolleys to Shibe Park and made the team. Beginning his twenty-two-year career, he was so appalled at the almost daily changing of the guard that he would ritually introduce himself to his infield mates every day.

Once Mack's spirit was reignited, he started rebuilding. When he added several new starters, including Joe Hauser, the quintessential good-hit, fair-field minor-leaguer, the A's crawled to seventh in 1922. The curveball specialist Rube Walberg helped Philadelphia inch ahead to sixth in 1923.

In 1924, Mack added crack Baltimore second baseman Max Bishop for $25,000 and got left fielder Al Simmons (*nee* Aloys Szymanski) from Milwaukee. Known as Bucketfoot Al for standing at the plate with his left foot facing the third-base dugout—the water bucket was traditionally placed at the far end of the bench—Simmons feared Mack would change his stance. "You can hold the bat in your teeth," said Mack, "provided you hit safely and often." Simmons batted .308 with 102 RBI, and the '24 A's climbed to fifth.

The offseason moves before the 1925 season had A's fans in a tizzy. Grove came along with his fabulous numbers in Baltimore. Mack wanted .333-hitting Portland, Oregon, catcher Gordon (Mickey) Cochrane so much that he bought an interest in the franchise for $132,000 and later acquired Cochrane for $50,000 and five players. The greatest battery in baseball history was forming. Teenager Jimmie Foxx was another addition to spring training. Four future Hall of Famers—Grove, Cochrane, Simmons, and Foxx—had joined the club in two seasons. Mack was a genius. The fans were talking pennant.

Grove was delighted finally to pitch in the majors, over-joyed to be riding a pennant express, pleasantly surprised by the fan support. For all intents and purposes, baseball was the only game in Philadelphia. And the mighty A's, no small contrast to the pathetic Phillies, were the only team in town. Corner stores carried canvas banners displaying inning-by-inning totals and highlights. Covered uncritically, their private lives respected, the players were gods. "When I was pitching in street ball, I imagined myself as Lefty Grove," says Bob Partridge, who lived near the park and was later a prep school and college coach and teacher. "When I was hitting, I became Jimmie Foxx."

Grove holding his daughter Ethel Doris, and seated next to his son Robert Gardner Grove, called Bobby. Young Bobby, himself a high school and college pitcher, threw righthanded but was often called "Lefty."

Ever impervious to the thrusts of American culture, Lefty Grove neither understood nor particularly cared about the social faults shifting below him. The Philadelphia he knew was the Philadelphia he saw in front of him. Literally.

Like most of his teammates, Lefty lived in town, eventually renting a house within half a mile of Shibe Park, at 2938 West Lehigh Avenue. The area's major east-west artery, Lehigh was lined with churches, shops, and offices. Many of Lefty's teammates lived close by. Max Bishop hooked up with a dentist and his family on Somerset Street. Jimmy Dykes and Joe Boley hung out at a dance hall on Twenty-Second and Clearfield. Mack would drive up and down Lehigh to check on his players. He often found rookies drinking cherry Cokes in Don Hoffman's restaurant. Once he discovered Grove leaving a speakeasy, bottle in hand. "Robert, I'll have that delivered to your house so no one will think you've been drinking," Mack told him. Al Simmons was easy to find. He constantly overslept at Mrs. Cromwell's on Twentieth Street, directly behind the right-field stands. Upon her signal, a local kid would wake the great star with the words, "Hey, Al ... you got to get your batting practice if you're gonna win the batting title."

The neighborhood was officially North Penn, although residents usually called it North Philly, and it was largely Irish. There were some better-off English and Germans and worse-off Italians within its boundaries, a Jewish district began west of Thirtieth Street, and a black community sat across Broad Street to the east, but North Penn was quintessentially Irish. Perhaps the greatest success story in American ethnicity—for some reason, WASPs are never counted as ethnics—the Irish have succeeded in everything, especially charm. In 1925, the Philadelphia Irish had made their mark as policemen, politicians, priests, construction workers, printers, and in many other occupations. The more successful lived on the tree-lined wider streets, owning three-story houses with porches covered by awnings. The less successful rented two-story houses on side streets. Sidewalks were so clean that dirt was even swept out of the cracks. Everyone knew the social center: It was Kilroy's tavern, catty-cornered from the ballpark.

Railroad tracks and industry clearly delineated North Penn. Herman Belmont, now a retired child psychiatrist, was growing up near the park. "You didn't see many cars— most of them were tin lizzies," says Belmont, the son of a shoemaker. "The milkman would come in his horse and buggy. There were row houses everywhere, and I would range down the alleys behind them yelling 'Strawberries! Strawberries! Ten cents a quart!' We lived in the 4000 block, and I could ride my bike all the way downtown safely." Only Prohibition bootleggers were not safe. With bars being driven underground and bootleg hooch surreptitiously sold, residents heard sirens when police entered the neighborhood on an arrest, or gunshots when gang warfare erupted.

★　　　★　　　★　　　★

At least all sides could coexist at the ballpark. Named for baseball manufacturer Ben Shibe, who introduced the cork-center baseball, Shibe Park had opened on Lehigh Avenue in 1909 as the first concrete-and-steel ballyard in America. A French Renaissance façade with columns, arched windows, and a domed tower housing Connie Mack's office behind home plate. By today's standards, Shibe Park was intimate; by yesterday's measure, impersonal and imperial, with a distinct separation of players and fans. On the other hand, among the twenty thousand seats when the place opened, there were thirteen thousand twenty-five cent seats, because Shibe believed in baseball "for the masses as well as for the classes." More than anything, Shibe Park was a showcase.

In 1925, the place had just been double-decked everywhere but right field, and new stands were erected in left field. Beyond the twelve-foot right-field wall, North Twentieth Street fans could sit in their front rooms or on the roof and see the game for free (until Mack built a high wall in 1935). Street urchins could watch the game through knotholes in the right-field fence. The fences carried no advertisements, the diamond-shaped playing area, sharply angled in center field, was deep green, and the mounds and basepaths were groomed like show dogs. All in all, it was some contrast to broken-down Baker Bowl, the Philadelphia Phillies home all but invisible in a neighborhood of warehouses and train sheds six blocks to the east.

The pitching mound was baseball's highest at twenty inches. (The fifteen-inch requirement was haphazardly enforced until 1950.) The 1925 dimensions were spacious: 334 feet to left, 468 to center, 380 to right. Nonetheless, players felt that the ball carried well, and it certainly took weird caroms off the corrugated iron fence in right. Shibe Park "inflated offenses by about five percent," Bill James wrote in his *Historical Abstract*.

Every park has a special ambience. The aura of Shibe Park was captured to perfection by Bruce Kuklick in his book *To Every Thing a Season: Shibe Park and Urban Philadelphia 1909-76*:

> When the team was home, hordes of fans walked up Lehigh, the street alive with the hum of baseball talk. Other rooters pushed out of packed streetcars at the corner of Twenty-first and Lehigh.

Frequently coming to work by public transport, ballplayers who did not live in North Penn might rub elbows with the Athletics' socialite devotee Henry Savage, a familiar spectacle on the trolleys in dingy clothes and battered straw hat. At the entrance to the stadium the clanging bells of the streetcars blended with the ooh-gahs of automobile horns, the blasts of police whistles, and the cries of vendors. The ballplayers would thread their way through the crowds to the clubhouses while the fans poured through the turnstiles of the main entrance.

The sounds inside as the hawkers made their pitch for peanuts, ice cream, and scorecards were loud but friendly. Once the game started, however, the noise of food sellers would compete with louder and less amicable cries. Fans screamed at umpires, and boos echoed from all over the park. Partisans razzed opposing players, of course, but reserved some of the nastiest assaults for the home team—someone in a slump, a pinch hitter who struck out, a pitcher having a bad day. Even from outside the stadium people could hear the famous "Huckster." He never seemed to shout, but his deep powerful voice coming from the lower grandstand was relentless against the visiting pitcher. The Huckster was so adept at rattling Jimmy Dykes on third base that Connie Mack unsuccessfully tried various ways to have him silenced.

The Huckster was around for years. Who was he? Did he actually sell vegetables from a truck? Did he have a megaphone? Long after his day

Shibe Park regulars wondered about him. Was he different people at various times? Was he the peddler Charlie Dougherty? Or the same huckster as "Bill" Kessler and his brother Eddie, who were famous for conducting stentorian conversations across the field?

At the beginning of an A's rally, the Huckster might briefly stop. Fans would ignore the cries of "Hot dog here" as everyone concentrated on the action. Then other sounds would take over—the steady beat of thousands of hands clapping, and a similar rhythm of stamping feet. The Huckster would return, adding his lungs to the Athletics' efforts.

The excitement carried outside the park. On Twentieth Street opposite right field and right-center, spectators frequently crowded onto the roofs of the houses. Toward the Somerset end of the block, fans on the roof often called play-by-play for folks hanging around the right-field wall. Those outside with a practiced ear—Quill the cop, Charley Score Cards, Peanut Mike, or any habitué—did not need help. Their voice was the noise of the crowd outside.

When a batter was waiting out a walk, there is a feeling of suspense or recklessness. It is followed by the sound of relief as thousands of people suddenly let out a breath and by a smattering of applause. A sharp roar means a single. As it eases off, an afficionado on Lehigh Avenue could imagine the runner rounding first, holding up, then walking back to the bag. A longer roar, broken off, indicates a long hit. When the break is followed by a tremendous cry, it tells the outsider that the ball has fallen safely and that the batter is scampering around the bases. A gasp of exhilaration from the crowd inside says that the runner has made it safely to second or third. A solid smack and relative quiet mean that thousands of pairs of eyes are watching a baseball soaring through the air. Next a crescendo of shouting, foot stamping, and clapping of hands can mean only one thing. Just the sound of bat meeting ball tells experienced listeners that it is a home run.[2]

Into this extraordinary park would eventually step a ready-made legend. There is something mythical about a new fireballer in town. In the 1800's he would ride into town on a horse. In 1925, he stepped out of a train. His reputation first preceded him, invariably exaggerated, to spring training. Grove could throw the ball at speeds of one hundred and fifty miles per hour, people may have been saying. Most of the time his fastball was invisible, they would have added. And it was always feared: a pitch that could kill. Remember, Carl Mays, trying to pitch inside, had dispatched Ray Chapman to some field of dreams in the sky just five years earlier. The following story told to the old ballplayer Bill Werber by A's scout Ira Thomas was almost certainly apocryphal, but it says something about the Lefty legend:

> As Thomas told it, he found the Grove home in Lonaconing at almost dusk. He knocked on the door and was greeted by Grove's mother, who told him that her son was squirrel hunting but

---

[2] ibid, pp. 55-57

The 1927 Philadelphia Athletics are pictured at the Thomas Edison home in Fort Myers, Florida. Edison is front and center. Grove is over his right shoulder, back row, bow-tied.

would be coming down the railroad right of way towards home "any time now."

Thomas elected to stroll up the rail tracks and soon saw the tall angular Grove approaching with squirrels swinging dead, their tails fastened under his belt. Introductions over, Thomas inquired as to the absence of a gun.

"Don't use no gun," was Lefty's response. "I kill 'em with rocks." Noting the incredulity on Thomas's face, Lefty took from his coat pocket a large smooth stone and, throwing with his right arm, busted a glass insulator on a telephone poll some sixty feet distant. Said the thoroughly astounded Thomas, "But I was told you were a lefthander."

"Am," said Lefty, "but if I throwed at 'em left-handed I'd tear 'em all up."[3]

Though Cochrane and Foxx had boarded the train from Baltimore to Florida with Grove, Lefty's name was on everyone's lips. The A's fairly screeched about their $100,600 acquisition. In one batting practice, he told the regulars what pitch he was going to throw. "Facing his delivery, which he preceded with a combination St. Vitus dance and acrobatic stunt, the batters were fortunate indeed if they saw the ball occasionally," the *Evening Bulletin* reported.

"His freak windup consists of a rapid double arm overhead motion," a writer gushed. "Then he raises his right foot high in the air and goes through a contortion apparently watching the center fielder with his left eye while the right optic seems glued on the batter.

"The ball is delivered in a sweeping half arm and half overhead swing. The secret of Groves' success lies in the strength of his left shoulder. He has hands that are smaller than the average person's, there is no special muscular development in the arms, but the left shoulder is a solid hunk of iron and beef.

"Groves has terrific speed. Some say his dazzling shoots can blind batters better than Walter Johnson did in his prime." The same writer said Grove was "a quiet youth, affable and easy-going and has made a big hit with his teammates."

---

[3] From an unpublished manuscript tentatively entitled *Memories of a Ballplayer: Bill Werber and Baseball in the 1930's* by Bill Werber and C. Paul Rogers. Copyright 1998 by C. Paul Rogers and Bill Werber.

When Grove four-hit the Phillies over five innings in his final preseason warmup, the *Inquirer* blared, "Lefty Groves gave an exhibition of spellbinding which convinced the fans he is some pitcher. Lefty worked free and easy, and did not attempt to chuck his arm off and consequently he was the finished hurler that dazzled the International League last season."

On Tuesday, April 14, Grove sat on a stool in front of his wire-mesh locker in the cramped clubhouse, donning the heavy flannel uniform of the day. It was cold and threatening outside. Lefty probably felt nervous, apprehensive, excited. And for good reason. It was opening day, and he was starting against Boston before twenty-five thousand fans, Mayor W. Freeland Kendrick, and Kendle's Band. Bunting and other opening day paraphernalia were everywhere. His Honor threw out the first ball to catcher Cy Perkins. Then came what a writer on hand called "the dismal failure of Robert Moses Groves."

In a pattern that would repeat itself all season, he dug himself in before he could dig himself out. "I'm too strong," pitchers say. "I'm overpowering the ball." When a pitcher is too pumped up, he will rush his delivery. In practical terms, that means that the elbow comes through too quickly, the hand trails, and the throw often sails high.

"Nervous as a deb," in one wag's words, Grove gave up five runs, six hits, and four walks before being mercifully lifted with two out in the fourth. Immediately, he grabbed his sweater and disappeared under the stands en route to the clubhouse.

The press descended on Grove, who was still calling himself Groves, with writing like this: "The weather was chilly and damp, and the Mackmen cavorted like bushers for five rounds. Lefty Groves, the $100,000 beauty, couldn't weather the Red Sox attack and the fans razzed the A's at every opportunity."

Fortunately, Lefty wasn't the whole story. Cochrane grounded out as a pinch hitter in the eighth, but contributed a key single in the tenth to help the A's beat the Red Sox, 9-8. Years later Grove incorrectly remembered losing his first big-league start to Walter Johnson. Having taken trains from Lonaconing and Baltimore to see the great man, Lefty had been obsessed with the guy for years. (In fairness, he did lose his first decision to Johnson a week later.)

It is doubtful Grove had anything to say after the game, which apparently soured him for the season. All year he "growled, grumbled, said 'No' to many requests with the finality of an earthquake or atom bomb," according to pitcher Stan Baumgartner, a teammate who later became a Philadelphia *Inquirer* sportswriter.

Grove was again undone in the fourth inning of his next outing. For the first—but not last—time people were calling him a six-figure lemon. "The juiciest lemon ever picked," to be precise. His third start, on April 21, was especially telling. While the Senators waited him out, he walked six men, twice lobbed the ball over, paid little attention to baserunners, and lost, 6-2. Though Grove had pitched eight innings, Mack was furious. "Wildness and weakness in the clutch" was an apt newspaper summary.

Soon word got around. He was too pumped up, as he had often been in the Little World Series. Batters would wait out Grove before swinging. Often behind on the count, the nervous rookie obliged them with rushed deliveries, walks, and meatballs. Not even veteran catcher Cy Perkins could harness Grove, who in addition to everything else, took his eye off the plate during his windup, failed to back up bases, criticized teammates on the bench, and locked himself in his room when Mack tried to speak with him. *You Know Me Al* had been published in 1914, and Grove had apparently adopted the persona of Jack Keefe: a pitcher so sure of his own ability that every loss must have been someone else's fault. One can imagine Lefty saying—or thinking—"The only reason I walked so many was that my fast one was jumping so. Honest, Al, it was so fast that [Billy] Evans the umpire couldn't see it half the time and he called a lot of balls that was right over the heart."

Theories abounded about Grove's struggles. Some said he wasn't sufficiently poised. Others cited Lefty's inability to hold runners on base or his catchers' struggles to throw them out. Grove said he always struggled in cold weather.

"Grove had speed ... and more speed," Cochrane many years later told columnist Frank Graham, on assignment from *Sport*. "In the beginning he was very wild. Catching him was like catching bullets from a rifleman with bad aim."

Pining for Baltimore, Grove wore two diamond-studded emblems honoring the Orioles' 25- and 27-game winning streaks in 1920 and 1921, respectively. "I'm going to hypnotize myself into believing I'm back in the International League," Grove said, "and if Ruth or Cobb comes to bat I'll call him Jones or Smith."

Connie Mack refused to panic. On May 8, notwithstanding three losses and six poor efforts, he supported Grove. Promising to stick with him at least three years, Mack said, "Remember about fifteen years ago. The Giants bought 'Rube' Marquard, called the $11,000 pitching beauty, from Indianapolis. It took Marquard two years to arrive. A newcomer in this league must get acclimated. Some get acclimated very quickly, others take time.

"I have every confidence in Groves and will stick by him to the finish. I'll bet a new hat he'll be a great pitcher yet, because he has the nerve and pluck to surmount all obstacles."

At some point during Lefty's struggle, Perkins got Grove to step off the rubber between pitches and slap the ball in his glove three times. A coach, Ira Thomas, told Grove to count to ten before each pitch. Philadelphia fans got into the act. "One, two, three, four, five, six, seven, eight, nine, ten!" they would chant as he wound up.

On May 9, Grove threw three strong innings to save a game in Cleveland. On May 15, he struck out six Tigers in four innings of relief to win, 8-7, the first-place A's eighth straight victory. Twice he worked out of trouble by striking out batters with runners on second and third. "Connie Mack has finally hit upon a scheme which uncovers the latent ability of 'Lefty' Groves," the *Evening Bulletin* crowed.

"Groves laughed and kidded in the pitcher's box. Perkins compelled him to pitch slowly and with less effort. 'Lefty' was like a wild colt who had to be held back. Some of his speedy pitches burnt clean through the catcher's glove and chafed Perkins' hands.

"Although it was ticklish in the last four rounds, Groves and Perkins engaged in comedy repartee and the usually nervous and fidgety pitcher actually laughed in two tight pinches.

" 'I think Groves will come through now,' said Perkins. 'I never saw such a speedy pitcher or such hooks as he showed today. No pitcher in baseball has as much. He's been nervous and unable to get started.

" 'He realizes he must win and has been overdoing himself. Hereafter he is going to laugh and tease the batters. When he laughs he wins and when he doesn't he's nervous and blows up.' "

Although Grove stopped George Sisler's 34-game hitting streak on May 20, too often he blew up. A noted hot-weather pitcher in Baltimore, Grove had one win in July and August. For a while, the team seemed to compensate. Two-thirds of the way through the season it was neck-and-neck with the Washington Senators. One writer gamely compared the 1925 A's with the 1911 pennant winners, citing nine .300 hitters, including the real rookie sensation, Cochrane, hitting .336 at the time. The pitching was similar, too, the writer added, with Sam Gray (12-6 at the time), Ed Rommel (20-6), and Slim Harriss (14-11).

The A's dropped out of the race by losing 12 straight in late August and early September, and Grove was by no means the only villain. They eventually finished second at 88-64, 8-1/2 games behind the Senators. They had won seventeen more games and improved three places in the standings. It was a season with much to recommend it: Cochrane's .331 rookie year; Al Simmons' league-leading 253 hits, plus his 24 homers, 129 RBIs, and .387 average; Ed Rommel's league-leading 21 wins. Alas, the fact that the A's came so close with Grove doing so poorly merely focused attention on him. Grove had an 8-10 record for the only losing season in his career. He led the league with both 116 strikeouts and 131 walks in 197 innings, the highest walk-per-inning ratio until 1938. Never again would his walks top his strikeouts. Old Walter Johnson, the pitcher historians most often compare with Grove, outdueled him, 2-1, on September 7 and went on to win two games in a World Series the Senators lost to Pittsburgh in the eighth inning of Game 7. At thirty-seven, Johnson (second in K's with 108) was two years from retirement. At twenty-five, Grove was two years from becoming a big winner.

There was a silver lining in the gray depression, little noted at the time but long remembered later. Before fifty thousand appreciative fans in the Bronx on July 4, Grove went head-to-head with the Yankee veteran Herb Pennock, a future Hall of Famer pitching "undoubtedly the finest game of a long and distinguished career," according to the New York *Times*. Inning after inning goose eggs were strung across the scoreboard. It was the best kind of baseball: taut, suspenseful, fast-moving. Pennock four-hit the A's, with no walks in what he later called his greatest game. Grove allowed 14 hits and five walks and pitched out of trouble six times, including a bases-loaded, no-out start in the thirteenth.

He would have taken the lead two innings later if Jimmy Dykes hadn't been thrown out by several feet—"open water," in newspaperese—trying to stretch a triple. The Yankees' Bob Veach singled to open the bottom half of the fifteenth, and was sacrificed to second. Grove fanned Lou Gehrig for his tenth strikeout of the long afternoon, but Steve O'Neill singled, scoring Veach on a "dusty slide." Grove had been beaten, literally, by inches. Oh-so-much drama wrapped into two hours and fifty minutes.

It was no fluke performance, either. On September 11, Grove beat the Yankees, 3-2, with a walk and three strikeouts. In the words of a *Times* headline, "Grove Hypnotizes The Yanks In Pinches." He was in control, literally, "pitching within himself," as ballplayers like to say.

There was also good long-range news for the club. Though farmed out most of the season, Jimmie Foxx was promoted to Philadelphia late in the season. In nine appearances as a pinch hitter, he had five singles and a double to hit .667.

A few days before Christmas, the *Evening Bulletin's* John J. Nolan took the eleven-hour train and "motor-ride" route from Philadelphia to Lonaconing, or "Lacone," as the inhabitants called it then. He found the population, which he described as hard-hit miners and "small storekeepers"—a three-year strike had devastated the area—defensive about their boy. "Them empires all need glasses," was a typical refrain.

"Huh, so I'm the wild guy of the league?" Grove roared at Nolan. "I'll show 'em something next year. See that chalk mark on the barn door? I measured off sixty feet. I reckon it is, and at six o'clock every morning I hit the chalk mark twenty times before I quit. Then I tramp the hills hunting and cover about twenty miles a day." Exercise freak Grove often toasted the evening by playing center for the town basketball team.

All winter Grove was usually up doing chores by 5:30 a.m. and asleep by 9 p.m. In his day, many players went to spring training to sober up. In 1926, Lefty arrived in perfect shape, with a mission.

DAYS OF GLORY

★　　　★　　　★　　　★

"I had a fixation about the Yanks. To put it exactly–I hated them. I always played my best against them. They never stopped. They were remorseless, rabid. They drank our blood. They kept right on hitting until they were weary and we were flat."

–Jimmy Dykes,
You Can't Steal First Base

Just when, how, and why Lefty Grove dropped the "s" from his name is unclear. In 1926 the Philadelphia papers were calling him "Groves" and the New York *Times* was referring to him as "Grove." According to one account, Lefty simply corrected reporters who were misspelling his name. That hardly seems right, since they were using his correct family name, Groves. More likely, he gave different versions to different writers, and the name evolved over time. One baseball figure who didn't absorb the change was Lefty's own manager Connie Mack, who never stopped calling him "Groves."

During March of 1926, Lefty was more concerned with his pitching. He warmed up with Earle Mack for twenty minutes a day. "I put nothing on any pitch," he said years later. "I merely concentrated on hitting different spots of the plate, and I finally got so I could throw strikes blindfolded."

Lefty tried a change of pace, slow ball, and a curve. "He's got the stuff, and the batters should be duck soup for him," Kid Gleason, once the Black Sox manager, then an A's executive, told the *Evening Bulletin*. "But to get by in modern baseball, a pitcher needs more than speed. He must watch the bases, have a change of pace and continually outguess the batter."

The A's were favored to win the pennant in 1926. First baseman Joe Hauser, who had missed the entire 1925 season with a broken kneecap, was back. The pitching looked good, the hitting solid. No one tried to read too much into the season opener, a stirring Eddie Rommel-Walter Johnson duel that the Senators won in fifteen innings.

Alas, neither Grove nor the A's could live up to such high expectations. The pitchers had the league's lowest ERA at 3.00 but couldn't seem to win close games. Hauser proved to be a bust. Too much rode on Foxx, who played just twenty-six games, and Cochrane, who dipped to .273. Al Simmons, with nineteen homers, was the only Athletic in double figures. If second baseman Max Bishop led the league with a .987 fielding percentage, Chick Galloway, a .240-hitting and .935-fielding shortstop, took the shine off the keystone combination. As a result, the A's went 83-67 and dropped to third, six games behind the Yankees and three behind the Indians.

Grove's improvement was notable if somewhat misunderstood: strikeouts up from 116 to a league-leading 194, walks reduced from 131 to 101 (no doubt contributing to innings up from 197 to 258), earned-run average down from 4.75 to a league-best 2.51 (in a year when the ball was juiced up). But what stuck in most observers' minds was his record: a

mediocre 13-13. Anyone looking deeper would have understood the apparent contradiction. Before the season was two
months old, the A's had been shut out in four of his starts.
Grove allowed only seven runs in those games. He had to
work for his club-leading 13 wins.

After beating the Red Sox, 3-1, on April 19, Grove struck
out eleven in a 3-0 loss to the Yankees' Sam Jones on April
28. He beat the Yanks five days later and fanned another
eleven in a 6-2 win over the White Sox' Urban "Red" Faber
on May 11. On May 15, Grove shut out the Tigers before
thirty-five thousand Philadelphians, and on May 28 he beat
the Yankees, 2-1, striking out nine batters before another
crowd of thirty-five thousand people in Yankee Stadium.
Even cynical New Yorkers stood up to cheer him; he had
fanned 26 pinstripers in twenty-six innings to date. In May,
he completed seven of eight starts and won five of them.

On June 2, Grove relieved John Picus Quinn with the
bases loaded, no outs, and one run in, struck out the side,
and retired all six Red Sox he faced to preserve a 5-1 win.
Quinn gave Grove a box of cigars. Three days later Lefty
mowed down 10 Browns in a 10-1 win. Then Lefty's support
took three weeks off. He lost, 1-0, to both the White Sox on
June 8 (on a squeeze) and the Indians on June 12 (in eleven
innings, when Tris Speaker scored from second on an infield
single), then allowed no earned runs but lost, 5-3, to the
Tigers on June 19. Five days later he allowed four more
unearned runs in a no-decision against Washington.

"Supported at Last!" the *Evening Bulletin* said when
Grove beat the Yankees, 7-1, on June 28. But mostly he
supported himself that afternoon: 10 strikeouts (including
Babe Ruth twice), only seven hits and, incredibly, not a
single three-ball count. "It's not a nice thing to admit,"
Yankee manager Miller Huggins said, "but I wouldn't want to

Lefty Grove in 1928: a lean, mean machine.
Westbrook Pegler called him "a straight line with ears on it."

face Grove every day he's feeling right. That boy has been taught a lot since last season. Formerly we only looked for speed—he has three different shades, fast, faster and fastest.

"Now he has wide, bending curves, better control, is mentally fit, has a lot of confidence and plenty of natural ability. He mixes his speed and curves and he's the speediest pitcher in baseball." Everyone was on the bandwagon, praising and overstating. Mack actually claimed that Grove had the same disposition after wins and defeats.

Seven days later Grove struck out 12 Yankees—his career high[1], as it turned out—and scored both A's runs on errors in a 2-1 win. Even the opponents were supporting him. Oh, and Lefty had enough left to pitch the last three innings, striking out two, in the second game of the doubleheader. "I trained my eyes during the winter," he told John Nolan. "I knew I could see a deer or bear at five hundred yards and if I could aim a shot at a vulnerable point on that animal at such a distance I certainly should be able throw a ball at a target which is sixty feet, six inches from the pitcher's box."

The Yankees especially must have felt like deer in a headlights. In five starts against them between April 28 and July 5, Grove went 4-1, allowing seven earned runs and fanning 48 in 44 innings. For the season, the Yankees had the league high with four K's a game. Grove more than doubled that total when he faced them.

On September 22, he set down the White Sox, 3-2, in the first Sunday game the A's ever played. (A state supreme court decision delayed the next one for eight years.) And so

---

[1] Why did Grove never strike out more than twelve batters in a game? First, because he was not pitching in a big-strikeout era. Although some batters swung from the heels in imitation of Babe Ruth, most knew that their job was to put the ball in play. Second, Grove was not obsessed with strikeouts. With a superb defense behind him, he was content to let batters hit the ball. Finally, he had no effective set-up pitch to speak of, and batters could expect his heater with two strikes.

DUTCH GROVE?

★   ★   ★   ★

While Grove was learning how to pitch, he may also have been learning about his roots. On a trip to Detroit, Grove got a call at the Statler Hotel from fourteen year-old James (Boyd) Grove, who insisted they were cousins. Lefty was skeptical but had breakfast with the kid and gave him two tickets for a game. Later, Grove, with a box of Sanders chocolates in hand, took a trolley to the Grove house on Cherrylawn Street for Sunday dinner.

Lefty sat with Boyd, his parents, and his four brothers. "We had roast beef with peeled, boiled, browned potatoes," says Boyd Grove, a retired insurance and membership salesman for the Automobile Club of Michigan (AAA). "Mom made lemon and chocolate pie, Lefty's favorite. He had the reputation of being ornery. To me, he was temperamental and a perfectionist. I would congratulate him on his pitching, and he'd shrug it off. It was just his job, and he expected everyone to be as good as he was. At a couple of games, I saw him shake his fist, throw his hat, and stomp on his glove. In the field, if someone dropped a ball or something, he'd blow his top!

"At dinner he was a perfect gentleman. I thought he looked elegant. He had a firm mouth and a good vocabulary. He never smiled much, but he had a deep laugh, showing his teeth."

Afterward, Grove and Boyd Grove's father, Philetus, an ordained Presbyterian minister, sat on the porch, smoked cigars and talked. Reverend Grove gave pitcher Grove the lowdown on the Bible, and some family history, too.

Lefty listened respectfully, always addressing his host as Reverend Grove.

Lefty's known relatives were Maryland miners; his unknown relatives, according to the Reverend, had traveled from the East in the mid-nineteenth century and worked in education, farming, and the ministry. Descendants of Dutch settlers (when Grove isn't an English or Welsh name, it often comes from the Dutch name Groff), they had some epic stories.

Boyd Grove's first cousin and Lefty's cousin once removed was Sally Rand, the fan dancer. Sally was Lefty's age, according to Boyd, though she claimed to be four years younger. She was raised in Hickory County, Missouri, and spent much of her time imitating the movements of swans on the Grove farm pond. First introduced as a nearly nude dancer at the 1932 World's Fair in Chicago, she did her famous fan dance, using ostrich plumes to conceal her body. She always wore spike heels, even on her slippers, not having the Grove family height. Though Sally was a heavy smoker, she danced from 1932 to 1979, when emphysema killed her at age seventy-nine. Another of young Boyd Grove's cousins, Goldianne Guyer Thompson, wrote a noted biography, *Pioneer Living with Mama.*

The Dutch side of the Grove(s) family is not mentioned in Mae Winne's family genealogy, and no definite connection has been established in this research. Nonetheless, anyone meeting Boyd Grove immediately suspects kinship. There are simply too many similarities between he and Lefty: the high forehead; the thick white hair (combed straight back, as was the Grove fashion); the all-arms-and-legs height and trademark lankiness; the broad toothy smile; the long nose.

it went: pitching generally well, splitting decisions. Grove beat the Yankees four of five times. He twice fanned 10 batters, twice fanned 11, once fanned 12, for a career-high five double-figure strikeout games. Only once did he allow more than four earned runs.

This was a mediocre season? Well, yes and no. Lefty was winless, clueless, and probably sleepless in September. In another pattern that would repeat itself, Grove and his teammates faced the Yankees in a late-season series that would determine Philadelphia's year. On August 31, the A's and Yanks began playing seven consecutive games: a series in Philadelphia, a series in New York, then back to Shibe Park. The A's stood in third place at 70-57, nine games behind the Yankees with twenty-four to play, but by no means out of contention. Philadelphia had beaten New York ten out of fifteen times. For his part, Grove was 4-1 against them and due to start twice in the series.

The A's beat Yankee ace Pennock, 8-5, in Yankee Stadium. Then it was Lefty's turn to open September. And he was awful. The Yankees scored twice in the first on a single, a walk, a single, a force, and a sacrifice fly. In the second, Grove walked the bases loaded—two runners would score—and was lifted. "Grove was wild, ineffective and apparently nervous, although why he should be nervous against the Yankees is a mystery," James R. Harrison wrote in the New York *Times*. "Lefty tried to stall his way through trouble and drew the ire of the umpires and fans on his head." Grove didn't take the loss in the 6-4 game, but he may as well have.

The next day's game was rained out, and the teams played a doubleheader at Shibe Park on September 3. With the Yankees comically bad in the field, the A's won the opener, 7-2. Grove was leading the nightcap 3-0 in the fourth, when Mr. Ruth came to the plate. The memory of the 1924

Grove with his Hall of Fame battery mate, Mickey Cochrane.
Black Mike rarely had his pitch selection overruled, but he sometimes
had to anger Grove to get the best from him.

brushback pitch intact, Grove disobeyed Mack's orders and challenged Ruth. Whereupon the Babe homered into the right-field stands. Mack lifted Grove at inning's end, and the Yankees rallied to win, 7-4. They ended the day leading Philadelphia by eight games instead of six.

Pennock shut out the A's, 3-0, the next day. "I used to hate to see Herbie Pennock coming in," Grove's wife Ethel said years later. "My heart used to sink right down to my boots." Well, imagine how she felt two days later, when the Yanks and Athletics played another doubleheader at the Stadium. Philadelphia's Rommel, leading the opener, 2-0, in the seventh, walked Ruth and threw three balls to

Gehrig. At this point Mack summoned Grove. Let's pick up Harrison's account:

"Calling on this flighty pitcher with three and nothing on the batter and two right-handed hitters coming up almost ruined the afternoon for the A's. Grove whirled two strikes over on Gehrig, but the next was ball four. The temperamental southpaw then walked Lazzeri, filling the bases with none out, and tossed one ball to Joe Dugan when Mack yanked him for Howard Ehmke."

It mattered not that the Yankees only scored twice, and the A's won, 5-2. New York won the series closer, 2-1, took the series four games to three, and left town ten games up on fourth-place Philadelphia with seventeen left. On the whole, the A's would have rather been anywhere but in Philadelphia that night.

And our boy? Reflect on Harrison's adjectives: nervous, flighty, temperamental. Not to mention disgraced against the Yanks and ridiculed by New York's paper of record. Grove had little time for beat writers, apparently less for powerful columnists like Grantland Rice, John Kieran, and Joe Williams who shaped public opinion. They retaliated by either ignoring him or slighting him. "He told me his temper originated when he had a conversation with a reporter on a train to Detroit," says Jim Getty, the judge who grew up with Grove's son Bobby. "He said that most of what they discussed didn't appear in the article. Maybe there were things he said or shouldn't have said. Maybe he was misinterpreted. Connie Mack called him into his office and said there would be no more long-distance conversations with reporters."

Grove's teammates were aware that he struggled under pressure and did their best to help him. Grove later said he shook off Cochrane maybe five or six times in the nine years they were together. From the beginning Cochrane had extraordinary physical skills. He handled Grove's fastball, Rube Walberg's curve, Rommel's knuckleball, and Quinn's spitter. He also knew how to handle men. Cochrane rarely socialized with his pitchers, so as to better preserve their professional relationship. He knew whose ego needed massaging, and who needed a kick in the butt. As Bob Broeg wrote, "He inspired great performance out of the mediocre and he also steadied some pitchers whose potential for greatness was sometimes obscured by their erratic temperament."

"Many times in my career I asked pitchers whether they did not think they needed a little help, [only] to get the surprised look of an insulted artist," Cochrane wrote in *Baseball—The Fan's Game*. "Once I asked it of Lefty Grove when we were kids breaking in.

" 'Get back there and do the catching. I'll do the pitching,' he snapped.

"I went back and he nearly tore my hand off with fireballs that the hitter hadn't seen. Lefty had been unconsciously letting up, and when he got sore at me he wanted to knock me out of the park with every pitch."

At other times Cochrane hurled insults at Grove, getting the expected rush of fastballs in return. "Sometimes I was a lot madder at Cochrane than I was at the hitters ..." Grove said. Occasionally, Cochrane's biographer Charles Bevis wrote, the two needed to be separated when Cochrane came to the mound. "Don't put a finger on him," Mack warned Cochrane. "If you do, you'll regret it."

Cochrane wasn't the only teammate to harness Grove's fury. Sometimes when Grove began working too quickly, third baseman Jimmy Dykes went out to slow him down. "When I saw that Grove's temper was rising and his blood pressure going up, I'd go close to the mound (not too close) and hold the ball in my glove," he told *The Sporting News* in 1969. "Lefty would be tense, his eyes narrow. 'Gimme the damn ball,' he would say. But the delay would steady him."

In 1927, the A's had nothing to be ashamed of. They went 91-63, the exact record of the first-place Yankees in '26. They just happened to be favored by most of the writers in spring training, and they just happened to finish second behind the '27 Yankees (110-44), one of the most famous legends in sport.

Violating his policy of building with youth, Mack signed Zack Wheat, Eddie Collins, and Ty Cobb—a six-legged, one-hundred-and-sixteen-year-old veteran with sixty-one years of experience. All hit well, and the .357-hitting Cobb gave the fans a thrill in his penultimate season by stealing home and by catching a fly in short right, then racing in to double up the runner.

Cobb also learned to appreciate someone else as much as himself. In a game with Washington, Mack motioned with his rolled-up scorecard for Cobb to move fifteen feet back on Goose Goslin. Cobb stood still until the infielders shouted, "Go back! Go back!" He finally relented.

Goslin's line drive went directly into Cobb's glove. Running back to the dugout, Cobb was grinning. "That's the first time anyone's told me where to stand," he said upon entering the dugout. "Mr. Mack, you had it exactly right."

Meanwhile, Mack was laying a foundation for the future. Dykes replaced Jim Poole at first and batted .324. Sure-handed Joe Boley (né John Peter Bolinsky), a $65,000 purchase from Baltimore, succeeded Galloway at short. Simmons hit .392.

Grove went 20-13—the first of seven straight twenty-win seasons—with a 3.19 ERA and a league-leading 174 strike-outs. His season did not, however, start well. Mark Koenig went five-for-five and the Yankees racked Grove for eight runs in six innings, winning, 8-3, before sixty-three thousand New Yorkers on Opening Day. Lefty beat New York in his next three decisions, however, and finished strongly with a six-game winning streak in August and September.

A 1-0, four-hit shutout over the Yanks on September 3 deserves special mention. The Yanks went one-two-three over six consecutive innings. In the second, Grove struck out Bob Meusel, Tony Lazzeri, and Joe Dugan on ten pitches, an unparalleled performance against the Yankees, at least as far as the ballpark statisticians of the day could tell. Naturally, the feat grew into a legend in which Grove struck out Ruth, Gehrig, and Meusel on *nine* pitches.

Even John Drebinger of the mighty *Times* was impressed: "A gathering of twenty-five thousand staid Philadelphians sat spellbound here this afternoon as Robert Moses (Lefty) Grove, tall and lean, turned in a performance that no other pitcher in the American League has been able to accomplish this year. In short, he shut out the Yankees, and as the final reckoning showed the Mackmen to have won by 1 to 0, those twenty-five thousand staid Philadelphians became just so many frenzied souls the while they howled a mighty paean."

The win was technically meaningless, because it cut the Yankee lead to seventeen games. However, Drebinger waxed: "The Yanks not only found themselves in the peculiar position of not being able to hit safely, but there were times innumerable when they were unable to connect with the ball at all. Nine of them struck out, the Babe himself being one of the victims, while Lou Gehrig, his eminent rival in the Home Run handicap, closed out a hitless afternoon by fanning for the third and final out of the ninth."

Nonetheless, Grove's most lucrative performance of 1927 was in an exhibition. It was not unusual for major leaguers to pitch in industrial leagues, sometimes under assumed names. In a kind of tacit agreement that ballplayers were underpaid, the big-league clubs willingly cooperated. With the season over for the second-place A's by September 30, East Douglas, the Blackstone Valley champion, met Holy Name of Clinton for the Worcester County, Massachusetts, championship at Worcester's New England Fairgrounds. A highlight of the 109th New England Fair—other treats included whippet and harness races, fly and bait casting, fireworks and vaudeville—it was a serious game, with professionals on both rosters. The East Douglas team used Al Nixon of the Phillies and Johnny Cooney of the Braves, with Washington coach Nick Altrock the designated clown. Soon-to-be Red Sox pitcher "Deacon Danny" MacFayden started for Clinton. Hall of Fame outfielder Jesse (the Crab) Burkett shared umpiring duties with local favorite Billy Summers.

The real catch, of course, was Grove. A millionaire manufacturer named Walter E. Schuster approached him on behalf of East Douglas. "About how much would my services be worth?" Grove asked. The conversation, complete with stilted phraseology the principals probably didn't use, was reported years later by the Philadelphia *Evening Bulletin*'s Raymond A. Hill.

"I was thinking five hundred bucks would be fair, considering the short hours and all."

This was phenomenal money, more than ten percent of an average player's salary. "Sounds fair to middling," said Grove. "But I thought I was through with baseball for the year, and I'm not so keen about putting on the monkey suit before training camp time. Still, a little bonus agreement might make me change my mind—so much, say, for every strikeout, on top of the five hundred bucks."

"How would ten bucks a strike-out hit you?" said Schuster.

"Right on the button it would hit me. Mr. Schuster. You've rented a pitcher."

Grove gave up a bunt single in the first inning. Then he was perfect. In a 4-0 win, Grove struck out 18, at one point whiffing nine straight without allowing a ball. "You gave me a break," Schuster said, handing over $680, "by not bearing down all the way. You're a good-hearted young fellow, by gosh."

"I try to be regular," Grove replied. He was in very regular form—steamed. Even as he pocketed his payoff, Grove began calculating what would have happened in extra innings.

"I'm sorry that guy MacFayden couldn't have held our side scoreless so that the game might have gone fifteen or sixteen innings," he said. "Boy, it was soft mowing them down, and I'd have made a regular cleanup only for Danny Mac." Evidently, Grove had visions of striking out thirty!

★ ★ ★ ★

In 1928 the name Grove was finally used universally. That aside, 1928 was one of the most disappointing years in Grove's career. It was certainly a sore point for the Philadelphia Athletics. Cobb and newly acquired Tris Speaker played their last seasons. Cobb, forty-one, somehow hit .323 in 353 at bats, while Speaker, forty, hit .267 in 191. Foxx was moved around too much—sixty games at third, thirty at first, nineteen at catcher—hitting .327 with 13 homers. Fortunately, Cochrane was the league's Most Valuable Player, rookie George (Mule) Haas—a clutch performer in the future—hit .280 and right-fielder Edmund (Bing) Miller[2], back from the Browns after a 1-1/2-season fur-

---

[2] Miller was a well-tanned farm boy from Vinton, Iowa. When he walked to his position, black fans in Shibe Park's fenced-in right-field stands greeted him warmly. According

lough with the Browns, reestablished himself as a popular favorite. Getting 42 wins from Grove (24-8), and the forty-five-year-old Quinn, (18-7) the A's won 98 games. They weren't enough. Losing was bad enough. What really hurt was losing the pennant by 2-1/2 games to the *Yankees*.

"They were terribly disliked in Philadelphia," Allen Lewis, an eleven-year-old Philadelphian at the time who later covered baseball for the Philadelphia *Inquirer*, told *Sports Illustrated*'s William Nack. "The papers used to write 'Noo Yawk Yankees.' It was ridiculous, but they did."

Boston had been the nation's first city in early colonial times, then Philadelphia in the eighteenth century (beginning, it says here, on the day in 1723 when Benjamin Franklin disembarked at the Market Street Wharf). In 1828, the Erie Canal opened the hinterlands to New York as no other metropolis, and there was no turning back. Philadelphia was reduced to second city.

"The battle between New York and Philadelphia in baseball was symbolic of that battle for urban supremacy," Bruce Kuklick told *SI*'s Nack.

And who was most responsible for losing this heartbreaking pennant to the Yankees and New York? Well, Lefty was once more the convenient scapegoat. The Yankees and A's made a two-team race of it. On July 4, the A's were 13-1/2 games out. After winning twenty-five of thirty-three games in July, they climbed to first, half a game ahead of New York, on September 8. Next day the A's and Yankees opened another critical late-season series with a doubleheader at Yankee Stadium. The problem was not merely Stadium mystique; visiting teams had to go through the Yankee dugout to reach

---

to the fevered imagination of AP sportswriter Edward J. Neil, who probably never visited the black section, they called out, "Looka that black boy playin' with them white folks. Now ain't he sumpin?" Teammates called Miller "Black Man" and "Dark Folks."

their own. As the A's passed through, young Leo Durocher, cocky as ever, glared at them. "You bums!" he shouted. "So you're in first. By the end of the day you'll be back in second." He was predicting a doubleheader sweep, and he got it. The Yankees won 3-0, 7-3, before an announced 85,265 fans— the Yankees later corrected the figure to seventy-five thousand—the biggest crowd, as the media pointedly noted, ever to watch baseball in the United States, Australia, Mexico, or Tierra del Fuego. On Monday, September 10, now 1-1/2 games out, the A's called on Grove to win what could only be described as a must game.

Going into the season, Grove had a 10-6 record against the Yankees. After getting shelled by them on Opening Day, he five-hit them on April 20, but neither the Yankees nor their writers were especially impressed. "It seems to me that Grove makes a mistake in not experimenting more with a change of pace and a less-trying delivery," Dan Daniel wrote. The Yankees beat Grove the next four times out. But by September 13, Grove had won 14 straight, just two short of the American League record held by Walter Johnson and Smokey Joe Wood since 1912. While beating the Indians, 3-1, on August 23, Lefty struck out three battters on nine pitches in the second, then needed eight deliveries to fan the first two hitters in the third. Eighteen days later, he was primed for the Yanks.

Grove took a 3-0 lead into the seventh. Bob Meusel led off by singling and was forced at second by Tony Lazzeri. After a double by Mike Gazella, the Yankees had two men in scoring position and their biggest threat of the game. A Ben Paschal groundout scored Lazzeri, but that was all the damage. The score was 3-1, still Lefty's game to win or lose. The numbers looked good: six more outs, fifteenth straight win, a mere half-game deficit at day's end.

After Babe Ruth's running catch prevented the A's from scoring in their half of the eighth, Grove walked to the mound. It was a moment that would be recalled endlessly as the years passed: the great man at the peak of his powers, ready to take his team down the stretch. And then....

Earle Combs walked on a 3-2 pitch. Third baseman Dykes knocked down Mark Koenig's smash, holding him to a single, then threw wildly past first, allowing Combs to reach third. Things were starting to unravel. Grove never threw at Gehrig because he didn't want to awaken a "sleeping dog." But his control, not to mention his self-control, was gone. He threw a wild pitch past Gehrig, Combs scoring and Koenig advancing to second. Then Grove threw unintentionally close to Gehrig. The Iron Man ducked and the ball hit his bat, looping into left for a single scoring Koenig to tie the score at 3-3. Gehrig took second on the throw home.

Curse the luck! With Ruth batting, Lefty's history with the Yankees may well have flashed before him: the brush-back pitch in 1924, the riding, the frustration of pitching generally well against them yet trailing them constantly in the standings. And now the Yankees had tied the score. Been handed two runs, really. What more? Ruth, with his wonderful sense of theater, bunted on the first pitch—foul by inches. Just think of it: Babe Ruth giving himself up to move Gehrig ninety feet. Or beat out a bunt. The Babe was saying simply this, "I can beat you every which way, busher."

Ruth took a ball. Then, on a 1-1 fastball—*mano-à-mano* combat, you give me your best, I'll give you mine—Ruth homered deep to right to give the Yankees their final 5-3 margin. Not even old Ty Cobb, popping out in his last official at bat, could bring the A's back.

When Grove lost, it was nothing for him to rip open his shirt, with buttons flying. Here he had lost more: his game, his streak, his season, his composure. "He suffered the agonies of the damned every time he lost a ball game," Dykes wrote. "His morning sulks annoyed us, but we stood 'em for we knew that Lefty would always give his all to win."

The morning after this particularly excruciating loss, the New York media staged an in-your-face celebration. "It was the Ruth, the whole Ruth and nothing but the Ruth," Richards Vidmer wrote in the *Times*. "The Babe stepped out of a story book and with one colossal clout broke a tie score, Bob Grove's winning streak and the Athletics' hearts."

Vidmer fleshed it out: "His big bat swung, a crackling sound split the tense silence. A ball sailed high and far toward the bleachers and then the thunder broke loose. A scream of delight went up from the multitude that echoed and re-echoed while the mighty busters of the Bronx trotted around the bases. Straw hats rained on the field, mingling with the torn and tattered bits of paper that had fluttered down when Gehrig had driven in the tying run with a single a moment before. The Yankees had beaten back the enemy for the third straight day."

It was all part of a piece. New York governor Al Smith was winning the Democratic nomination for president. New York mayor Jimmy Walker was getting to meetings on time, a real stop-the-presses event. And now this. The cocky bastards. The ignominy of it all. Noo Yawk, Noo Yawk.

Down 2-1/2 games, the A's never caught up. They finished at 98-55, a great team beaten by the greater Yankees (101-53). Grove lost six of seven decisions to the '28 Yankees, including four losses to one Henry Johnson, who baffled Lefty as no other pitcher did in one season. Lefty was now 11-12 lifetime against New York. Even in seeming disgrace, however, he had built up his legend. While beating Chicago 5-3 on September 27, he fanned Moe Berg, Tommy Thomas, and

*He was not called the Tall Tactician for nothing. Connie Mack
always appeared erect in the dugout, his suit and hat in place,
pencil and scorecard in hand.*

Johnny Mostil on nine pitches in the seventh inning. His 24 wins and 183 strikeouts led the league, and his 2.58 ERA placed a close third.

Nonetheless, Lefty Grove had a very bad winter, and memories of the Yankee humiliation were only part of it. Early in November, Grove was hunting in Middle Ridge, West Virginia, with Roberdeau Green Annan, twenty-four, a refractories broker. Reportedly, Annan came over the top of a wooded hill and Grove mistook him for game. Birdshot lodged in his left eye, leaving him partially blind and completely litigious. He went to court and charged $100,000 worth of damages.

According to Annan, Grove ignored a basic hunting rule. "When two hunters are paired," Annan told a jury in Cumberland, Maryland, at the trial two years later, "it is a rule for the one on the right to shoot only the birds which fly to the right, while the man on the left shoots only the birds which fly to the left." Grove declared himself unfamiliar with the rule and got two experts to agree.

On February 5, 1931, Grove was found not liable. A's teammates Bill Shores, Bing Miller, Rube Walberg, and Jimmy Dykes were in the courtroom. Visibly relieved by the decision, Grove said he had been unable to pitch effectively in 1929 and 1930. You be the judge.

In 1929, Mack's fifteen-year pennantless streak ended. The A's went 104-46, whipping the Yankees, who were saddened by the death of manager Miller Huggins, by eighteen games. Another of Lefty's old Orioles teammates put the last piece in the championship puzzle. He was nerveless, fun-loving George Earnshaw, a high-kicking fastballer with a sharp-breaking curve who led the league with 24 wins in his first full season. Foxx was finally given a place in the lineup, at first base, and hit .354, with 33 homers and 118 runs batted in. At twenty-one, he was finally on the way to becoming arguably the greatest righthanded slugger in American League history.

There were five other .300 hitters with at least 400 at bats—Haas (.313), Dykes (.327), Simmons (.365), Miller (.335), and Cochrane (.331). Miller stole 24 bases. Second baseman Bishop, the underrated catalyst, walked a league-leading 128 times.

The Yankees had Ruth, Gehrig, and Lazzeri as their three-four-five hitters, the A's had Cochrane, Simmons, and Foxx. Let's consider the Philadelphia A's Murderers Row.

After starring in baseball, football, basketball, track, and boxing at Boston University, Mickey Cochrane became the greatest catcher in baseball history. An exceptionally fast runner and a superb hitter for his position, he fanned less often—only eight times in 606 appearances during the '29 season—than any full-time catcher in history. Benefiting from Cy Perkins' catching instruction, Cochrane was midway through eleven consecutive seasons of 100 or more games. Mack considered him the key to pennants in 1929-31.

In 1929, Black Mike played in 135 games, hit .331, and drove in 95 runs. The Yankees' Bill Dickey played in 130 games, batted .324, and drove in 65.

Bucketfoot Al Simmons attracted notice by stepping down the third-base line—into the bucket—as he took his stance. Nonetheless, he stepped forward while swinging, kept his left shoulder perpendicular to the mound, and sprayed balls all over the park with one of the longest bats anyone had ever seen. He had tremendous power to left, but the wickedly slicing balls he hit to right gave fielders even more trouble. Ty Cobb called him "the gamest man in baseball with two strikes on him." After both men left the A's—Simmons was with the White Sox, Lefty the Red Sox—Lefty found him the toughest righthander he ever faced. Far from fearing pitchers, Simmons held them in contempt. "They're trying to take the bread and butter out of my mouth," he'd say.

A strong-armed left-fielder—he twice led all AL outfielders in fielding percentage—Simmons was the Athletics' Gehrig. In 1929, he had 34 homers and a league-leading 157 RBI while batting .365. Gehrig had 35 homers, 126 RBIs, and an anemic (for him) .300 average.

With his broad shoulders, shirt-busting biceps, and square jaw—he was six feet tall and weighed 195 pounds, gargantuan numbers for the age—good-natured Jimmie Foxx was called the Beast. To others, he was the A's Ruth. In 1929, Foxx's .364 average, with 33 homers, and 118 RBIs gave Ruth (.345, 46, and 154) some competition for a change. The Babe was king, yet many observers considered Foxx the strongest hitter in baseball history. "I never saw anyone hit a baseball harder," said Ted Williams, later a teammate of Foxx's in Boston.

"He even has muscles in his hair," an opposing pitcher said. In Shibe Park, Foxx homered over the two-tiered left-field stands. In Chicago, he hit a ball an estimated six hundred feet. With a prodigious blow off Lefty Gomez, he shattered a seat three rows from the top of Yankee Stadium. Foxx considered that shot his longest homer ever. Years later Gomez and his wife, watching the men on the moon, saw one astronaut pick up a strange white object. "I wonder what that is," said Mrs. Gomez.

"That's the ball Foxx hit off me in New York," said Lefty.

Philadelphia's Lefty—the fourth Hall of Famer on this extraordinary team—had no peer on the Yankees or anywhere else in baseball. By 1929, he had turned the corner and rounded the bend. He was walking tall. More than earning his $20,000 salary, Grove went 20-6 and led the league in winning percentage (.769), strikeouts (170), and ERA

*In 1929, the A's broke through and won their first pennant in fifteen years.
Virtually an all-star lineup, they fielded (uniformed, from left) Eddie
Collins, Jimmy Dykes, Max Bishop, Jimmie Foxx, Mickey Cochrane, Al
Simmons, Lefty Grove, and George Earnshaw.
Their well-dressed attendants were not identified.*

(2.81). Indeed, that big-bopping season he was baseball's
only pitcher with an ERA under 3.00. Of supreme importance to the Gotham jinx, he beat the Yanks in their Bronx
opener, 7-4, on April 21—and beat his old nemesis, Henry
Johnson, who lasted just two-thirds of an inning.

On May 17, Grove beat the Senators, 4-1, throwing his
first ever complete-game victory ever over them. One jinx
down, another to go.

"I've been catching Lefty for five years, and I don't think
he ever hurled a better game," Cochrane insisted, even
though Grove yielded seven hits and six walks. "He was wild
because he was trying so hard to win. Imagine Washington
with 13 men left on base."

After Grove, now 11-1, held the Yankees to one run on
June 21, striking out six and walking none, Ruth conceded,
"When that guy is right, there isn't a team, and never has
been a team, that could lick him....Today he was the greatest
pitcher I ever faced. He had everything."

"The fast one looked like a marble and the curve broke as if it were running on a track." ("As if it were"? The media protected the Babe day and night.)

Added another shellshocked Yankee, Lyn Lary, who normally had so much success against Lefty he called him his "cousin," "If there is a man in baseball who can throw a ball faster than Grove, he must have a cannon up his sleeve."

On July 4—always a big day for Grove—he struck out 10 batters in the first five innings and 11 overall in a 3-1 morning win over the Red Sox. Cochrane supported him with three doubles and a solo homer. John Picus Quinn beat the Sox, 8-1, in the afternoon to put the A's, already an otherworldy 53-17 (.757), 9-1/2 games ahead of second-place New York. Grove was 13-2.

But he was only human—all too human. On July 16, Grove was facing the Indians in Cleveland's League Park when things began to go bad in the fifth inning. "I was playing short and Max Bishop was at second," Dykes told the Cleveland *Plain Dealer*'s Hal Lebovitz years later. "Grove was pitching. First Bishop fumbled a grounder. The next batter hit one right at me, an easy double play ball. I fumbled it.

"Grove was so put out he began to toss the ball to the batters. Luckily we got out of the inning without any damage.

"All of us came back to the bench mumbling about Grove. We were only two games ahead of the Yankees at the time [actually eight] and it meant a lot to us. Mr. Mack heard us grumble and he said, 'Boys, do you want me to take Robert out?' He always called him Robert.

"All of us said, 'Yes.'

"Mr. Mack looked down the bench toward Grove and said, 'Robert, that'll be all today for you.'

"Grove stood up and yelled, 'To hell with you, Mr. Mack.'

"Mr. Mack got up, walked all the way over to Grove, pointed

his finger at his chest and said quietly, 'And the hell with you, too, Robert.' You know, Mr. Mack never cussed. We had never heard him use that word before. The way he did it made all of us laugh. Even Grove. He picked up his glove and walked out of the dugout, laughing all the way."

With Grove at 17-2 on July 28, a New York *World* writer wondered if he'd win 30 and speculated on the reasons for his success. "This year the leftsider has slowed up a bit, with the result that he is pitching to the batters instead of at them."

And pacing himself, as he did on August 14. Breaking a twenty-day winless streak, he beat the Indians, 5-3, in the longest outing of his career, a seventeen-inning, sixty-eight-at bat marathon. Sustained excellence will make you a Hall of Famer, but an epic performance—a called-shot homer, a shot heard 'round the world—will make you a legend. Pitching seventeen innings didn't grab enough headlines, and it may have drained Grove. He was only 2-4 from there on, but he finished the season with three scoreless innings against the Yankees in a Series warmup. Overall, he was 2-1, with two saves, against them.

Oh, Philadelphians were enjoying their triumph. Describing a Shibe Park doubleheader between the teams, a *Times* man marveled:

"The overflow crowd outside the park was the largest in the club's history, according to police officials. Mounted policemen were employed to control the surging masses, and police reserves had to be summoned. The thirty-six thousand seats in the stands were filled an hour before the game. Perhaps ten thousand more fans clogged every aisle, clung to steel girders under the grandstand roof around three sides of the field, and mounted even the roof of the left-field stand, a thousand strong.

"Across the street from the low right-field wall the roofs of a

DAYS OF INFAMY

☆   ☆   ☆   ☆

At the Hall of Fame one day, baseball historian John B. Holway asked Grove about his record in all-star games against teams from the Negro leagues. "I have never," Grove said, staring at his questioner, "played against blacks in my life."

Actually, Grove had no objection to integrated games and routinely played in them. His problem was that he often lost. Negro leagues data were haphazardly reported, especially by the white press, but box scores uncovered by Holway substantiate Lefty's frustration.

In 1926, a black team composed mostly of players from the Homestead Grays and Philadelphia Hilldales played a six-game series against an American League all-star team with batting champ Heinie Manush and MVP George Burns. In the second game, at Shibe Park on October 2, Grove and Nip Winters, the best black left-hander of the time, squared off before nine thousand spectators. Behind Oscar Charleston's three hits, including a triple, Winters beat Grove, 6-1.

Grove pitched a scoreless tenth inning in game three, won by the white team, 11-6. In the sixth game, played October 7 in Bloomsburg, Pennsylvania, spitballer Phil Cockrell shut out Grove, 3-0. The blacks won the series, five games to one.

On October 14, 1930, in Baltimore, Luther (Red) Farrell and the Baltimore Black Sox faced Grove, who did not have a complete all-star team behind him. He did have A's second baseman Max Bishop (.316), Braves first baseman Johnny Neun (.213), and Phils catcher

Virgil (Spud) Davis (.280). Though Grove struck out 10 Black Sox, he walked seven, allowed 11 hits, and lost, 9-3.

If Grove was embarrassed by his record in integrated play, his opponents didn't lord their victories over him. To the contrary, they showed him nothing but respect. Outfielder Norman (Turkey) Stearnes, a prodigious power hitter, told Holway:

"Lefty Grove and Satchel Paige are about the two hardest pitchers ever put on a glove. I've hit at a lot of people, I've hit at George Earnshaw, Red Ruffing, a lot of them, but I don't think anyone threw as hard as those two boys. I'd sit and watch them when I wasn't playing and they were in town. Grove could throw hard like that all day long."

row of buildings were terraced with a thatchwork of humanity extending the whole block. The right-field wall, though fortified with barbed wire, was stormed by the overflow just as the first game started. Perhaps a thousand dauntless fans cascaded over the wall into the park without paying before the police organized a successful counterattack."

Most great World Series are best remembered for a single contest: Game Six in 1975, Game Seven in 1960, Game Five in 1956, to name a few. The 1929 Philadelphia-Chicago Series should be remembered for at least three.

It began with the most famous managerial decision in postseason history, one that directly concerned Grove. Connie Mack didn't announce his Game One starter until minutes before the game. "Hey, Jim, look who's warming up!" Simmons exclaimed to Dykes.

It was Howard Ehmke, a thirty-five year-old journeyman who at the time had a 166-165 record over fourteen seasons, had pitched 54-2/3 innings all season, hadn't started in seven weeks, and had been told he'd be released at season's end.

"What's the matter with you two?" Mack scolded.

"If Ehmke's good enough for you, he's good enough for us," Simmons said, recovering quickly.

In neither his next-day column in the Philadelphia *Inquirer* nor his memoir *My 66 Years in the Big Leagues* did Mack explain his decision. Newspapermen at the Series and historians have concluded that Mack feared the Cubs' righthanded hitters, especially Hack Wilson, Kiki Cuyler, and Rogers Hornsby—hence no starts for lefties Grove and Walberg—and felt Ehmke's sidearm collection of curves and off-speed fastballs would keep them off the plate, off-balance, and partially blinded by the white shirts in the Wrigley Field stands. Latter-day speculators point to Grove's recent ineffectiveness; he had failed to complete his past four starts and had ripped skin on his throwing fingers. The fact that neither Grove nor fellow lefty Walberg started in the Series would seem to confirm the first theory. It should be noted, however, that Mack meant to use Grove in relief every day if necessary.

In any case, Mack told Ehmke to scout the Cubs when they visited the Phillies. He did his homework well. Using a curve, a fastball, and a changeup, he had the Cubs flailing wildly, 13 of them striking out for a Series record that would last twenty-four years. Foxx broke the scoreless tie with a seventh-inning homer, the A's got two unearned runs in the ninth, and a Chicago last-ditch run was wasted. A's 3, Cubs 1. "The long right arm of Howard Ehmke, the Philadelphia veteran, sounded the drum beat of woe to fifty-one thousand Chicago rooters this afternoon as it fell across the back of the Cubs like a whip," Grantland Rice wrote. Rice described "a fine, slow curve." *Inquirer* reporter S. O. Grauley, referred to a "sharp-breaking hook." The writers were as baffled as the hitters.

There was a delicious subplot. Cochrane teased the Cub bench so mercilessly and profanely during Game One that Commissioner Kenesaw Mountain Landis threatened to suspend him. "Hello, sweethearts," Cochrane subsequently greeted the Cubs. "We're gonna serve tea this afternoon!"

In Game Two, George Earnshaw struck out seven Cubs but fell apart after 4-2/3 innings, and left Grove to protect a 6-3 lead with two men on base. He promptly struck out pinch hitter Gabby Hartnett on five pitches. "He took savage lunges, but it was like a befoozled chap trying to hit a fly with a swatter after an all-night party," wrote Grauley.

"If Grove was nervous, so was Bismarck before the French diplomats in the 1870 Treaty," Grauley metaphored on. Like a fire hose in a wastebasket, Grove simply smothered the hitters: six strikeouts, three hits, one walk, and no runs over 4-1/3 innings. The A's won 9-3, Foxx again contributing a key homer. Though Earnshaw failed to complete the fifth inning, the official scorer gave him the victory. Grove was left to enjoy the greatest long-relief save in Series history. "I want to say that when Grove goes into a game that has only five innings or so to last that there is nobody in his class," Mack wrote in his daily Series column.

Mere numbers don't convey Grove's effect on the Cubs. Catcher Hartnett, who fanned both times he faced Grove in the Series, wailed an old refrain. "How can you hit the guy," Hartnett asked, "when you can't see him?"

The Cubs had been baffled by the A's starter in Game One. They were overwhelmed by the A's reliever in Game Two. A's pitchers had struck out 13 Cubs in each game. A's hitters had homered three times (the Cubs were having trouble getting the ball out of the infield). A's fans were talking sweep.

No such luck. The Series moved to Philadelphia. Earnshaw lost Game Three, 3-1, and the Cubs had Game

Murderer's Row South. In 1929, Jimmie Foxx, Mickey Cochrane, and Al Simmons combined for 74 homers, 370 RBIs, and a .350 batting average. Up in New York, Lou Gehrig, Bill Dickey, and Babe Ruth had 91 homers, 345 RBIs, and a .320 average.

Four wrapped up, leading, 8-0, in the seventh. Cub pitcher Guy Bush, the winner of Game Three, wrapped himself in a blanket and started doing a war dance. When Simmons hit a terrific home run to the roof over the left-field pavilion, the A's were satisfied they wouldn't be shut out. Then came singles by Foxx, Miller (misplayed by center fielder Hack Wilson), and Dykes (scoring Foxx).

Mack told Joe Boley, "I think he's losing his stuff. Just swing at the first pitch." Boley did and got the A's fourth straight single, scoring Miller.

One out later. Bishop scored Dykes with a single to center, and Cubs manager Joe McCarthy summoned Art Nehf to replace starter Charlie Root. The score was 8-4.

Each time the A's tallied, a crowd in Philadelphia's City Hall Plaza, hearing the piped in play-by-play and watching steel figures moved on a magnetic scoreboard, cheered mightily. They were growing louder and louder.

Mule Haas hit a line drive to center. Poor Hack Wilson, entering the personal hell of people who would be too often remembered for a single embarrassing moment, lost the ball in the bright sunshine. While he raced back in search of it, Boley and Bishop scored. Embarrassment enough, until Haas also scored on the inside-the-park homer. It was now 8-7.

Dykes, on the bench, shouted "We're back in the game!" and pounded the man next to him. It was Connie Mack.

"Sorry," said Dykes.

"That's all right, Jimmy," said Mack, a scrawny sixty-six. "Wasn't it wonderful?"

Everyone at City Hall Plaza was convinced the A's would win. After walking Cochrane—more raucous cheers from afar—Nehf was taken out for Sheriff Blake.

The A's shot the sheriff. Simmons singled. Foxx rifled one through the box, scoring Cochrane and making it 8-8. At Philadelphia's Franklin Field, young Allen Lewis was watching Penn play Virginia Poly in football. The scoreboard said, 8-0. "And then the crowd erupted," Lewis told *Sports*

Illustrated years later. "In the bottom of the seventh they put '8' up on the board. Play on the field stopped, and all the players turned around and looked up."

The A's shot the deputy, too. Pat Malone replaced Blake. Pitching inside to Miller, Malone grazed him. The bases were now loaded. Dykes came to bat. In his memoir he described what happened next:

"Malone set me up with a strike across the letters. I knew what was coming. Malone was a fastball pitcher. Another fast one was coming. I got set. I swung. The crack of the bat was sweet music for my ears. As I rounded first I saw [Riggs] Stephenson chasing the ball. I headed for second, slid, made it. Simmons and Foxx were home!"

While running for first, Dykes never saw the ball glance off leftfielder Stephenson's glove. Many felt he should have had it. Two goats in one Series! Two goats in one inning! The score was now 10-8.

When Lefty Grove appeared in the top of the eighth, A's fans everywhere celebrated the win. It was as sure a bet as ever existed in sport. Three up, three down in the eighth. Like clockwork: Charlie Grimm grounded to short, Danny Taylor and Hartnett struck out. Three up, three down in the ninth. Norm McMillan struck out. Woody English struck out. Hornsby flied to right. Over and out.

In his two appearances, Grove had struck out 10 batters in 6-1/3 innings. Heywood Broun's quote is worth repeating. "When danger beckoned thickest," he wrote, "it was always Grove who stood towering on the mound, whipping over strikes against the luckless Chicago batters."

Down three games to one, the Cubs took a 2-0 lead into the ninth inning of Game Five. With one out, the crowds in Shibe Park began walking to the exits, watching the game over their shoulders. With two strikes on him, Max Bishop singled over third, and some in the crowd of thirty thousand began returning to their seats. Even President Herbert Hoover, who had buttoned his overcoat while his wife Lou donned her suede gloves, paused in his bunting-wreathed box down the third-base line. Mule Haas planted him there with a two-run, game-tying homer over the right-field wall. Mayor Mackey plunged from the stands and embraced Haas as he was mobbed by teammates.

Again, a sense of inevitability reigned in the A's dugout, a sense of dread in the Cubs'. Cochrane grounded out but Simmons doubled and Foxx was intentionally walked.

Miller, a noted breaking-ball hitter, looked for a curve, got a fastball, and doubled to the scoreboard, Simmons streaking home with the Series-winning run. Mayor Mackey again vaulted over the railing, this time tossing his hat in the air.

Commissioner Landis made his way around the clubhouse, using hand-to-hand combat to advance from one locker to another. At length he spotted Cochrane. "When are you going to serve that cake and tea, Mike?" Landis kidded.

Mack won the city's Edward W. Bok Award for service.

☆   ☆   ☆   ☆

Ten days later, on October 24, 1929, Grove was honored by the Junior Order of the United American Mechanics:

LEFTY GROVE SILENT AT FESTIVE BOARD

MECHANICS TENDER HURLER DINNER,
BUT HE FAILS TO MAKE AN ADDRESS

There were two hundred and fifty members at Degenhardt's Banquet Hall to honor their brother—one assumes honorary—member Lefty. He just said "Thanks" many times.

Perhaps Grove was focused on a homecoming banquet in his honor at Lonaconing's Central High School scheduled for six days later. Sponsored by the Lonaconing Business Men's Association, the event included a meal of Maryland baked ham with apple sauce, prepared by the school home economics club and the Lonaconing Nutrition Group of the American Red Cross. Someone wrote a song in Lefty's honor, with the rousing chorus:

> *How do you do, how do you do*
> *Here's to you, here's to you*
> *How do you do, how do you do,*
> *Here's to you, here's to you;*
> *From the far off Western plain,*
> *To the rocky coast of Maine,*
> *They are singing loud your fame,*
> *Hurrah for you, you, you.*

Not even the stock-market crash one day before the banquet could have spoiled the fun. Besides, Lefty handsomely survived the crash, thanks at least in part to Connie Mack.

"Robert, where do you have your money deposited?" Mack asked him earlier in his career.

"In a local bank," said Grove.

Whereupon Mack asked him to move the money to a Philadelphia bank that didn't close down during the panic. He apparently moved some but not all of his money there. According to reports, he also invested in government bonds. He did not gamble on the stock market, though he was certainly affected by how the great crash affected others. "I do not have to remind you," he said years later, "of those dark days when the banks closed down."

After the 1929 World Series, Lefty might have taken stock and considered his career. Notwithstanding five seasons in the minors, he was lucky to be discovered in Midland, lucky to be discovered in Martinsburg, exceptionally lucky to be sent to two excellent professional teams, both with managers who could handle him.

And lucky to be liked in Philadelphia. "I never did get his autograph," says Mickey Vernon, a Philadelphia-area youngster who later became a two-time American League batting champion. "He would walk right by you."

Despite his occasionally embarrassing public appearances, Lefty was viewed as both an icon and an idol. "His arm looked twenty feet long," says Wayne Ambler, another Philadelphia kid and later an A's infielder after Grove left for Boston. "He just threw it by them."

Especially popular in his hometown, Grove spent $5,700 to open his own establishment, Lefty's Place, a nifty hangout housing three bowling alleys, a pool table, and a counter with cases of cigars, cigarettes, candy, and soft drinks. Lonaconing's first citizen employed his out-of-work brother, Dewey, who had lost his job when the glass factory burned down, and his physically challenged brother-in-law, Bob Mathews.

In 1930, the A's went 102-52, topping the Senators by eight games and the suddenly woebegone Yankees by 16. Lefty was unchanged in personality as well as pitching. When rookie Doc Cramer doubled off him in an intrasquad game, Grove hit him in the ribs the next time he came to the plate. "I thought it was an accident," Cramer said, "until a few days later, when I bounced a ball off Grove's shins in a pepper game. Sure enough, the next time I hit against him, he bruised my ribs again."

Grove underwent another name change. In fact, two. The word Lefty was no longer being put in quotes. He was now referred to as Robert Moses (Lefty) Grove. Gamblers called him Man O'War. And he pitched like one. In his best season by far—some called it his best ever—he went 28-5 and led the league in wins, strikeouts (209), and an ERA (2.54) fully .77 ahead of the league's next-best pitcher. Wins, ERA, and strikeouts are considered a pitcher's Triple Crown.

(He also led the league with nine saves, although the figure wasn't tabulated until years later.) This in the supreme live-ly-ball year—"There is no other plausible explanation [for so much hitting]," George Will wrote in *Bunts*—when the National League hit .303 and the American .288.

★　　★　　★　　★

Some memories:
April 15: Grove beat the Yankees' George Pipgras, 6-2, with Henry Johnson pitching mop-up for the losers. Starts against New York, however, and quickly became the exception rather than the rule. When Mack decided to rest Grove in games he might conceivably lose, Lefty pitched just 38-1/3 innings agains the Yanks in 1930-31.

May 18: Grove shut out the Senators 1-0, the A's getting their run when Al Simmons broke up a possible double play witha a hard slide at second.

May 30, June 1: First, Grove survived an exhausting no-decision game in which he faced thirty-five batters, yielding nine hits, four walks, and six runs, while fanning six in nine innings. Two days later, after battering poor coach Earle Mack in a thirty-minute pregame warmup, Grove trudged out of the bullpen and after a walk struck out the last two batters of the game to preserve a win.

June 23: Grove beat the White Sox 2-1, with 11 K's.

July 25: While Lefty beat the Indians, 14-1, his teammates executed two triple steals.

August 4: Grove beat the Red Sox, 13-4, and homered.

August 12: After Grove's 9-1 win over the Indians, Cochrane told the *Evening Bulletin's* Nolan, "The dope on Lefty is that he now saves himself and doesn't bear down all the time, just when he has to."

August 25: Joe Cronin and Sad Sam Jones destroyed what would have been a 16-game winning streak—Lefty had won eight straight before, and won another seven straight to finish the season—while Washington beat Philadelphia, 3-2.

September 1: In what the *Inquirer's* Isaminger called "a copyrighted situation," Grove faced Ruth with the A's leading 5-2, two on, and two out in the ninth. With a 2-2 count, the great man threw and the great man missed. Some seventy-four thousand voices in Yankee Stadium were hushed. [Grove appreciated the whoosh of silence. Like a Jamesian Englishman, he was never so happy as when holding his tongue.]

September 3-16: Grove won four games in seven days, five games in eleven days, and six games in fourteen days, including one relief performance in which he retired all nine batters he faced and beat the Red Sox for the seventh time of the season. "Grove relishes the job of being assigned to toss up his fireballs and squelch a rally," Nolan wrote.

Sept. 18: "I don't know how we possibly could have won without Grove's remarkable work," Mack told the *Record's* Bill Dooly. "Grove has worked harder than any pitcher I recall of recent years."

An athlete succeeds for three reasons. First, he has a body capable of great athletic feats—or of being trained to produce them. Second, he has good training habits. (O.K., the Babe didn't train, but the Babe was the Babe.) Third, perhaps most important, is his mental approach. Lefty's rules for success, widely circulated and posted:

1) Attend to business.
2) Eat regularly, get at least eight hours' sleep—especially from 10 p.m. to 2 a.m., when sleep is soundest—and observe moderate habits.
3) Don't "know it all"—give the other fellow credit for a little knowledge.

His baseball persona established, Lefty left his fans hungry for more personal details. What was Lefty like at home? Ethel, whom the newspapers always referred to only as "Mrs. Robert Moses Grove," shed light on his life in an interview with the *Evening Bulletin*'s Helen O. Mankin before the 1930 World Series.

Lefty was superstitious, his wife reported. He spat when he saw a load of hay, saying, "Now we'll win one today." He wore hairpins in his coat lapel for good luck. At 6-foot-2-1/2 inches and 174 pounds, according to the story, Grove ate sparingly and was usually halfway through his meal by the time his wife got her own food on the table. "He is said to feel more at home with thousands of baseball fans looking on, than in a parlor where there are a dozen people," Mankin reported. "Lefty drives his wife to the theater and calls for her, but seldom goes to see a show." The car? "The Groves have a new automobile, a big blue one, an expensive make. It has a small white elephant on the door [honoring both the A's logo and Lefty's political party of choice], with 'Lefty' underneath it and is equipped with a radio."

For her part, Ethel "is friendly, her brown eyes dance, and she seems to have the best time over trifles." She pronounced herself content to run a seven-room home, bake cake and chocolate fudge for Lefty, and embroider pillow cases and centerpieces at the G.T. Club (secret name), where members paid ten cents a week dues and invited their husbands to parties there twice a year.

" 'The ladies have known each other all their lives,' said the wife of the well known hurler. 'We sew and talk, then somebody plays the piano and the lady who is hostess serves refreshments. No—nothing stronger than tea. None of the ladies drink or smoke. We have a grand time, just good, clean fun. All the members are married except one, Ollie Eichhorn, the secretary who takes care of the dues.' "

Showing a streak of independence, Ethel insisted on calling herself Mrs. Groves—the family name, after all. "We were married as 'Groves' and the children were christened as 'Groves' and Groves is it for us," she said.

Whatever may be said of Lefty's professional behavior, he was piling up credits with friends, neighbors, and relatives. "One day we were out of flour," said a niece, Mae Winne of Baden, Pennsylvania. "He drove to the store and cooked us all a batch of buttermilk pancakes."

Grove brought a box of batting practice balls home every year. He gave his nieces and nephews fifty cents at Christmas and a $5 watch at graduation. "Every time he won a game or hit a homer, a case of Wheaties containing fifty little boxes would come to our house," said Lefty's niece Betty Holshey. "I used to think, 'Is this the only cereal there is?' "

The Groves settled at 89 Douglas Avenue in a two-story, seven-room, yellow wood house with green steps up to a porch, only a quarter-mile from Main Street in Lonaconing. Lefty installed a six-tube radio set and worked on his huge gun collection.

The 1930 National League champion Cardinals had a .300

hitter in every spot, a late-inning rally in every pot. They finished with a 21-4 run to oust the defending champion Cubs and win their third pennant in five years.

In Game One, Grove matched his fastball with Hall of Famer Burleigh Grimes' spitter, Grimes being one of the few players grandfathered when the wet one was banned in 1920. The Cardinals actually outhit the A's, nine to five, but the A's outslugged St. Louis. All five hits were for extra bases, in different innings, and telling. Dykes doubled, Foxx and Haas tripled, and Cochrane and Simmons homered. Completely in control, if not overpowering (five K's), Grove threw 119 pitches, including just 39 balls. The A's won, 5-2.

In personality, second-game starter George Earnshaw was Grove's opposite. A party boy, Earnshaw was as relaxing as bathtub gin. In style, however, he and Grove were bedfellows. Earnshaw had a great fastball, a few miles an hour slower than Grove's. Earnshaw's curve broke more sharply. Both were tireless. Going the distance, Earnshaw won Game Two, 6-1.

Despite a 5-0 defeat in the third game—Rube Walberg was the loser—the A's were up two games to one. Alas, Grove lost Game Four, 3-1, to Jesse Haines' "dipsy" pitches. Lefty was victimized by teammates, too. With two outs and two on in the decisive fourth inning, third baseman Dykes elected not to tag the runner coming from second and threw the ball past first for an error, enabling the Cards to eventually score two unearned runs.

Back to Earnshaw in Game Five. After matching zeroes with Grimes for seven innings, Earnshaw was lifted for a pinch hitter. Grove came in. You knew he would do his part, and he did: a walk and a single in two innings. Jimmie Foxx came to bat in the ninth, and you knew he would do *his* part. With Cochrane on first and one out, Foxx homered way back in the left-field bleachers. Everyone at Sportsman's Park sat numbly as the Beast rounded the bases. The A's went on to win, 2-0, with Grove getting the decision.

On just one day's rest, Earnshaw pitched a complete Game Six, five-hitting the Cardinals, 7-1. Series to the A's, four games to two, and an unprecedented fifth world championship for the old man. Concluding the Year of the Hitter, Series MVP Earnshaw went 2-0, with 19 strikeouts in 25 innings, and an 0.72 ERA. Grove was 2-1, with three walks and 10 strikeouts in 19 innings, and a 1.42 ERA. Forget about Spahn, Sain, and pray for rain. This was a gravy train.

Could the white elephants rumble on? Simmons held out before the '31 season. On Opening Day, Mack announced that Bucketfoot Al would not play for Philadelphia. When Mack's cab arrived at Shibe Park, he reached into his pocket. The driver declined payment. "If you can't afford Simmons, you can't afford me," he said.

A few hours later, Simmons signed a three-year contract for a reported $100,000. Rumble, young men, rumble.

TRIUMPH AND TANTRUM

★　　★　　★　　★

"He is a little chimney, and heated hot at the moment."

–Henry Wadsworth Longfellow,
The Courtship of Miles Standish,
Part III

Relaxing in his St. Louis hotel room on the night of August 22, 1931, Lefty Grove *should* have felt on top of the baseball world. He was already certain of his fifth consecutive 20-win season, with an otherworldly 25-2 record. Connie Mack told the St. Louis *Post-Dispatch* that Grove was better than Mack's previous prize lefties, Rube Waddell and Eddie Plank. Grove was indisputably the best active pitcher in baseball. Even Giants manager John McGraw, who despised the junior circuit so much he refused to play its pennant-winners back in 1904, said so.

Three days earlier Grove had tied the American League record of 16 straight wins in one season established by Smokey Joe Wood and Walter Johnson, both in 1912. The following afternoon Grove would surely pass his co-holders. In the first game of a doubleheader at historic Sportsman's Park he was facing the fifth-place St. Louis Browns—fully 35-1/2 games behind the first-place A's. His opposite number was one Dick Coffman, a 5-9 pitcher the Browns had considered releasing three weeks before.

Actually, there were storm clouds in the air, if only anyone had been looking for them. Al Simmons, out of the lineup since August 16, was in Milwaukee getting treatment for a sprained, infected, and blistered left ankle. Utility outfielder and pinch hitter Handsome Jimmy Moore had replaced him the five previous games, homering from the cleanup position on August 22. Centerfielder Mule Haas was down with a fractured wrist, while shortstop Joe Boley and third baseman Jimmy Dykes were sidelined with charley horses. Coffman had won three straight, allowing only four runs, and volunteered to face Grove. Nonetheless, the A's, defending world champions two years running and now an incredible 82-31, thirteen games ahead of the second-place Senators, couldn't imagine their ace losing. So what if there were injuries? So what if Coffman had a modest winning streak of his own, including a one-hit shutout of the White Sox? Surely, the opposition was trifling. Surely, Lefty Grove would need little support. Just give him a run or two. He'd take care of the rest.

Nonetheless, Grove could not have been overconfident as he pondered the assignment. He knew that baseball is the least predictable of sports, a game's outcome hanging on as little as which pitches move an extra inch, which bounces are true, which way the wind is blowing. Even in this, his most spectacular season, he had been unpleasantly surprised a number of times.

Lefty's words, moods, and actions were so predictable that we can make an educated guess how he behaved before the biggest game of his career and the day he would remember more vividly than any other.

Grove followed his normal night-before procedure. Around 6 p.m. he took the elevator to the ground floor of the Kingsway Hotel, originally called the Buckingham Hotel when it was built for visitors to the 1904 World's Fair, now a residential/guest establishment. A steak dinner awaited him in The Grill, a noted ground-floor restaurant, and the service, as advertised, was "dignified and exact." After a cigar in the lobby, Grove headed for his room at 9 p.m., a detective-story or shoot-'em-up western magazine awaiting him. He took the receiver off the hook and turned out the lights at 10 p.m.—a vintage early-to-bed-early-to-rise American, he. As Joe Cronin, who later managed Grove, put it, "Ten in the morning is the middle of the day for him."

On dates he wasn't pitching, Grove was up at 6 a.m. This being a game day, he slept late. Stretching by the bay window, he looked across the street to Forest Park, site of the old World's Fair. Grove was less interested in the view than in the weather. The sky was clear, with a hot, sweltering day in the offing—weather certain to vex players in their flannel uniforms, but not the indefatigable Grove. Smiling, he said aloud his favorite expletive, "Yes, sir!"

After "whistling and splashing around in the bathroom," in the words of Boston newsman Bill Cunningham, who roomed next door to him after he was traded to the Red Sox, Grove headed downstairs to take a walk. That accomplished, he dined in the cream-colored main dining room, eating his cereal and fried eggs and reading the sports section. Afterward he relaxed in a lobby seat—this one, he noted with satisfaction, an elegant and upholstered easy chair— watching people go by and keeping his thoughts to himself.

You could see him now as he was then, with his watch fob

and white suit. One leg crossed over another, Grove sat with an enigmatic smile suggesting a personal secret. Every so often, he blew smoke that flew across the lobby like clouds racing down a corridor of sky. Red Smith called him "one of the great lobby-sitters of his time, a graven image shrouded in cigar smoke."

Occasionally, considering some memory or other, Lefty frowned like a man who has eaten bad fish. Briefly, he reviewed the season.

In the preseason, it should be noted, the American League, whose teams had batted .288 in 1930, introduced a new, heavily stitched ball. Grove said it would give him better control and more speed. "With the new American League ball and nothing to worry about, I feel I can win thirty games this season," he said in February. Feeling his oats, Grove held out briefly, resembling "a little boy with a peeve—having fun while pouting," in Boston columnist Harold Kaese's words. On April 14, before President and Mrs. Hoover in Washington, Grove pitched three innings of one-run relief and beat the Senators, 5-3. Four days later, saving his first start for the Shibe Park opener, he threw a five-hit, ten strikeout complete game against the Senators but lost, 2-1, the winning run scoring when right-fielder Bing Miller bumped into second baseman Max Bishop as he was about to field Ossie Bluege's fly ball. Raging in the clubhouse, Grove grabbed the sides of his shirt and ripped it open, buttons rat-tat-tatting across the floor.

He stomped Washington, 5-1, on April 22. Following a bad relief performance in a no-decision on the 24th, Grove was then idled for fifteen days with what he told Mack was a "severe cold." It is fruitless to speculate whether he was depressed, or whether he'd have won the three likely starts he missed. What's noteworthy is that Connie Mack accepted

Grove's explanation without comment or question, the fatherly manager allowing the tempestuous pitcher his long leash. "He hasn't felt like pitching and for that reason I permitted him to treat his cold in his own way," Mack told reporters in early May. "He is all right now and will probably work one of the games against the Browns."

As went Grove, so went the A's. Playing only 7-7 ball through May 4, they stood in fourth place. It was unrealistic for the defending champions to languish long, but no one expected them to rebound so dramatically. On May 5, Earnshaw beat the Red Sox 4-1, and Philadelphia was heading into a 17-game winning streak. After another Athletics win on May 6, Grove returned to pitch two innings of relief, striking out four while saving a 6-4 win over St. Louis May 9. On May 12, in his first start since April 22, he four-hit the White Sox, 5-2.

Grove won again as a starter May 16, beating Cleveland, 12-5, while hitting safely twice, saved games as a reliever the next two days, took a day off, then shut out the Tigers, 3-0, on three hits. On May 25, he beat New York, 4-2, despite having to face Ruth and Gehrig with one out and runners on second and third in the ninth. Let John Drebinger of the *Times* describe what followed: "He fanned Ruth and he fanned Gehrig, and the crowd, bathed in perspiration, fanned itself." (Yet another opportunity to create a three-strikeouts-on-nine-pitches legend.) By the time the A's finally lost one, 6-2, to the Yankees on May 26, they had a 24-7 record and a five-game lead over second-place Washington. Lefty, still streaking, won twice more in May on two innings of relief against New York and a twelve-inning shutout over Boston, and beat the White Sox, 2-1, on June 3. An unearned run ended a thirty-inning scoreless streak. His eight-game winning streak ended two days later, when Grove pitched six

strong innings of relief before Chicago's Lew Fonseca homered in the twelfth to beat him, 7-5. A six-inning stint after
just one day's rest hardly seems fair, but without a full-time
reliever on his six-man pitching staff, Mack expected his ace,
now 9-2, to be both a workhorse and a winner.

Grove didn't mind the labor, just the losing. "He was so
mad [after the June 5 loss] he didn't talk to anyone," Dykes
told Cleveland sportswriter Hal Lebovitz years later. "He got
in his Pierce Arrow and drove to his home in Lonaconing,
Maryland. He didn't show up at the park for three days."

When Grove started his record-seeking streak on June 8,
the A's stood 33-11, five games ahead of Washington. After
returning to Philadelphia, unpunished by Mack, Grove said
nothing to anyone, went back to work, and won 12 straight
by August. All pitching and batting streaks are accompanied
by some luck. Grove trailed in five of the 12 wins, including
three times after the fifth inning. In each of those nail-biters
shortstop Dib Williams, who had won the job from Joe Boley,
bailed him out. The score was tied, 3-3, on July 1 against
Cleveland, when Williams drove in the game-winner with a
single. On July 13, the Indians reached Grove for 13 hits
and seven runs to take a 7-5 lead after eight innings. The A's
rallied to score seven times in their half of the inning, the
crucial blow a grand slam by Williams, who was pinch-hitting
for Grove. With a scoreless inning of relief from Earnshaw,
Philadelphia won, 12-7. Cleveland led, 3-2, in his eleventh win
on July 25 before the A's scored three times in the seventh—
two players coming home on a Williams single—and went on
to win, 6-3.

But mainly Grove helped himself. In his best start, on
June 23, he shut out the Browns, 3-0, with a nifty two-hitter.
Pitching on July 4 after only two days of rest, he beat
Boston, 9-7, with 10 strikeouts in seven innings of relief to

George Earnshaw, Eddie Rommel, and Grove in 1930 or 1931.
Rommel was at the end of his career. His bookends, one unflappable
and fun-loving, the other irascible and serious, dominated baseball.

win again. On July 28, Grove entered the game with the
score tied, 3-3, a man on third and no one out in the eighth.
He retired the next three hitters, and a three-run ninth,
started by Foxx's homer, gave him a 6-3 win.

With Grove's winning streak at 12 by August the baseball
world began counting down toward the record. Grove beat
the Senators on 11 well-spaced hits, 3-2, in game thirteen
(August 3), the Browns, 8-1, in game fourteen (August 11),
and the Indians, 4-3, in game fifteen (August 15)—all, naturally, complete games. The record-tying contest was no
gimme. On August 19, Lefty squared off against the Hall of
Fame spitballer Red Faber, forty-two, in Chicago's Comiskey
Park. The suspense didn't last long. The A's struck for two
runs in the second, another in the third, and one more in

the eighth. Grove conceded two runs in the ninth, largely because Bishop first booted a grounder, then failed to tag a runner on a non-force play. Truly in form, Lefty yelled at Bishop after the second blunder. Then he settled down and got two grounders to win, 4-2. "He blended his devastating fastball with a snapping curve that knocked off opponents like tenpins," the Philadelphia *Inquirer*'s Isaminger wrote. The time of the game was vintage-baseball—one hour and forty-two minutes.

During this streak, Grove pitched complete games in thirteen of fourteen starts, won in two of four relief appearances and beat every team in the league but the Yankees, whom he faced only once, in 2-1/3 innings of scoreless relief. The patsy Browns fell three times. At this point Grove had a 25-2 record, with a 2.02 earned-run average in a season noted for strong hitting, and only 57 walks in 227-1/3 innings. He seemed in control by any definition of the word.

Still, sitting in the lobby on the record-challenging day, Grove fumed anew. Lefty had an uncanny way with numbers. If he hadn't been summoned to relieve against the White Sox back on June 5, he thought, he would already have won 24 straight. He'd have easily passed the major-league record of 19 set by Tim Keefe in 1888 and tied by Rube Marquard in 1912, and the all-time record of 21 set in 1904 by minor-leaguer Baxter Sparks of the the Delta League's Yazoo City club. "That Lew Fonseca ..." he may have thought, clenching his fists and tensing his body. Ah, well, Grove likely comforted himself, he would surely meet and beat the AL record in St. Louis.

The bus ride to Sportsman's Park was a quiet one. You didn't mess with Lefty before he pitched, and certainly not before he set records. Teammates tiptoed around him while he took his celebrated ten-minute nap and hour-long rubdown in the upstairs trainer's room. Photographers didn't even think of approaching him when he warmed up. "On the day he was pitching," Dykes told Lebovitz, "it was suicide for a photographer to take his picture. He'd throw the ball right through the lens." By the time he walked to the mound in the last half of the first inning, Grove probably hadn't spoken to anyone all day but his breakfast waiter.

Asked to describe their participation in history, most people say they were so enmeshed in matters at hand that they can't flesh out the scene. Grove remembered every detail of the game but probably ignored the locale.

If Lefty had looked around, he would have seen a park that had a "garish, county-fair sort of layout," as Red Smith wrote in 1929. A portly baritone named Jim Kelly announced the lineups to infield-area crowds through a megaphone, then trudged to the outfield where, exhausted from his efforts, he announced only the batteries. "Call for Phil-ip Mor-rees," Johnny the Bellhop bellowed in a recording attached to an outfield wall sign. Topping the bleachers was a hand-operated scoreboard laden with ads and a clock.

The flagpole stood in fair territory. Standings for both leagues were listed in the outfield. A concrete left-to-center wall rose eleven feet, six inches. From the 354 mark in right-center to the right-field line, another concrete wall of the same height was topped by a twenty-one-foot, six-inch wire screen that kept the ball in play. In an ode to a long-gone age when parks were really parks, a goat grazed the spacious outfield to help the grounds crew cut the grass before games.

On August 23, 1931, the park looked as spacious and ornate as a coliseum, with seventy-five feet between home plate and the backstop, and second decks stretching from foul line to foul line. Few noted the rickety, rotting Depression-era wooden seats and the tired-looking grass field bent out of shape by its two home teams, or denounced the disgrace of a blacks-only, screened-in section in right field—the only fair-territory seats in big-league ball where you couldn't catch a homer.

Built asymmetrically to suit roads and buildings, the park was bordered by 3623 Dodier Avenue behind first, Spring Avenue behind third, 2907 North Grand Boulevard behind right, and Sullivan Avenue behind left. The field measured 351 feet to left, 379 to left-center, 426 to a deep corner just left of center, 424 in center, 422 just right of center, 354 to right-center, and 310 to right. The dimensions slightly favored lefthanded pitchers.

It is not necessary to speculate about the rest of Lefty's day. With twenty thousand sweltering spectators on hand for the 1:30 p.m. game—a huge audience come to see history, not the home-team sluggards—Grove breezed through the first two innings. The Browns' designated sacrificial lamb, Coffman every bit as effortlessly blanked the A's. A quiet, good-hearted fastballer of Grovian size (6'2", 195 pounds), Coffman would last fifteen years in the big leagues without ever winning 10 games in a season. He did pitch decent relief with the 1936-39 Giants, leading the National League with eight relief wins in 1936, seven relief wins in 1937, and 12 saves in 1938. However, there was no indication whatsoever back in 1931 that he might outduel Lefty Grove, breaking history as it were.

After Fritz Schulte's two-out bloop single against Grove in the third inning, Oscar (Ski) Melillo hit what appeared to be a routine liner directly at substitute left-fielder Jimmy Moore. Unfortunately, "at-'em" liners aren't easy to judge. A player has little trouble gauging a ball hit to the side, because he can triangulate it and determine how far it has traveled and how fast. A drive hit right at him is just a blob

145

growing bigger; it's initially as easy to track as the distance to the moon. At-'em liners usually appear headed a shorter distance than they actually travel, and racing in is a nearly universal urge.

Many fielders start wrongly but recover in time. Not poor Moore, a guileless fellow out of Paris, Tennessee, who had the sun to contend with in addition to the difficult angle. In a sequence that would haunt him forever, Moore moved in, saw a baseball in no hurry to descend, and retreated in panic. The ball tipped off Moore's glove and rolled to the fence, Schulte scoring on the double.

Grove was reduced from smirking dandy to exasperated rube. He stood on the mound, squinty-eyed, red-faced, slapping his glove against his leg in disgust. The A's on the bench, who could see the play perfectly from their first-base-line dugout, probably covered their eyes. Only Connie Mack, sitting erect in his suit, starched collar and hat, undoubtedly showed no emotion.

Moore never blamed the brilliant sun in a cloudless sky— a hindrance to everyone that day—as an excuse. "If I'd stood still, I'd have caught it," Moore told the Boston *Globe*'s Kaese thirty-four years later. "If I'd been sitting on a chair, I'd have caught it. But Melillo was a light hitter and I moved in two steps. The ball was hit harder'n I thought, and it just nipped off the end of my glove."

What an indignity to Grove: a run built on a bloop and a bumble. At inning's end, he glared at Moore, then seated himself on the wooden bench in the dugout below the playing field. Grove probably didn't fume long, though. There was a game to be played. The A's would rally. He would pitch shutout ball for the duration.

He was only partly right. Yielding no more runs, Grove completed a seven-hitter with six strikeouts and no walks.

Grove with the Most Valuable Player award for 1931.
To win it he had to beat out teammate Al Simmons (.390 average)
and the Yankees' Lou Gehrig (184 RBIs).

Alas, Coffman was better. All his pitches seemed to have come down from a higher league. His fastball and changeup, always good, were even better, and his problematic curve was breaking sharply. The blond righthander allowed only three hits: Foxx's bunt in the second inning, Moore's two-out single in the fourth, and a leadoff single to right by Cochrane in the seventh.

Cochrane's hit ignited the closest thing to a rally the A's staged all game. Moore sacrificed him to second (scoring position!), but then Foxx took a called strike three, Miller reached base on Coffman's only walk, and substitute third baseman Eric McNair ended the threat with a short fly to right. After retiring the side in the eighth, Grove threw down his glove in the dugout. "Let's go," someone said. They went...down in order. The A's lost meekly and quickly, 1-0, in one hour and twenty-five minutes. It was the only game all season in which they'd been shut out.

"No one mistake made by a ball player this season hurt another as Moore's misjudge did to Grove today," Isaminger wrote. "The chance open to Grove comes only once in a lifetime. It is the remotest and most forlorn possibility that the mighty sidewinder will ever win sixteen straight games again in any future season."

After the last out, Mack went directly to Moore. "Now, James, you're going to feel bad," Mack said (and Moore recounted to Kaese), "but I've seen Cobb miss easier balls than that. Another thing. We're going to be in the World Series and I don't want any fights or anything or anybody getting hurt." Mack advised Moore to remain on the bench for awhile before heading back to the clubhouse to change.[1]

---

[1] Mack was fond of Moore, nicknamed "Hollywood" as well as "Handsome" for his good looks and fancy clothes. When a fan asked Mack after the game why he was playing Moore, he said, "I'm glad you asked me. It's because he dresses so well, he's an inspi-

With no exit door on the visitors' dugout, the A's were forced to walk across the field to the Browns' third-base dugout, making them easy targets for autograph seekers and boo birds alike. Grove's teammates plodded across the diamond and through the Browns' dugout, clattered down a hallway in their cleats, and disappeared into the visiting-team clubhouse. A grubby, low-ceilinged room with peeling paint, wooden lockers, and a few showerheads, it was but temporary sanctuary. Mount Grove was about to erupt.

Fortunately for his teammates, Grove blasted only the inanimate and the absent. Old ballplayers' memories are fuzzy and selective. They tend to forget details and rewrite history to glorify themselves and their time. To compound historical inaccuracy, Depression-era baseball writers rarely entered clubhouses immediately after games. With little competition from magazines and electronic media, they described the action, finished their stories at game's end, and walked downstairs to the clubhouse, if at all, many minutes later. In the event of some team embarrassment, they usually protected the offenders. More team employees than disinterested chroniclers—their travel expenses were usually paid by the clubs they covered—the writers defended their see-no-evil reporting as "good for baseball." Accordingly, there were no on-the-scene reports of disturbing postgame events on August 23, 1931.

Nonetheless, later accounts from different sources confirmed perhaps the most complete clubhouse demolition in baseball history. "Too bad, Mose," said catcher Cochrane, addressing Robert Moses Grove by his familiar nickname as he entered the clubhouse. Ignoring him, Grove tried to tear

---

ration to the rest of the boys around the hotels." His baseball embarrassment notwithstanding, Moore later became a successful Memphis politician responsible for the existence of an airport, a stadium, a coliseum, and the Liberty Bowl football game.

off the clubhouse door and shredded the wooden partitions separating the lockers. He ripped off his shirt with both hands, the buttons flying by Doc Cramer three lockers down, and stomped on his uniform. "Threw everything I could get my hands on—bats, balls, shoes, gloves, benches, water buckets, whatever was handy," Grove told Donald Honig. They could all be picked up, more or less intact. Not so the banged-in lockers and broken chairs left in his wake.

Ending his day-long silence, Grove ignored Moore but raged at his absent leftfielder Simmons, and at Mack for giving Simmons the day off. "If Simmons had been here and in left field, he would have stuck that ball in his back pocket," Lefty yelled, and historians subsequently recounted. "What the devil did he have to go to Milwaukee for?"

Grove's teammates sat silently. No brave soul reminded Grove that Bucketfoot Al had been sidelined all week and would be out for two weeks as well, yet had volunteered to play. Nor did anyone point out that Coffman had outpitched Grove, that even a flawless Lefty couldn't have won without some A's runs in extra innings, that he might have been out of the game by the time they scored.

After Lefty's twenty-minute tirade, the A's took the field for the second game. Now Grove reportedly began demolishing the showerheads. Meanwhile, his teammates were routing the Browns, 10-0, supporting Waite Hoyt with 17 hits. When news of their scoring rampage reached Grove, his raging almost surely swelled.

It remained for the avuncular Connie Mack to soothe him. Grove normally celebrated his wins with a twenty-five cent cigar. Post-Coffman, he was surely puffing on a ten-cent stogie that could barely be described as a smoke. "Robert," Mack said when he finally cornered Grove in the hotel, "that boy pitched a great game, and if we had played them all night we still probably wouldn't have scored." Mack kept pounding away until Grove conceded that Coffman had pitched "all right." Mack's words must have been at least temporarily therapeutic, because that same evening Grove was able to chuckle about Moore's misjudgment with Philadelphia writer Cy Peterman.

On August 29, Grove pitched against the Yankees. Nervous enough on his first start after his winning streak's eclipse, he was scarcely consoled to be facing the happier, more popular, and more quotable Hall-of-Fame southpaw he was later confused with, Vernon (Lefty) Gomez.

The Yankees, as expert in their bench jockeying as their playing, began riding Grove as he warmed up. According to one report, some of their kinder calls were "Kicked over any water pails lately?" and "That was a bush stunt, Grove, but you are a busher, aren't you?" From there, they doubtless added reminders about his appearance, his origins, his mother.

In response, Grove gripped the ball harder and threw it faster. First inning: He struck out Sammy Byrd, Joe Sewell, and the Babe. Second inning: Grove walked Lou Gehrig, then fanned Ben Chapman, Lyn Lary, and Bill Dickey. Third inning: Grove whiffed Tony Lazzeri and Gomez before getting Byrd to pop up. Ten batters, eight K's.

It was a great beginning, but a costly one. In gripping the ball so firmly, Grove tore some skin off his left index finger. He survived two more innings before surrendering a grand slam to Gehrig with one out in the sixth. Fortunately, the Athletics had kayoed Gomez and were leading 7-0 at the time. With help from Jimmie Foxx's five RBIs and Rube Walberg's fine relief, they hung on to win, 7-4, and give Grove his 26th victory.

Generally, Grove was pitching without discomfort. In earlier seasons, his vicious wrist jerk had cracked fingernails and blistered his hand, limiting his late-season starts. By easing the snap in '31, Grove's limb stayed healthier. Throwing more breaking balls, he beat the Senators six of seven times after losing eight of thirteen decisions against them in previous years.

After stopping the Yankees, Grove won another five straight. Before only twenty-five hundred fans in Shibe Park, he beat the White Sox, 3-1, on September 18 to become the first 30-game winner since the Indians' Jim Bagby won 31 in 1920, the first lefthander ever, and the century's first 30-game winner with under 300 innings (288-2/3). Hell, everyone knew it was going to happen—why bother showing up? Six days later he beat the Red Sox, 9-4, to go 46-4 since July 25, 1930—still the best fifty-decision run of the century. Grove's 31-4 season included winning streaks of eight, 16, and six games. His 31 wins were nine ahead of runner-up Wes Ferrell and haven't been topped. Discounting a five-run, three-inning Series warmup loss on September 27, when he barely tried, he yielded six runs in three defeats.

Not since Ed Reulbach in 1906-08—and never again—had a pitcher led the league in winning percentage three years running. Grove's percentage of .886 was the best for pitchers with at least 20 decisions until Ron Guidry went 25-3 (.893) in 1978. Lefty's 2.06 earned run average, baseball's best from 1919 to 1943, was .61 ahead of the second-place Gomez and 2.32 below the league average. (Without the Series warmup, Grove would have bested Guidry's percentage and a 2.00 ERA.) Grove also led the league in complete games (27), shutouts (four), and strikeouts (175), and added five saves to place sixth in the league. He won his second straight Triple Crown (wins, ERA, strikeouts); only Pete Alexander (1915-17) had previously done so, and only Sandy Koufax (1965-66) and Roger Clemens (1997-98) have done it since.

Was there anything else Grove could possibly do? Well, good fielding always accompanies good pitching, right? Lefty had his first errorless season.

Notwithstanding Simmons' hitting (.390), and Gehrig's run production (184 RBIs, 301 runs produced), Grove was named Most Valuable Player by the writers. The A's were baseball's best team for the third straight season. A Murderers' Row of pitchers, led by Walberg (20-12) and Earnshaw[2] (21-7), worked on Lefty's off-days. A's pitchers allowed 65 fewer runs than any team in the league, and A's fielders committed 141 errors, fewest in the majors. By contrast, the second-place Yankees set a major-league scoring record of 1,067 runs and finished 13-1/2 games back. The argument over the relative merits of pitching and fielding vs. hitting ended in 1931. It is raised anew by fools.

The 1929-31 A's broke even with a better-known team, the 1926-28 Yankees. The A's had a 313-143 (.686) record, the Yankees 302-160 (.654). The Yankees outscored the A's by all of six runs, 2,716 to 2,710. The A's allowed 1,992 runs, the Yankees 1,997. Both teams won three pennants and two World Series. For his part, Grove's .840 winning percentage over three years was the best run of the century, .067 ahead of Christy Mathewson in 1908-10.

In the 1931 World Series Grove unveiled the rubber stamp with his facsimile autograph, leading some to believe he was an illiterate rube. The A's had beaten the Cubs in the 1929 World Series and the Cardinals in 1930. Again, they faced the Cardinals. If you were to believe the *Evening*

---

[2] Earnshaw had six saves to Grove's five. Both could throw 95-miles-per-hour fastballs. If the score was tied or the A's had a one-run lead in the eighth, the two big men would walk slowly to the bullpen, as frightening an image as Goose Gossage in the 1970's. Most regular-season games started at 3 pm, and the skies were darkening and the shadows lengthening by the time Grove and Earnshaw pitched relief. There were not many homers in the gloaming. And they were ready to start two days later.

Bulletin's John Nolan, Mack waited until the last minute to start Grove in the opener. Mack walked to the breakfast table and said, "Good morning, Mrs. Grove. What sort of humor is your husband in today?"

"Oh, Lefty feels fine," she said. "I know he is ready for any job you have. Look at the big breakfast he is eating."

"That's great," said Mack. "Lefty, have one more cigar and take a rest. You're working today."

"O.K., boss," said Grove.

With a blister on a throwing finger, he mixed curves with slow balls and gave up four hits and two runs in the first inning and 12 hits overall. Fortunately, he walked none, struck out seven and got bailed out repeatedly by the left side of the infield—Dykes and Williams. Grove held on to win, 6-2.

"Naw, the blister didn't hurt," he said, "but them dinky hits they made got me mad. I started thinking that maybe my control was too good. You know I was putting them right over the plate.

"I started thinking, and you know what happens when a lefthander gets to thinking. Well, I began to chuck up slow ones and a little curve. Every time I tossed one the Cards got a hold of it. From now on, they won't see nuthin' but fastball pitching."

Afterward, according to writer Nolan, Grove unaccustomedly ate frog legs and went to the movies before retiring. The Cards won the second game, 2-0, behind their ace, Bill Hallahan, who had been held back rather than wasted against Grove. When a rain delay gave Grove three full days to heal his blister and rest his arm, he started Game Three. Though he allowed only two earned runs in eight innings, Lefty surrendered 11 hits and lost, 5-2, to the old spitballer Grimes. Earnshaw two-hit the Cards in Game Four, 3-0, but the next afternoon Pepper Martin got three hits and four RBIs in a 5-1 Cardinal victory. With the A's a game from elimination in Game Six, Grove—"pitching at the very peak of his form for the first time in this intersectional warfare," according to AP writer Alan Gould—won, 8-1, permitting only five hits and one walk while fanning six. He left 39,401 Cardinal fans sitting on their hands and walked out of World Series play forever.

Unfortunately, the Series was not to be remembered for Grove's pitching. It was Martin's showcase. The Cardinal centerfielder batted .500 and stole five bases. In Game Seven, with the bases loaded, two outs in the ninth, the Cardinals nursing a 4-2 lead, and Grove warming up on the sidelines, Hallahan relieved and Martin raced in to grab Bishop's sinking line drive and become a national hero. Like the '26 Cardinals, the '31 version had beaten their American League rivals in seven games.

Grove was not the only A's player to feel the sting. His catcher, worried over financial losses, batted .160 and blamed A's pitchers for failing to hold runners. He primarily meant Earnshaw, who gave up four of Martin's steals.

In the 1929-31 World Series, Grove had a 4-2 record, a 1.75 earned-run average, six walks in 51-1/3 innings, and two saves. Over the same seasons, he won 79 games and lost 15. Grove's spectacular string was much appreciated in its time but soon forgotten. Evidently, it didn't stand out in boldface type. Coming in the years 1929-31, the streak couldn't be included intact in write-ups of the 1920's or 1930's. It coincided with gaudier, catchier batting numbers. It ended with all eyes on Pepper Martin.

After the Series, Grove headed for Japan with a major-league all-star team that included Cochrane, Gehrig, and Simmons. On one occasion, fifty thousand Japanese cheered wildly when a university team got three hits off Grove, but they were equally appreciative of "Grovesan," who reportedly ended one game by striking out six batters on nineteen pitches, chuckling all the while. "G'vove! G'vove!" they yelled, at least according to U.S. newspaper reports. Actually posing for a picture, Grove brandished an oversized righthander's glove with a Rising Sun/Old Glory logo that adoring fans gave him. Cochrane, who found the trip therapeutic, posed with him holding a large glove of his own. "We had the time of our lives," said Grove, "and every place we visited the natives tendered us a royal reception."

During the 1931-32 off-season, however, Grove probably mused little over his sensational year, his team's Series loss, the trip to Japan, or a snub by another temperamental star, Babe Ruth, who left him off his traveling all-star team. Proud, ultracompetitive, egocentric, Grove obsessed over that dog day of August in St. Louis. He had no problem with Moore, to whom he sent a Christmas card. Instead, Lefty raged over the imagined slight by an absent Hall of Fame teammate. Lefty never, ever forgave Al Simmons.

FAREWELL TO PHILLY

★　　★　　★　　★

"Scattered to the four winds, the once-proud Athletics."

–Cy Peterman,
Philadelphia *Evening Bulletin*

I n 1931, Lefty Grove had a great year at the bank as well as on the field, thanks to an incentive clause in his contract. According to one account, he was paid a base salary of $20,000, plus $1,000 for each win over 20. That added up to $31,000. Another source reported that he had been paid a $19,000 salary, with a $500 bonus for each win over 20. In short, $24,500. Since he signed a two-year deal for a reported $50,000 following a brief holdout before the 1932 season, the second figure seems more accurate. He wouldn't have wanted to take a substantial pay cut from a $31,000 season.

After a slow start in '32—he lost consecutively to New York, Boston, and Washington in April—Grove regained his old form. On May 5, he beat eventual 193-game winner Wes

Ferrell and the Indians, 15-3. "The sky was overcast and his fastball was zooming," Ed Pollock wrote in Philadelphia's *Public Ledger*.

"When planes take off a ship, people say they catapult," says Frankie Crosetti, a rookie shortstop for the Yankees in '32. "That was what his fastball did halfway to the plate. He threw just plain fastballs—he didn't need anything else."

Grove then shut out Chicago and St. Louis, building up 24 straight scoreless innings. By mid-June he had won eleven consecutive games, and Mack, remembering how a relief loss ended an eight-game winning streak the previous season, refused to send him into tight games he might lose on a fluke. The A's were only 32-24, seven games behind the Yankees, and a reason often cited was relief pitching and Mack's failure to use his number one fireman. The great Connie Mack was actually being criticized by the hometown press.

Cy Peterman of the *Evening Bulletin* asked him: "Suppose he [Grove] goes in with a couple of men on base, one or none out, and the A's two runs or less ahead?"

"He probably would pull out of it all right," replied Mack. "But—he might not. He might be cold, he might not have enough warmup. The two runs might score, the game is tied, and then should they hit and our boys fail to score again, the loss is charged to Lefty, when it really isn't his fault. I won't do it. No, sir. If he loses now, it'll be his own game and his own fault, not mine."

Backtracking rapidly, Peterman wrote, "Pretty decent of the old man, don't you think? We do."

On June 15, Grove sprained his ankle shagging flies in his private hell, Sportsman's Park. Lefty put his leg up and read westerns until his next appearance.

It was no fluke when the White Sox beat him on July 9. Grove lasted six innings and surrendered seven earned runs in a 7-0 loss. Then he really tailed off. On July 12 he gave up a career-high 18 hits in a 7-6 loss to Cleveland. In a thirty-day period he lost six of ten decisions. Yet one of his four wins was a game he remembered fondly the rest of his life.

On July 31, Grove opened Cleveland's brand-new Municipal Stadium before the governor, mayor, commissioner, both league presidents, and 81,179 other fans, the largest crowd in baseball history to that date, and shut out Mel Harder, 1-0, on four hits, two walks, and six strikeouts. The A's got their eighth-inning run when Max Bishop worked a base on balls from an 0-2 count, Mule Haas sacrificed him to second, and Mickey Cochrane scored him with a single. Grove himself squelched an Indians rally, with men on first and second and no outs in the seventh, when he fielded a bunt and threw perfectly to third without looking. Then he struck out catcher Luke Sewell and threw out second baseman Bill Cissell. In a showcase event, Grove gave a showcase performance. The *Inquirer*'s Isaminger referred to Municipal Stadium as the "leviathan of baseball parks" and Grove as the "monarch of moundsmen."

In another memorable day during the 1932 season, Grove was presented the 1931 Most Valuable Player Award, a splendid trophy prepared by silversmiths, with a pitcher atop a globe-like baseball. The family, including Lefty's wife, children, and mother-in-law, gathered in his Philadelphia house at 2938 Lehigh Ave. "I guess this is one night Robert can drop his cigar ashes all over the house if he wants to and I'll never say a word," Ethel said. Lefty's redheaded daughter Ethel Doris, nine, was asked if she was excited about attending the presentation in Shibe Park. "Unhun [no]," she told local writer Betty Starr, " 'cause I'm not going to the game. Baseball is only for boys, not for girls. I'm going to the movies, where they give you free cushions this afternoon, and

Bobby's going too. I made him 'cause I want his cushion!"

On August 5, Grove relieved in accursed Sportsman's Park. He should have stood in bed. After homering in the top of the tenth inning to give the A's an 8-7 lead, he committed a costly error and allowed two runs in the bottom half, losing, 9-8, to the Browns. "Mose Grove signed his dinner check, rose from the table, and with his good left arm hurled the pencil clear through the dining room door," Cy Peterman wrote. "Then, as the missile went skimming into the lobby, he stalked through the Kingsway courtyard, sought a secluded corner and read the details of his latest and toughest defeat."

Nonetheless, Grove won nine of his last 10 decisions— beating Ferrell for the fifth straight time in the process— again completed twenty-seven of thirty starts, and went 25-10, with a league-leading 2.84 ERA, to make *The Sporting News* Major League All Star team for a then-unmatched fifth straight year. After seven consecutive years of leading the league in strikeouts, Grove fell to second, two K's behind Red Ruffing, with 188. With Jimmie Foxx getting 100 extra-base hits—one of only eight players ever to hit triple figures—slugging 58 homers, driving in 169 runs, and batting .364, the A's won 94 games.

Alas, the spirit wasn't entirely winning. Or so said third baseman Jimmy Dykes. The club had the same eight regulars and the same top three starting pitchers, yet seemed to give up after matching the Yankees through mid-July, Dykes wrote in *You Can't Steal First Base*. In fairness, Mack's relief strategy was wanting and it is doubtful any amount of effort would have caught the competition. The Yankees, destiny's darlings redux, won 107 and swept the Cubs in the "called shot" World Series.

Grove was not forgotten. Giants manager John McGraw, no doubt wishing he'd landed Lefty some ten years earlier, placed him at the top of his annual All-America team. "Grove, of course, is still the game's foremost pitcher," he wrote in Philadelphia's *Evening Bulletin*, "this despite the fact that his record this year suffered no little from a sprained ankle that kept him on the sidelines for almost four weeks. Gomez, too, has been very good, but my choice goes to Grove because of his greater experience." At last: someone who could distinguish Lefty Grove from Lefty Gomez.

☆   ☆   ☆   ☆

There was plenty of hot air during the Hot Stove League. The A's, according to Mack, had the highest payroll in baseball. When Simmons, Haas, and Dykes were sold to the White Sox for $100,000 during the World Series, rumors abounded that Mack was selling off the club because of Depression debts and investments gone sour. Previously, attendance was waning because, "Who wants to see a team that wins every year?" Now the excuse was, "Who wants to see a team that's past its prime?" In fairness, Athletics fans, as hard hit as the owner, were deserting Shibe Park for legitimate financial reasons. Attendance had declined for three straight years, bottoming out at four hundred thousand in 1932. The club claimed a $500,000 loss.

People wondered if Mack would show up for opening day in 1933. Oh, he did. Showed up and marched straight to the flagpole, "eyes front and shoulders straight like a Sinn Fein leader dodging British bullets," in Wilfred Sheed's words. He wasn't criticized in town for years to come. But the Philadelphia A's were through, through like the Roaring Twenties, through like the Republicans.

But not Grove. With the club reeling after a 13-14 start, Grove was summoned for extensive relief work. From May 20 through May 30, he worked eight times in ten games over eleven days, winning four, saving four, allowing one run in 23-2/3 innings. In a whirlwind climax to the streak, he pitched 3-2/3 innings against the Red Sox to win the opener of a Memorial Day doubleheader, then threw two innings in the second game to save one of Gowell Sylvester Claset's two career wins.

Lefty not only did the job but did it pleasantly, a fact Cy Peterman found especially newsworthy in a June 3 column:

> "The greatest change in a man I ever saw."
>
> Some time ago a man who knew him when, said that of Lefty Grove. And no finer compliment was ever paid. The Grove who has been pitching his heart out for the A's this last two weeks is no more the grumpy fellow who came to the club nine years ago, than your scribe is a Chinese war lord.
>
> Here's just a flash of the Grove of today.
>
> The boys were all sorry that Lefty didn't get credit for both those Memorial Day games. His heroic work in the ninth and tenth innings of the second encounter really deserved more, and we mentioned it to Mose on the way home that night. He rode the same train with us and chatted in the smoker.
>
> "I'm satisfied with one," said Mose without hesitation. "Besides, that win'll do the big fellow more good than me. I'm glad it went to Claset."

Not that Grove had mellowed on the mound. "I have no great admiration for Grove," Hank Greenberg, a rookie in '33, wrote in his autobiography, "though I respected his pitching. He was kind of a grouchy guy. He tried to intimidate you when he was on the mound. Of course, he was older than I was; he was a veteran when I broke in. He treated every rookie with disdain and tried to intimidate him, and I guess that was his psychological ploy. He was the best left-hander I ever saw."

In Cleveland on June 22, Grove entered the game with the A's up 2-0, but allowed two runs to score when left-fielder Bob Johnson misjudged a line drive. Grove threw his glove into the dugout at inning's end. "That's the last blinking relief pitching I'll ever do for this blankety-blank ball club," Grove yelled. "You guys save your own games after this."

"Don't talk like that," said Mack.

"Don't tell me how to talk!" Grove screamed back, throwing down his jacket and kicking it.

Mack got up and kicked the jacket himself. "I'll tell you how to talk," he said, turning to Walberg. "Go down and warm up, Walberg, and we'll get a real pitcher in this game."

"Yah, and send down your whole staff," Grove said, "and you can put 'em all in, because you'll need 'em all to get anybody out."

Nonetheless, Grove eventually picked up his glove, resumed pitching and allowed no more runs, preserving an 11-6 win. Mack and Grove had met eyeball-to-eyeball, and Grove had blinked.

When Grove apologized to Mack that evening, Mack said, "Oh, that's all right, Robert, we all get worked up sometimes, but you must try to control your temper."

Lefty won eight of twelve decisions in June and July, pitching into extra innings in three straight victories. At the All Star Game in Chicago, Grove worked three scoreless innings. With the American League ahead, 4-2, two runners on and two out in the ninth, he threw three fastballs by Tony

Cuccinello. "Aspirin tablets," muttered Cuccinello. By August, however, Grove was rumored to have lost his speed.

"Has Grove's arm gone bad?" a Phillie asked the *Inquirer*'s Baumgartner.

"What makes you ask that?"

"Oh, young Connie Mack [Connie's son, Connie Jr.] told me a few days ago. He said Grove was pitching and winning with his head these days, nothing else. He said he has lost a lot of his stuff."

Really? On August 3, Grove beat the Yankees, 7-0, for their first blanking in a record two years, one day, and three hundred and eight games. The Yankees had averaged 6.5 runs per game during the streak. Against Grove, Babe Ruth and Lou Gehrig went zero-for-seven, with five strikeouts.

Grove yielded only five singles and thrice pitched out of trouble. In the fourth inning, Earle Combs singled and went to second on Joe Sewell's out. Grove walked Ruth, then struck out Gehrig and induced Ben Chapman to fly out. In the sixth Combs singled and Sewell walked, but Grove struck out both Ruth and Gehrig. Finally, in the eighth, Frankie Crosetti led off with a walk. Red Ruffing, pinch-hitting for fellow pitcher Herb Pennock, flied out. Combs got his third single of the day, with Crosetti advancing to third. Working conservatively, Grove walked Sewell to load the bases for Ruth and Gehrig. Memories, memories. Good memories, for a change. Grove fanned the Babe for the third time of the afternoon and got Gehrig to fly out. "The crafty calls of Cochrane and the control of Grove saved the day for the A's," wrote Charlie Bevis in Cochrane's biography.

On a given day anyone can shut out anyone, but there had been no given days for two Yankee seasons. During the streak Ruth and Gehrig stood tall. Gehrig was the most productive Yankee, with a .335 average, 69 homers, and an incredible 310 RBI, followed closely by Ruth (.334, 84, 270). Grove brought them to their knees. "New York writers said that never before, in the same game, were Babe Ruth and Lou Gehrig, Colonel Ruppert's twin howitzers, subdued as completely [as] Lefty subdued them yesterday," the *Inquirer's* Isaminger wrote the following day.

In the last inning of an August 30 exhibition game against the Markson's Furniture semipro team in Syracuse, New York, Grove took the ball, hitched up his pants, turned his back to the plate and waved in his outfielders. They trotted in, two to vacant spots in the infield, one directly behind Grove. It was a repeat of a stunt Rube Waddell is said to have pulled years earlier.

All baseball "hot dogs" are good players. You cannot pull a risky stunt and fail, or you will be reduced to ridicule. Grove delivered. With the hitters scared of getting hit and the umpire so intimidated he called balls and strikes from behind the mound, Grove struck out the side on nine pitches as if the semipros had merely been, oh, the Yankees.

The one major-league player Grove couldn't strike out was Joe Sewell, who was finishing his career as the Yankee third baseman. "Tell me, how did you strike him out?" Grove asked Rube Walberg during an August 29 game. The conversation was recapitulated by Hugh S. Fullerton, Jr. of the AP.

"Who, Joe Sewell?" Walberg said. "I don't know. Just lucky, I guess. Maybe some resin got in his eyes."

"Wish I'd get lucky," said Grove. "He's one guy I've never been able to fan." Well, no one else had much luck with the keen-eyed contact hitter, who struck out just 114 times in 1,903 games over a fourteen-year career.

Despite Grove's 24 wins (against only eight losses), 21 complete games, and .750 winning percentage, all league highs, his strikeouts declined from 188 to 114, a personal low. He worked 275-1/3 innings, third in the league. Another indication of his weakening condition may have been his hitting. After four good years (for a pitcher)—.216 (1 homer, 15 RBI) in '29, .200 (2, 17) in '30, .200 (0, 12) in '31, and .168 (4, 12) in '32—he batted an anemic .086 (1, 7) in '33. Notwithstanding Foxx's Triple Crown, the A's faded to fourth with a 79-72 record.

Sore arm or not, on October 1 Grove returned to central Massachusetts for another exhibition against a semipro team, his 18-strikeout one-hitter from 1927 still fresh in everyone's minds. Before the game Grove chatted with Spencer club reserve Frank (Dodo) Bird, a catcher (17 games) for the 1892 St. Louis Nationals. Then Lefty threw to his catcher for the day, a nervous Providence College student named Birdie Tebbetts, later a big-league receiver and manager. Time hadn't dulled Lefty's fastball. "[Former A's shortstop] Jack Barry, who was managing Grove's team and scouting the game, told me, 'Don't take your eye off it,' " Tebbetts said. "I called for a fastball, and the first pitch went right through me. I only caught the third strike against the first three men he faced. The ball was rising and moving around so much that I just fought them off. I was protecting myself."

Grove pitched a no-hitter for eight innings and struck out 15 batters altogether (there's no record of how much he was paid per K). Unfortunately, fielding mistakes by teammates cost him dearly in the ninth and tenth innings, and Spencer lost to visiting North Brookfield, 3-1, before thirty-five hundred fans crowding O'Gara Park.

Though Birdie Tebbetts committed two errors, he had a even bigger day than Grove. For his success in fighting off Grove's fastballs, he was signed by a big-league scout.

Mack, now seventy, wanted to cut Grove's salary, which

family members have said was his all-time high of $28,000. Grove asked to be traded. *Après ça, le déluge.* On December 12, at the winter meetings in Chicago's Palmer House, Mack sold Grove to the Red Sox for $125,000. In the same breath, he traded Walberg and Bishop to Boston for one Harold (Rabbit) Warstler, one Robert G. Kline, and $35,000. Mack traded Cochrane to the Tigers for $100,000 and second-string catcher John Pasek. (Cochrane was immediately named manager.) While Mack was at it, he sent Earnshaw and Pasek to the White Sox for $25,000 and catcher Charlie Berry. In what the AP called "the biggest deal in the history of baseball," Mack had disposed of five stars mostly for warm bodies and $285,000. At least he had wiped out the club debt, reported at $200,000.

Lefty heard the news while having lunch at Marshall's in downtown Lonaconing. His friend Milt Hout came in and told him, "I just heard on the radio that you've been traded."

"Oh, I don't believe that. No one told me," Grove said. Then someone else came in with the same news. Lefty was not surprised, and reasonably pleased to be joining an up-and-coming team. "I'll like it a lot to be over there with such good fellows as Eddie Collins [the general manager] and Bucky Harris [the manager], both of whom know their stuff," Grove told a reporter, who quoted him in stilted language he probably didn't speak. "I've known Collins [a former A's teammate] long and intimately. He certainly knows his baseball.

"I'm sure I'll have more enthusiasm for my pitching next year, and the years thereafter then for some time. That's no reflection on Connie Mack, but merely the idea that change is good for some of us after we've been in one place for some time.

"I'm sorry that I'll no longer have Mickey Cochrane catching me. There's a great lad. But Rick Ferrell, as everybody knows, is one of the greatest catchers in the game ..."

Mack later said that he had never put up with so much grief from any player as he did from Grove. It was not just a question of tolerating Lefty's excesses. Mack knew when to console and cajole him, as he did after the 16-game winning streak was broken. The old man could also stand up to Grove when he went around the bend.

Asked what it was like being managed by Mack, Grove said he didn't know, because he never paid attention to him. He was exaggerating, of course, but Grove's role in their *pas de deux* was underrated. At times the relationship was a veritable chess match. Arthur Daley, the Pulitzer Prize-winning New York *Times* columnist, described one memorable game:

> Old Mose once had the Yanks beaten by a run with two outs in the ninth inning and runners on first and second. The hitter was Gehrig. Grove wanted to walk him. Connie wig-wagged no. Lefty stood on the mound, fuming. He fired one in, a deliberate wild pitch. Both runners advanced and first base was open.
>
> "Walk Gehrig," signaled Connie, which was what Grove had wanted to do originally. So he struck out the next hitter to win the game.
>
> "Nice managing, Mr. Mack," said Lefty, a glint of amusement in his eye.
>
> "Thank you, Robert," said Mr. Mack, not quite appreciating that Grove had set up his victory with a wild pitch.

Grove had to feel he was doing well. He had ridden the crest of the wave with two of history's greatest teams, the

Baltimore Orioles of 1920-24 and the Philadelphia Athletics of 1929-31. Now he was joining a promising new club, one rebuilding under a dynamic young owner who was about to open an impressively reconstructed ballpark. Everything would be sparkling and green.

BOMBING IN BOSTON

★　　　★　　　★　　　★

"The Red Sox are a religion. Every year we reenact the agony and the temptation of the Garden. Baseball child's play? Hell, up here in Boston it's a passion play."

–George V. Higgins

High noon, March 2, 1934. In the 1930's, spring training didn't begin for the Red Sox the moment they pitched camp in Sarasota, Florida. It started when the official Red Sox travelling party, complete with diehard fans, officials and equipment, pulled out of South Station. This year the team's ritual sendoff looked for all the world like the start of a politician's whistle-stop tour, or maybe the next leg of a papal visit. On board the *Senator* were "royal rooter" George Murphy, other prominent Sox boosters, a minor-league player, and nine newsmen, the largest press contingent the *Herald's* Burt Whitman could remember. Two extra sleeping cars, the *McDougal* and the *McCausland*, had been added. More than one hundred well-wishers crowded the platform. "No less an authority than travelling secretary Phil Troy claimed that this was the first time in his two decades of connection with Boston ball clubs that a departing squad has been given an honest-to-goodness cheer as it pulled out of South Station for Dixie," Whitman wrote. His story was headlined: "Hose Given Royal Send-off;/Travel Like Prima Donnas."

Why did the lowly Red Sox produce so much enthusiasm? The city of Boston and its woebegone sports teams needed resuscitation, and Boston's thirty-one-year-old owner, Tom Yawkey, looked like the doctor. In only thirteen months at the helm, he had acquired the best pitcher in baseball, turned an also-ran team into a projected contender, and transformed a ballpark into a pleasure palace. The sight of all that hope pulling out of South Station was not only inspiring, but Depression-lifting.

Smiles soon faded. *The Curse of the Bambino*, a book written by Boston *Globe* columnist Dan Shaughnessy, refers not merely to the trail of also-rans and last-place teams that succeeded Babe Ruth's departure to the Yankees after the 1919 season. The Sox have been hurt by something far worse than mere failure: the sensation of reaching for the brass ring, only to see it snatched away. All too often the promise of spring has become the betrayal of summer. Boston has lost championships on the last day of the season, on the day after the last day of the season, and four times in the seventh game of the World Series, often with designated scapegoats. Nineteen thirty-four was the first of the cursed seasons, with spirits raised and dropped like a wrestler repeatedly lifting and slamming his opponent to the mat.

In Depression Boston, a winning team could give a huge boost to the civic psyche "It was an act of faith," says Boston historian Phil Bergen. "Religion, sports, and politics—things you thought you could trust."

Then as now, teams that spent were teams that won. The pre-Yawkey Red Sox and the National League Braves had endured the 1920's and early '30s trying to stay out of last place and bankruptcy court. The hockey Bruins failed to make the 1934 playoffs, while the football Boston Redskins were two years from an unfortunate date with destiny. In 1936, they would, uniquely for their sport, play a "home" playoff game on the road. After losing to the Green Bay Packers at New York's Polo Grounds, the Redskins moved immediately to Washington, D.C.

No wonder Bostonians were turned off by their pro teams. For sporting satisfaction, they walked from work to twilight semipro baseball games that sometimes outdrew the majors, went to the race track, or attended boxing and wrestling matches where Irishmen like Steve (Crusher) Casey were huge favorites and the opponents were given descriptions like "dusky-colored grappler." Some of these ugly events degenerated into public brawls.

Public life was no more uplifting. If "Hub of the Universe" was an exaggeration, Boston was certainly the trading and transportation center of the region. Products passed endlessly in and out of the port of Boston. But with factories and mills dying in places like Haverhill, Malden, and Lowell, the goods weren't getting there. When plants wither, the garden dies.

Newspapers trumpeted murder stories. Old money sat in banks, and there was no new investment to speak of. In a languishing hourglass economy—what goes around comes around—Bostonians were overwhelmingly wealthy, working class, or poor. The social climate was established by a strange coalition of Irish Catholic and Yankee Brahmin Puritans. In the years before Yawkey's arrival, city officials had banned Theodore Dreiser's *An American Tragedy*, Upton Sinclair's

Oil, Eugene O'Neill's *Strange Interlude*, and Ernest Hemingway's *The Sun Also Rises*. According to the book *Boston, The Great Depression and The New Deal*, anything to the left of *Little Lord Fauntleroy* was fair game. "The Cabots and that crowd are so afraid of a left wing they won't go near one, even if it's on a chicken," Groucho Marx told the *Harvard Crimson* in 1929.

A provincial pretender, that was Boston. Not even the New Deal could bail it out. Boston was seventy-three percent Roman Catholic and had given Franklin Delano Roosevelt the largest majority of any city in the 1932 election. You'd think the Irish Catholic James Michael Curley, finishing his third term as mayor in 1933, would have taken the aid pumping out of an energized Washington and steered it to his ailing citizens. Unfortunately, Curley played the disingenuous politics of today. Nominally a Democrat, he owed his only allegiance to the Curley Party. A master of image, he won massive support by playing on ethnic and religious divisions. Lacking ideals and ideology, he practiced the politics of personal enchantment. Nonetheless, despite scandal and stagnation, he was adored. There are two statues of him behind Boston's City Hall. One shows him standing and speaking, the ultimate rhetorician. The other shows him on a park bench, a man of the people.

In his better days, Curley had created jobs by building parks, playgrounds, beaches, hospitals, bridges, tunnels, and schools. He literally lifted scrubwomen off their knees by giving them long mops. But by the first year of the Roosevelt administration, Curley the public servant had become Curley the power monger. In what should have been his shining hour, he travelled abroad and balked at federal relief, rejecting it altogether unless it went to his personal contractors, with major kickbacks to Himself. Though Boston was eligible for 22,800 jobs under the Public Works Administration (PWA), the city accepted only 12,500.

In *The Rascal King*, a definitive Curley biography, Jack Beatty describes a late 1933 walk through Boston by John Bantry, the pen name for editor and columnist Clifton Carberry of the Boston *Post*:

> Along Atlantic Avenue, facing Boston Harbor, stood a string of abandoned commercial properties. Block after block between Atlantic Avenue and Milk Street, the heart of the downtown business district, was entirely devoid of tenants . . . . Throughout the city large properties were not earning enough in rent to pay their ever-rising taxes. This residual effect of Curleyism was at the same time one of its continuing causes. With such little economic vitality in Boston's private sector, for many in the next generation of Bostonians the only career alternative would be a job "on the Gas Company" or "on the Edison" or "on the city."

In 1934, Curley turned over the city's misery to Frederick W. Mansfield and took his merry mischief into a successful run for governor and a term noted more for pomp than substance. No wonder Bostonians looked for relief in sports.

And there they were, the rebounding, resurgent Red Sox. A last-place (43-111) team in 1932, Boston had signed catcher Rick Ferrell and third baseman Bill Werber in 1933. Eddie Collins, late of the A's, arrived to wheel and deal as general manager. And, lo, the Sox rose to seventh and 63-86 in the first year under Yawkey, who had inherited a fortune of more than seven million Depression dollars when he turned thirty. Home attendance jumped from 182,150 to 268,715. During the winter meetings of December, 1933, Collins engineered the big deal for Grove, Walberg, and Bishop. Early in the '34 season Boston would add Cleveland pitcher Wes Ferrell, a 23-game winner two seasons earlier.

That wasn't all. Yawkey replaced manager Marty McManus with Detroit's Bucky Harris, a pennant-winning skipper with the 1924 and 1925 Senators. And Yawkey spent $1.25 million on union labor—a good political move—to turn Fenway Park from a wooden fire hazard to a cement-and-steel master-piece, complete with the most famous landmark in baseball: the left-field wall. Counting player purchases, Yawkey dis-pensed at least $2.25 million on the team. The Sox would surely become winners, if not contenders, and fans were dreaming of the first pennant since 1918. Indeed, Jack Doyle, the "well-known Broadway betting commissioner," rated the Red Sox 4-1, close behind the Senators and Yankees, each at 2-1 to win the pennant.

The focus of everyone's attention was Grove. Good reli-gious fans that they are, Bostonians have always looked for saviors, be they named Foxx, Williams, Clemens, or Martinez. In Grove they landed their first savior. He had won 172 games in his past seven seasons and was universally acclaimed the game's nonpareil pitcher. Understandably, fans were projecting wildly. Grove would lead the Red Sox, who had been wandering the wilderness for fifteen seasons, to the promised land of pennantdom.

★　　　★　　　★　　　★

Baseball is a sport best understood incrementally, as facts and feelings accrue over a seven-month spring and summer season. To understand how the extraordinary 1934 season unraveled for Lefty Grove and the Red Sox, let's follow the daily Boston newspaper headlines and deadline writing of beat reporters.

The Boston press was not quite the lair of selected head-hunters and hitmen it became when an unpolished Ted Williams came to town. Many of the scribes were outright "homers" who occasionally wrote in the first person about rooting the old town team along. They referred cordially to teams by the names of their managers—the Mackmen, the McKechniemen. The players were given all kinds of affection-ate nicknames; Lefty himself was variously known as Lefty Bob Grove, Robert Moses, Mose, and Robert Moses Grove. (Sometimes Lefty and Moses were in quotes, sometimes not.) The newsmen, journeying across the northeast quadrant of the country on the same trains as the teams, were viewed more as fellow travellers than foes.

To be sure, nasty writing crossed their typewriters. When their teams went bad, writers felt as betrayed as children losing their parents. Their printed reactions were often hyperbolic, just as their praise could be excessive. The scribes also wrote in telling, breakneck (they did not have much use for commas) detail. At their best, they went where the facts led them. And the Boston writers went everywhere, since Boston also had a National League team. ("Boston vs. Chicago" was an ambiguous schedule promotion.) Some of their best writing followed interviews with famous men from both leagues: Bill Terry, Walter Johnson, the Dean brothers.

Be alerted. You will not hear much from the Boston *Globe*. The Voice of New England, which currently has one of the country's finest sports sections, covered games far too succinctly at the time, the Harvard-Yale crew race and Boston College sometimes getting equal treatment with professional baseball. But you will hear from the *Herald* stylist Burt Whitman and Harold Kaese, then with the *Transcript*, and later a *Globe* columnist. A nut for research and detail, Kaese thought nothing of writing twenty-inch analyses of both Boston teams. In an age when sportswriters mostly typed about what was in front of them, Kaese's work foreshadowed the more critical and comprehensive coverage of today.

There were no negative stories filed when the team train picked up players and officials in Providence, Bridgeport, New York, and Washington. Arriving in camp on March 4, the great throng was thrilled when Grove, who had preceded the train to Florida, entered the Sarasota Terrace Hotel at 3 p.m. with fellow pitcher Walberg. The weather was blustery outside, with rain about to fall, and practice had been called off. The big story was arriving.

"It seemed that everything around the hotel stood still for several minutes, while Grove was given royal greeting," Whitman reported.

"Goodness gracious, Herbie," Grove teased forty-year-old Herb Pennock, his old Yankee nemesis, now a fellow Bosox. "You'll have to do a lot of running to get that stomach down." Everyone laughed. Pennock was as thin as a reed of grass.

"The ice was broken and everybody met everybody else," Whitman's dispatch continued. "Merely because you may have read that Grove is a taciturn, even grumpy fellow, who doesn't mix well, we hasten to add that he mixed beautifully with these Red Sox."

Grove announced that he wouldn't be practicing on Sundays because, "six days are enough for me, and always have been." Notice that he made the announcement without consulting anyone. Lefty and Lefty alone was given a single room in the road hotels. He expected carte blanche, and Tom Yawkey, several years his junior, was in thrall. The manager, general manager, and coaches could only follow.

The media seemed in step, too. Wrote Whitman after the March 5 opening practice, "He went into the bunting game like a trained acrobat, apparently without any stiff joints in his makeup."

On March 7, Harris sucked up his gut and announced that Pennock would replace Grove after six innings all season to conserve the great man's fastball. There is no record of Grove disagreeing, and Harris didn't follow through anyway.

Three days later Grove finally threw batting practice. His fastball certainly seemed normal, and teammates struggled to get the fat part of their bats on the ball. "It almost seemed that his glamorous reputation had them buffaloed," Whitman wrote.

"This Grove, with all his speed, throws the lightest ball I ever caught," said Joe Judge, the former Senators first baseman, who warmed Grove up while trying to make the Red Sox. "It fits your glove like a feather. He cut loose with a couple today that had whiskers on 'em, and they landed soft as a baby's kiss."

He went on: "A natural overhand thrower like Grove gets a cushion of air in front of his ball that makes a buffer when it lands. But these sidearm tossers hit like a hard rock."

Generally, Grove wasn't pushing himself too hard, restricting the bulk of his workout to playing pepper and doing some sprints. Back at the hotel, he lounged on a veranda, smoking big cigars, playing practical jokes. The *Evening Transcript*'s LeRoy Atkinson described him in detail:

> Grove is still a big country boy. Around the hotel he is a menace to life and limb. Usually picking on travelling secretary Phil Troy, who stands only shoulder high to Robert Moses, the

big Lonaconing, Md., southpaw will swing the protesting Phil around as though the two were performing an adagio dance.

"I'm all black and blue around here," complains Phil, rubbing his gunwales. "I guess I'll have to take out an insurance policy as big as we have on Grove if the big fellow doesn't lay off me."

Another favorite trick of Mr. Grove's is to come up behind a newspaperman and take the skin around both ribs and then pull. The flesh seems to come out a foot and then snap back against the bones like the crack of an elastic. The feeling cannot be described, and the Grove back-slap: ow!

In truth, it was a relaxed atmosphere all around–at least with the athletes. With relatively few youngsters in camp, Harris let the players set their own routines and adhere to the midnight curfew without supervision.

"I want all the work you can give me," Grove told Harris on March 13, "until the week before the opening game of the season, and then I don't want to work out at all until the first game of the season."

GROVE NURSES FIRST SORE ARM OF HIS CAREER

Too soon, he wasn't working out at all. Pitching thirty minutes of batting practice on March 14, Grove threw at half speed and virtually no speed, riling the batters. Immediately after the workout, Grove headed to trainer Doc Watson, who rubbed salve on him, massaged him, and put the offending arm under electric lights.

"You'll bake me browner than a goose, Doc," he moaned.

"Oh, that's nothing, and feels a lot hotter than it is," Watson

Grove and longtime Yankee nemesis Herb Pennock (far right) at the train station. They finished their careers together with the Red Sox.

said. "You've never had any of this stuff. I'll bring you around in no time at all. You are like a kid going to the dentist for the first time."

Within two days, Grove's arm had become a major concern. The trouble was diagnosed as a sore spot near the top of the left shoulder, somewhere behind the biceps muscle and various ligaments. Watson had to fight through them to knead the sore area. Grove screamed.

The Red Sox hadn't played an exhibition game, but the newsmen who had ballyhooed the season under headlines like "Red Sox Record Warrants Rising Pennant Chorus" began predicting a fourth-place finish—at best. The weather, in the thirties and forties, didn't help the team get ready. One day Grove felt fine, the next day he relapsed. Some teammates privately wondered if the injury was legitimate. Grove grimly ran sprints outside Payne Park and spent half an hour daily under the violet-ray lamp.

For all the gloom of the sportswriters, Red Sox fans were undiminished in their enthusiasm. Steeled by rough winters, New Englanders were accustomed to springs both actual and metaphoric. Lefty Grove was merely the first local hero ready to stage the Perils of Pauline. The adventures of Ted Williams, Carl Yastrzemski, Wade Boggs, and Roger Clemens would follow. Let's call the 1934 drama "Waiting for Lefty."

On March 30, Grove, with Collins and Yawkey in tow, stopped at the Athletics spring headquarters to see his old owner/manager Connie Mack and trainer E.E. Ebling. Denying rumors that Mack had knowingly sold the Sox damaged goods—the Sox G.M. would issue the same disclaimer all season—Collins said he was pleased with the trade.

"The loss of Grove is farther reaching than appears on the surface," Harris said. "Were he able to go, it would serve as an inspiration to the rest of the ball club. However, all we can do is wait and see what develops."

On April 4, still in Florida, Grove staged his first full-scale tantrum of the year. After warming up for fifteen minutes before a game against the Dodgers in which he wasn't expected to pitch, Grove caught a return throw from coach Tom Daly and suddenly threw down his glove. As the ball rolled past his feet, Grove walked past silent teammates and stationed himself beside the dugout.

Subsequently Grove headed to the bench, ripped a teammate's sweatshirt from a peg, and threw it down. Then he flung his glove off the wall and walked outside the dugout. "To hell with it!" Grove screamed. "I can't do the club any good! I might as well hang up the spikes!" Grove took his black windbreaker into the clubhouse, where he spent three innings before returning to the field, only to sit conspicuously apart from his teammates on the grass.

At least, this was the report in the *Herald* and *Globe*. The *Globe* beat man, Melville E. Webb, Jr., who had virtually ignored Grove's arm trouble except to report denials from Doc Watson, Harris, Collins, and Grove himself, did not file on April 5 and improbably claimed the stories were absurdities cooked up by "kid" reporters who weren't on the scene. Webb said that Grove threw down his glove, shagged some flies in the outfield, and sat *with* his teammates on the grass.

To Webb, the problem was entirely in Grove's head. He was simply too lazy to take spring training seriously, Webb strongly implied. "To express a personal opinion, I feel that the failure of Grove to get in shape to pitch in turn has had a negative effect on the morale of the ball club. The huge sum which Tom Yawkey spent for this outstanding pitcher of the league just naturally perked up the whole confidence of the Harris outfit at the start of the spring training season.

"Had Grove been right, there would have been no such steady turnovers such as the Sox have experienced as they have lost seven of the nine games already played with National League ball clubs. That's no excuse, but so far as things have happened to date, I am of the firm belief that there would have been better results had Grove never been added to the pitching staff at all."

Collins expressed no alarm over Grove's outburst, and Grove himself recovered quickly. "Say, it looks as if after this when I want to get a little peeved, I'll have to go lock myself in my room," he joked to the *Herald*'s Gerry Moore.

Ballplayers constantly return too soon from injuries. They are under pressure: from their teammates, from the club, from the fans, from the press, from themselves. So they return prematurely, get hurt, and earn praise from everyone: a real gamer, plays in pain. Ready or not, on April 7 Grove played his first spring training game, pitching four innings in Birmingham, Alabama, against the minor-league Birmingham Barons.

He tried to remember his old routine. After warming up for fifteen minutes on the sideline, Grove walked to the mound, threw his customary three pitches and announced he was ready. He was not. With a man on second and two outs, he surrendered a run-scoring single to Buzz Arlett, a former Phil now becoming a minor-league legend.

Grove was so discouraged by the third inning that he yelled to the umpire, "Where does the ball have to be?" Whereupon he lobbed the ball to the hitter, who doubled in the third run of the inning.

In the end Grove gave up eight hits and four runs in four innings. "The spirit was willing, but the flesh was not," an unidentified *Herald* correspondent began a story. ". . . Lefty didn't even have the ghost of his fastball."

"I couldn't get anything on the ball," Grove, the picture of dejection, told the writer back in the hotel lobby.

"There is still a knot in his arm," said Watson. "And the chances are, he won't be able to pitch until it's eliminated."

GROVE'S TROUBLE TRACED TO TEETH

As spring training unfolded, the drama of "Waiting for Lefty" got curiouser and curiouser. Perhaps the problem wasn't in his arm, or even in his head. After the Birmingham blasting, Grove took a dental exam that revealed three abscessed teeth and inflamed tonsils. On April 8, E.L. Sorrell, Yawkey's Birmingham-based brother-in-law, extracted two molars. After the second tooth broke and had to be cut out, Lefty decided to have the third one removed in Philadelphia. The tonsil problem was not disclosed at the time. Lefty thought he could take his chances with them as they were.

The doctors in attendance agreed that the teeth had affected Grove's pitching. If they didn't somehow bother the arm, they worsened his general physical condition. "One of the doctors at Birmingham said that he 'wished he had as much chance to go to Heaven as Lefty Grove's arm had to come back, following the elimination of poison from the general system,' " Webb wrote.

"I'm going to be ready—let the teeth fall where they may," Grove said from Atlanta. On April 10, in Philadelphia, another dentist took out the third abscessed tooth.

"Sore arm, sure I've got a sore arm," a notably cheerier Grove said. "But why all the uproar? Everything is coming along fine, and it won't be more than a week or so before I'll be in good shape.

Grove immediately segued to his teeth. "And he pulled a big one right out of my mouth right here—look." He showed the reporters. The fans' hopes must have soared like a thermometer on the first sunny spring day.

On April 11, Grove announced he wouldn't pitch for ten to fourteen days—the time, he said, it would take for the poison to leave his system.

His wife Ethel arrived from Lonaconing with the Grove car, and a few days later, they headed nonstop from Philadelphia to Boston. "I'll be out tomorrow, and I'm feeling right in the pink again," said Grove upon his arrival. "The dentist . . . told me not to stir up the animals too quickly."

So now we come to opening day. With a 154-game season and many doubleheaders—it was routine to play them every Sunday, plus Memorial Day, Independence Day, and Labor

Day—the regular season lasted 5-1/2 months, or two weeks shorter than the current schedule. With the off days, everything was compressed, giving each game greater urgency.

The April 16 Sox opener in Washington was rained out. Entering Fenway Park for the home opener the very next day was like driving down a road in rural Ireland. Everything was sparkling and green. There were new green signs over the enlarged grandstands, bright green paint on the cement walls, and green bullseye lights to mark balls (red for strikes) on the new sheet-metal-and-steel wall with its thirty-seven-foot-tall fence. Stretching from the left-field corner almost to dead center, the great wall was also long enough to hold updated scores from both leagues, as well as advertisements (later removed) for whiskey, razor blades, and soap. Fully 15,708 new seats were installed, boosting the park's capacity to 37,500, including box seats clear down to the field and bleachers "for forgotten men and small boys," according to the *Herald*'s Whitman. The seating areas melded into each other in a unified pattern. It was also considered an ultra-modern stadium for its time, the sixth largest in baseball. And it wasn't just useful. It was beautiful.

Fenway Park was a major story in Depression Boston. There were no tall ships being built, and no tall buildings either. Thanks to a height restriction, the thirty-story U.S. Custom House was the only skyscraper in town. Rebuilt Fenway was the product of heroic 'round-the-clock effort. It survived a five-hour, four-alarm off-season blaze that burned down the center-field bleachers and turned reconstruction into re-reconstruction. Finished on time in spite of it all, this gleaming gem—the city's largest private construction project of the decade—was to Bostonians what Yankee Stadium, Central Park, the Statue of Liberty, and the Brooklyn Bridge were to New Yorkers. In Boston newspapers, opening day was so important it shared page one with a hot murder trial.

The Sox looked every bit as spiffy as their park. Their new uniforms, simple but stylish, were more subdued with less red but more subtly ornamented. The pants and shirts were plain, with "Red Sox" printed in blue with red trim. (They said "Boston" on road uniforms.) The socks were especially elegant. A two-inch red anklet yielded to a one-inch blue stripe, a two-inch white stripe, another inch of blue, then white to the bottom of the knickered pants. The caps were blue, with a red "B" on front. The warm-up coats were red on one side, blue on the other.

Grove threw on the side with Tom Daly, purely as a sidelight. With pitcher Gordon (Dusty) Rhodes starting before 30,336 fans, the mayor, and the governor, the Red Sox rallied from a 5-0 deficit to tie the score. In the eleventh inning, erratic pitching and an untimely error cost them a run and the game, which they lost to the Senators, 6-5. But fans left Fenway babbling about the exciting team they'd seen. The fluke ending surely couldn't be a harbinger of days (and seasons and decades) to come.

"We want Grove!" the fans chanted when he warmed up in the Washington series. Grove did pitch five innings against Holy Cross in an April 27 dress-rehearsal exhibition at Worcester, Massachusetts. He fanned the first two hitters, then let up a little, allowing only one run and four hits in five innings. "I felt all right all day," he said afterward. Nonetheless, Harris held him out of a series in Yankee Stadium, the site of far too much Grovian discomfort already.

ARM FAILS: SOX WIN, 13-12

With the Sox in fourth place at 7-7, Grove made his first appearance on May 5, in relief, against the Browns. He began warming up in the second inning, when the starter, Johnny Welch, was struggling. Harris asked if Grove was ready for the third, and he said no. Rube Walberg worked the inning, and Grove entered the game in the fourth, with the Red Sox leading, 9-3. He walked from the bullpen, a lanky wraith in his white No. 10 uniform, while nineteen thousand Fenway fans cheered.

It was showtime, and he bombed in Boston. A walk, a triple, a single, a double, a walk on four pitches. Grove pointed to catcher Rick Ferrell, signaling for him to hold the ball. Without a look to the dugout, he walked off the field, carefully skirting the first-base line. He had surrendered three hits, two walks, and five earned runs without retiring a batter.

"The great southpaw was wholly without his famous 'smoke' ball, so named because of its amazing speed," the *Herald*'s Whitman wrote. "He merely was a thrower in there, and his control was not good."

Grove agreed. There was no pain, and no stuff, either.

Nine days later he threw 6-2/3 innings of one-run relief against the White Sox. Grove reported with the bases loaded, walked a batter to force in one run, allowed another to score on a fielder's choice, then ended the inning by inducing a ground ball.

Mopping up the loss until game's end, Grove yielded three hits and one unearned run in the following five innings, retiring 12 straight batters at one point. "The pronounced silver lining to the defeat was that Bob Lefty Grove staged a real come-back, impressive to a marked degree and indicative that soon he will be able to take his starting turn in the box for manager Bucky Harris," Whitman wrote.

"Certainly feels all right," said Grove.

Boarding an all-night train to St. Louis at 4:30 p.m, both Grove and Harris struggled to contain their joy. "Just give me a couple of days of rest and I'll be ready to start," Grove "war-whooped," according to the *Herald*'s Gerry Moore. "I was right yesterday and don't think that anyone is more pleased than I. Watch us go now."

"I believe he was hurried too much for that first appearance," said Harris. "When he had those teeth out, he had to start training all over again and I don't believe he was ready when I asked him to go in there against the Browns. Yesterday it was different. Lefty was right and I think he's right to stay. We are going places with his help."

☆   ☆   ☆   ☆

On May 19 in St. Louis, Grove got his first start. It was against Dick Coffman, who had ended his 16-game winning streak three years earlier. Long overdue for revenge, Lefty held tough in another pitching duel. Trailing 1-0 in the seventh, the Red Sox used an error by Ski Melillo—the same man whose single beat Grove in '31—and a three-run homer by Grove himself to score four times. Lefty went the distance and won, 4-1, on six hits. There was nothing more he could ask for. He celebrated the usual way, undoubtedly with even more gusto. It takes a big man to smoke a big cigar.

The press was impressed, but in a surprisingly restrained way. Grove had visibly tired in the ninth, but centerfielder Carl Reynolds, shortstop Lyn Lary, and third baseman Bill Werber made good plays. "The lefthander did not show the blinding speed he has possessed in the past, but he was good enough to stop the Browns," a *Herald* correspondent wrote.

"One watching him yesterday could not believe that he was the 'fireball' pitcher of old," one writer reported. "His work was labored and it was perhaps over-anxiousness on the part of the Browns that helped his effectiveness. He may win more games for the Red Sox this year, but the 'old Grove passeth.' It may be years before the fans again see his like."

On May 23, Grove gave up five runs and 10 hits early, then improved as the game progressed in a struggling win over the Indians. In a "conference of war," Grove insisted on batting for himself with the club down a run in the ninth. He singled, and the Red Sox went on to win, 7-5.

But this season wasn't just drama; it was melodrama. Grove proceeded to lose four straight, twice giving up eight earned runs and once seven. There seemed to be no question at all that the old Grove had passed. His speed waltzed off forever, and the backup dancers were nowhere to be seen. Was the problem his arm, his delivery, his confidence? Or something else? Grove had ended the 1933 season with severely ripped fingertips. Now the whole left hand was at risk. While he was being raked for eight runs in 5-2/3 innings during a May 28 loss at Detroit, he struck out a batter with no one on base and catcher Ferrell whipped the ball to Bill Werber at third. "Before throwing the ball to Lary at short, I noticed blood on it," Werber said. "Instead of letting the ball go around the infield, I took it to Lefty on the mound to inquire where the blood had come from. When I looked at the inside of the middle finger of his left hand, there was no skin there. He was pitching from raw meat.

" 'Mose,' " I said, 'you can't pitch like that.'

" 'Get the hell outta here!' he said. 'Gimme the damn ball. Get your ass back to third base.' " No one—not teammates, coaches, or the manager—stood up to him.

While other Red Sox pitchers blossomed, Grove didn't pitch between June 17 and July 3. "Little wonder that the Red Sox look their strongest of the season," Harold Kaese wrote. In a close race, they were 36-33, just 7-1/2 games behind the league-leading Yankees.

LEFTY GROVE OPERATED ON FOR TONSILS

———

RED SOX PITCHER, DESPERATE,
UNDERGOES MINOR OPERATION THIS MORNING

———

PHYSICAL CONDITION MAY BE IMPROVED

ORGANS FOUND TO BE BADLY INFECTED
—PROBABLY THE LAST REMEDY

Grove threw two innings of ineffective relief July 3 in New York and returned to Boston while the team headed to Philadelphia. Ending a closely guarded secret, Grove had his infected tonsils removed on July 5 by Dr. Harry P. Cahill at the Cardinal O'Connor House in St. Elizabeth's Hospital.

It was the Philadelphia connection, his hope in ages past, that changed Lefty's mind. "He told Connie Mack a few weeks ago in Philadelphia that he'd do anything to get in shape for 'those two fellows up in Boston [Yawkey and Collins],' G.M. Collins told Boston columnist George C. Carens. "When he came back, Lefty said: 'Cocky, shall I have the tonsils yanked?' We conferred with Dr. Eddie O'Brien, our consultant, and he had Dr. Harry Cahill remove them."

All Boston baseball seemed to hinge at once on the great silent one's vocals. "The very bad condition of his tonsils is encouraging," Kaese wrote, "for it means that they would be sufficient to rob Grove of his strength." In other words, good tonsils could equal a strong arm.

Kaese referred twice to Grove's "last chance" and linked it to the Red Sox' season. "The addition of a Grove in his old-time form may be the spur that will lift the Red Sox to leadership of the American League for the first time since 1918."

"A sore arm, or loss of confidence, will probably never be corrected entirely," Kaese concluded. "The question of Grove now depends on the question of the success of the operation removing his tonsils. It is baseball's biggest question of the year."

Grove missed the July 10 All Star Game in Chicago, where the Giants' Carl Hubbell struck out Babe Ruth, Lou Gehrig, Jimmie Foxx, Al Simmons, and Joe Cronin in succession. For the time being, the Meal Ticket was baseball's best and Lefty was a leftover. On July 15, the *Herald* reported that Grove would report to the team in Chicago the following day, possibly for service in the "Windy City series." False alarm.

On July 24, he did pitch two innings in a loss to the Tigers, a team he had terrorized all through his career. Grove produced a Tigers run virtually by himself by walking Billy Rogell, wild-pitching him to second, and serving up a single to Marv Owen.

Manager Harris, choosing New York as the locale to vent his grief, told an AP reporter that the Red Sox could blame their season—they had just lost a doubleheader to the Yankees and hit safely only 22 times in four games—on Grove's ineffectiveness. "Figure it out for yourself," he said. "We had every reason to expect Grove to win at least twenty games for us. He has won only four and it's a question of whether his arm will be in shape to start another game before the middle of August. Yet we are only nine games or thereabouts back of the leaders, neither of which has the stuff to make any runaway of the race this year. With Grove in shape and taking his regular turn, I don't think there's a doubt he would have fifteen victories by now, which would mean we would be right on top of the heap."

Grove pitched batting practice and proclaimed himself fit and ready. Skeptics far and wide expected little from him. "These hard-ball pitchers go fast when they go," Babe Ruth said. "They haven't got so much left when the old hop disappears. I wish him luck, but I'll be surprised if Grove is ever a twenty-game winner again."

Grove and Alvin Crowder, AL co-leaders with 24 wins in 1933, had won four games apiece by August of '34. Suddenly, Crowder was waived from Washington to the Tigers amid talk of leading them to a pennant. Grove was "fighting to stay in baseball with a throwing arm ailing so that he is about as near to the end of his rope as he can be without dropping into the void," Kaese wrote.

BABE WET-EYED AS 46,766
BOSTON FANS SAY FAREWELL

Attendance continued to soar. Fenway set a new record on August 12—this time not because of Lefty, but because of the Bambino. Babe Ruth, hoping to manage in 1935, came to Boston for what was supposedly the last time (his move to the Braves hadn't been concocted yet). He had obviously mellowed, because he now put Grove on his all-time all-star team.

The great man, forty, bid a wet-eyed farewell to an adoring overflow crowd of 46,766—the fire laws hadn't been changed yet—with at least ten thousand more turned back. For the unprecedented occasion, some twenty extra police, forty firemen, and one hundred and sixty other extra help cared for the crowd, and forty-five additional cars were added to the Boston elevated. Because of traffic, the Brookline Avenue bus line was re-routed away from Kenmore Square to Beacon Street.

People sat in the aisles or watched from nearby rooftops.

The field was roped off across the outfield. Ruth was always a double treat, and it seemed fitting he should part in a doubleheader. Playing left, he went two-for-six without a homer or an RBI. "The climax, and we never saw such a demonstration in any ball game before, came when the big fellow trudged off the field in the sixth inning of the second game," Whitman wrote in the *Herald*.

"Spontaneously and as one man, the huge crowd, all the way around the field, stood up and applauded. There was little shouting. It was hand clapping, steadily swelling in volume until the big fellow was lost to sight as he entered the Red Sox dugout—the one he first entered as a major leaguer twenty years ago—and passed out of sight to the intimacies of the Yankee clubhouse under the grandstand.

"The Red Sox said there was tears in Babe's eyes as he passed through the dugout on the way out because he was touched by the mass applause."

GROVE CHECKS A'S AFTER FERRELL FAILS
AND RED SOX COAST TO 11-9 VICTORY

Grove wanted nothing to do with his own pitching obituaries. On August 8, he returned from what, with the exception of that two-inning outing, was a five-week recuperation, to face the Athletics for the first time, in Philadelphia. With the Red Sox leading 10-6 in the third inning and Wes Ferrell too battered to continue, Grove walked to the mound and held the A's to six hits, two runs, and no walks over 6-1/3 innings. "Grove was as steady as a ship's chronometer," the *Herald* correspondent gushed.

On August 14, he got his first start since June 9. Again facing Dick Coffman and the Browns, Lefty thrilled the Fenway faithful by mixing fastballs and curves in a 7-3, six-hit win. Everyone agreed he had some speed, if not the old speed, and good "stuff." Harris promised to return him to the rotation.

With six weeks left, the Red Sox were fifteen games behind Detroit. Yet the fans, still storming Fenway, were enjoying "luscious little tidbits," in Kaese's words. One was the continuing drama of Lefty Grove. Again, hopes were raised. Again, he couldn't sustain them. On August 19, Grove faced Crowder in the first game of a doubleheader. Another Fenway-record crowd, this time 49,995, watched the game. Some attendees came to see a first-place team, others to watch two fine pitchers. Still others arrived to cheer Detroit's player-manager Mickey Cochrane, Lefty's old battery mate, a native of Bridgewater, Massachusetts and a Boston University grad; or to honor a Tigers coach and old Lefty mentor, Gloucester's Cy Perkins. In Boston, all sports are local, too.

The Tigers won, 8-6, with Grove giving up all the runs in his five innings. The writers said he didn't pitch badly and allowed some "soft" runs on four errors, two passed balls, and two more miscues that the official scorer called hits. "Pitching duels, after all, require some contributions by the other eight players on the ball club," Kaese tersely noted.

At about the same time, *Collier's* Bill Cunningham found Grove smoking and playing solitaire. "How's the arm?" he asked.

"Okay, it's coming along," said Grove.

Cunningham wrote, "If you don't think his heart was deader than those biceps, you don't know your baseball, or at least you don't know your Grove."

Cunningham shifted into high gear: "You hate to see a king prowling around without his crown, a champion suddenly stricken by a foe he can't fight back. Here was baseball's

Prometheus, and like Prometheus he seems doomed to be chained to the mound hurling impotency while, not vultures [sic], but the batsmen he once blazed down in droves gnaw the vitals out of his once indomitable delivery."

Grove won two of his last five decisions—dispirited, he was mostly pitching relief and making careless mistakes like moving slowly to cover first—to finish at 8-8. In all, he pitched just 22 times for 109-1/3 innings, threw five complete games in 12 starts, and finished with a 6.50 ERA, the league's sixty-third best and third worst. He surrendered 23 earned runs to his once-patsy Tigers in three starts lasting 16-1/3 innings. Hank Greenberg homered off him twice in one game.

Nonetheless, the Red Sox climbed to fourth at 76-76—their only first-division season since 1918—and more than doubled attendance to a franchise-high 610,640 fans. Ordinarily, an improvement of 13 wins and three places in the standings would be cause for celebration. Not in Boston, with its press and win-starved fans expecting a contender.

The fans spent September booing manager Harris. This was unfortunate, because he had motivated the players well. "The spirit was unusually high," says Werber. "We were always playing jokes, and Harris was part of most of them."

For some rooters and sportswriters, though, Grove was the whole sad story. So what if Wes Ferrell was the only pitcher in the rotation with a winning record? Who cared if Walberg and Bishop, the other ex-A's, were clearly over the hill? Did it matter that Yawkey hadn't developed a farm system, as critical to pennants then as now? In retrospect, the letdown owed less to poor performance than overblown expectations created by sportswriters and gamblers. But not to the Calvinist critics. With 16 more wins by Grove to equal his 1933 total, they said, the Red Sox would have won 92, two behind the second-place Yankees and nine behind Detroit. In other words, but for Lefty, Boston would have been in the race till September.

Here was a city that didn't blame James Michael Curley, who could have created jobs, but did blame Lefty Grove, who couldn't possibly carry the Red Sox on his back. "Boston runs to brains as well as to beans and brown bread," William Cowper Brann had written years earlier in his Texas newspaper *The Iconoclast*. "But she is cursed with an army of cranks whom nothing short of a straightjacket or a swamp elm club will ever control."

Actually, the Sox had something to cheer about. In the usual pattern, there was at least one player worth watching. With his .321 average, second-in-the-league 129 runs, and major-league-best 40 stolen bases, third baseman Bill Werber —"something that Boston has not had for years: a fast, aggressive natural infielder, hitter and baserunner," Kaese wrote—pumped up the large crowds at Fenway. Werber, a nonagenarian writing his second baseball memoir, was Grove's most sympathetic supporter. "When he had to leave the mound all season, he'd kick a bucket of ice water in the dugout and splash it everywhere," Werber said[1]. "He didn't unbutton his shirt in the clubhouse. He'd grab it on either side, give a yank or two and the buttons would fly by all over the clubhouse floor." A familiar pattern, but one that would last a whole season. "He never made excuses afterward," says pitcher Joseph (Crooning Joe) Cascarella, who played for the Red Sox in '35 and '36, "for which I admired him."

Was there any indignity too base for Grove to endure dur-

---

[1] Grove always kicked the bucket with the outside of his foot. Late in the season the team trainer, tired of replacing busted pails, produced what Werber called a "stout" one and circled it with a band of iron or steel. At one point Werber drop-kicked it, neglecting to use the Grove method, and fractured a toe.

ing the '34 season? Ray Robinson, a distinguished magazine editor and biographer of Christy Mathewson and Lou Gehrig, was a young autograph seeker in New York City at the time. He described one experience in the December, 1993, issue of *The Diamond*:

> Robert Moses "Lefty" Grove, the 300-game winning southpaw with the world-class temper, was sitting in the Alamac lobby one morning when we approached him. One couldn't mistake this living Grant Wood portrait for anyone but Grove. Decked out in his egg-white Panama suit, Grove could have been the dyspeptic master of a Southern plantation.
>
> Thrusting my autograph book (which I still have at home, its yellowed, crumbling pages fatigued by time passing), I politely asked Grove if he'd sign for me. I turned to a page featuring a few pictures of the incomparable pitcher, then handed him my fountain pen. Grove took it and signed. But as he returned the book and pen to me, he gazed down at his pants. A rivulet of dark blue ink had dribbled its way down from his fly to his right knee. The pen—not a ballpoint, remember—had betrayed me.
>
> The ashen-faced Grove, known to demolish locker rooms after a losing effort, grabbed me by the back of the neck. I thought he was going to toss me across the lobby at 100 miles per hour, a smidgen faster than his famous fastball. Instead he thought better of it. "I don't ever want to see you again!" he growled. I made certain he never did.

There were a few moments of levity, like the time Grove put a lizard down the back of Red Sox historian Ellery Clark. Overall, they were small compensation. As Werber puts it, "Nineteen thirty-four was a lost year for a very proud man."

OLD MAN MOSE

★　　★　　★　　★

"No man loves life like he who is growing old."

–Sophocles

Though Lefty Grove now worked in Boston, he retained strong ties to the Philadelphia Athletics. Therefore, it was no surprise to old A's hands to see Grove working out at the Philadelphia Health Club in January, 1935. Grove told a newsman he felt fine. "The old wing never bothered me after midseason," he said. "I'm coming to Philly for three or four weeks of preliminary work and massaging, starting February 3."

Grove was certainly aware that his idol, Washington's Walter Johnson, had recovered smartly. After returning home with a sore arm midway through the 1920 season, Johnson stumbled through three seasons—if 17, 15, and 17 wins constitute stumbling—then became a 20-game winner twice more while leading the Nats to pennants in '24 and '25. Hope springs eternal, and winters eternal too.

Grove spent three weeks in Hot Springs, Arkansas, before spring training. Every day he had breakfast at 10 and played thirty-six holes of golf, carrying his bag. If it rained, he used the rowing machine. He pitched very little in spring training –four innings against major-league opposition–but always without pain. The verdict: he could pitch again, but he certainly wasn't the fireballer of old. After an April performance against Grove, Russ Cassatt of the minor-league team in Charlotte, North Carolina, wrote home, "We couldn't do anything with a screwy lefthander they had out there and I can't see why because he didn't show me anything but a two-for-a-nickel curve. They called him 'Moses' something or other—a pretty fair country ballplayer."

"The fast one is hopping," Grove insisted on opening day. "There hasn't been a twinge in my shoulder all spring." He said he was so hungry he could eat two steaks at one sitting.

As the 1935 season opened, Red Sox hopes were higher than ever. Second baseman Ski Melillo arrived from the Browns with the league's best fielding percentage over the past two seasons. Eddie Collins convinced Tom Yawkey to send Bucky Harris back to Washington in exchange for $225,000 and player-manager Joe Cronin, the twenty-eight year-old Senators shortstop on his way to the Hall of Fame. Though Cronin was the son-in-law of Washington owner Clark Griffith, he was happy to leave. "Well, Mil," he told his wife Mildred, "it looks like good-bye Washington and hello Boston, and here's hoping we bring the pennant to Boston."

Well, why not? The Red Sox had improved three places to fourth. Now, with Cronin aboard and better seasons expected from Grove and Wes Ferrell, among others, how about three more places? Grove had to be especially encouraged, because he had struggled against the Senators (18-14) in general and Cronin in particular.

So how did the season go? Well, there was comic relief, at least. Trailing the Indians 5-3, on September 7 at Fenway Park, the Red Sox loaded the bases with none out in the ninth. Whereupon boy wonder Cronin hit a line drive down the third-base line. But instead of scoring two or three runners, it deflected off the glove of the nearly decapitated third baseman Odell Hale to the shortstop, who caught it (for one out) and threw to the second baseman (two outs), who relayed to first (triple play!).

It was a funny season, in a grim sort of way. Cronin, Ferrell, and Grove delivered, but the Sox repeated in fourth, with a 78-75 record. As so often happened, the Sox had the stars but not the spars. Though Cronin contributed his usual solid year (.295, 95 RBIs) and Ferrell's brother Rick hit .301, no one had as many as 15 homers and the team led the league with 194 errors. Wes Ferrell (25-14), who had the AL's most wins, and Grove (20-12, 2.70), who had the lowest ERA, might as well have been unaccompanied.

But what a story Lefty Grove was! It is not unusual for a pitcher to turn from speed to craft in his thirties—Frank Tanana is a good recent example—but what Grove did was unprecedented. Late in the 1934 season he discovered that his arm hurt less when he threw curves than when he threw fastballs. The curve was his main out-pitch in '35. The reason it worked so well, Grove said some years later, was that he had lost his fastball. "I actually was too fast to curve the ball while with Baltimore and Philadelphia," he told a writer for Newspaper Enterprise Association.

"The ball didn't have time to break enough because I threw what passed for a curve as fast as I threw my fastball. I couldn't get enough twist on it. So I used to break a comparatively slight hook into the dirt in a clutch and let it go at that.

"Now that I'm not so fast I can really break one off and my fastball looks faster than it is because it's faster than the other stuff I throw."

Then Lefty broke off a thought for all time: "A pitcher has time enough to get smarter after he loses his speed."

"It wasn't that Grove developed a curve ball after he hurt his arm," said catcher Moe Berg, a Red Sox catcher and intellect, "but that he improved the good curve he had to the point where it was almost a great curve."

Writing about the '35 season in the September, 1941, issue of *The Atlantic Monthly*, Berg positively gushed:

> In 1935, Lefty had recovered from his first serious sore arm of the year before. Wear and tear, and the grind of many seasons, had taken their toll. Now he had changed his tactics, and was pitching curves and fastballs, one or the other. His control was practically perfect. On a day in that year in Washington, Heinie Manush, a great hitter, was at bat with two men on the bases. The game was at stake; the count was three balls and two strikes. Heinie stood there, confident, looking for Lefty's fastball. "Well," thought Heinie, "it might be a curve." Lefty was throwing the curve more and more now, but the chances with the count of three-and-two were that Lefty would throw his fastball with everything he had on it. Fast or curve—he couldn't throw anything else; he had nothing else to throw. Heinie broke his back striking out on the next pitch, the first forkball Grove ever threw. For over a year, on the sidelines, in the bullpen,

between pitching starts, Lefty had practiced and perfected the pitch before he threw it, and he waited for a crucial spot to use it. Lefty had realized his limitations. The hitters were getting to his fastballs and curveballs more than they used to. He wanted to add to his pitching equipment; he felt he had to. Heinie Manush anticipated, looked for, guessed a fastball, possibly a curve, but Lefty fooled him with his new pitch, a forkball.

Here was the perfect setup for outguessing a hitter. Lefty Grove's development of a third pitch, the forkball, is the greatest example in our time of complete successful change in technique by one pitcher.

Berg was off on his Manusha. Grove did develop a forkball and may have thrown it to Manush on more than one occasion, but not with a three-and-two count and a game on the line. Grove pitched to Manush, pinchhitting, to lead off the tenth inning on June 5, and Manush grounded out. Perhaps Grove threw a forkball, and perhaps Heinie broke his back. The Senators then rallied to beat Grove. More remarkable is the fact that thirty-five year-old Grove was pitching in extra innings. He did so eleven times as an Athletic and fourteen more times as a Red Sox.

Remember, he was pitching his home games in Fenway Park, where The Wall, 315 feet down the left-field line, was supposedly death on lefthanded pitchers. It's a baseball given that a lefty must learn to pitch inside at Fenway. If he throws everything outside, a righthanded hitter will crowd the plate and still be able to pull the ball.

But let's be clear what "inside" meant to Grove. He didn't

With Philadelphia Grove would just as soon smash a camera lens as pose for a picture. He mellowed considerably with the Red Sox.

toy with the inside corner; he pitched *way* inside. As a fastball pitcher in Philadelphia, Grove hit twenty-eight batters in nine seasons. As a finesse pitcher in Boston—he called his new repertoire "curve and control"—he still hit another fourteen in eight seasons. By establishing the inside of the plate and driving batters back, he could use the outside part to get them out.

And yet, pitching in and out—the time-honored Fenway pattern—was not what made him a big winner there. By combining a still-effective high riding fastball with a sinking forkball that he eventually learned to throw more effectively than his curve, Grove throttled hitters more often by working them up and down.

"Pitchers at Fenway were reluctant to throw changeups, because batters would hit them out if they were too high," says Broadway Charlie Wagner, a sharp-dressing Red Sox pitcher in 1938-42 and 1946, who had been watching Grove since his days in Baltimore. "But Moses, who had great control and excellent mechanics, was a cute pitcher in his latter days. If you were a high-ball hitter, he'd work the ball down. If you liked low pitches, you'd never see one. He was also the greatest one-run-ahead pitcher I ever saw. By the ninth inning, with victory in sight, he put it in another gear. You could see some mustard coming up to the plate. You could wrap up the bats."

Grove was 77-22 in Fenway, including 55-17 with the Red Sox, and won 20 straight at home between 1938 and 1941.

On April 19, 1935, Grove beat the Senators, 10-4, retiring the last six batters he faced on only twelve pitches before leaving the game following the sixth inning. Babe Ruth's two-for-seven debut with the other Boston team and John Kelly's Boston Marathon win got more ink. A week later Grove lost to Washington, 10-4, but allowed just two earned runs while Cronin committed three errors. "A commendable and encouraging pitching performance," Gerry Moore wrote in the *Globe*.

"Yes, Grove's arm seems to be O.K., but we fellows feel that the old speed and zip and fire is not there any more," an opposing batter said. "In other words, we are not afraid of Bob as we used to be. We get in there confident that we can hit off him. The balls may come along like bullets sometimes, but at least at the present time, we figure that if we wait we'll get the ball that we can hit."

They were right; they just couldn't hit the ball hard or far. "I've got a lot of things now that I didn't have when I broke in," Grove told John Lardner after shutting out the Yankees on June 1. "Maybe I was faster then, but I didn't know the hitters. I didn't know when to let up and when to bear down. Right now my arm feels fine. By using it right, not trying to strike out every one of these fellas as they come along, I can win plenty of games this year."

After running up a 6-6 record in which he never failed to last at least five innings on starts, Grove won six straight from June 29 to July 21. "You can't take any roundhouse cuts at Mose," said his old teammate, Jimmy Dykes, now the White Sox manager. "He don't give you any more good balls. He's curving plenty these days and most of the time he throws his fast one it's going right by you, just as it did when we were with the Athletics." (In the 7-6, fifteen-inning loss to Philadelphia that ended the streak on July 27, the A's tried to throw a fast one by Grove after walking a batter to reach him. Grove hit a grand slam and wagged his finger at the opposing manager—"You shouldn't have done that, Mr. Mack"—as he rounded third.)

Jimmie Foxx, in his last season with the A's, agreed with Dykes. "Lefty throws past you with quite a bite this season. He has probably lost some of his terrific speed, but he has given his fireball a new touch that makes it as effective as ever. Nowadays the last six feet of Lefty's fast pitches seem to jump. This is probably an optical illusion, but it gives the batter a tendency to swing late."

Outfielder Bing Miller, back with his old A's teammate, said, "He's developed such a good change of pace that he can get by even when he hasn't much on his fast one."

Grove astounded everyone by staying strong all season. It took the Senators fourteen innings to beat him, 2-1, in the rain on September 1—they somehow won four of five decisions off him—and he went on to win his last four starts. Let's underscore the numbers: 8-8, 6.50 in '34; 20-12, 2.70 in '35. Name a more dramatic turnabout in baseball history.

In 1936, Yawkey continued spending freely to raid Mack's floundering A's. In his most celebrated deal of the offseason, he spent only $150,000 and a washed-up pitcher to acquire seventeen-game winner Footsie Marcum and Foxx, reuniting Grove with his old roommate. By now, the team was being called the "Gold Sox" and "Yawkey's millionaires."

It was the first of many times that Boston would trade for righthanded power on the assumption that peppering The Wall meant certain contention. Of course, this *was* Jimmie Foxx, and he *was* just two years removed from winning the triple crown, and he *did* deliver in his accustomed style (.338, 41 HR, 143 RBIs). Yawkey also put up $75,000 for two more A's: .332-hitting outfielder Doc Cramer and .270-hitting shortstop Eric McNair. Now the Sox surely would contend. And what happened? McNair (.286) and Cramer (.292) didn't disappoint, Ferrell repeated as a 20-game winner, and Grove won nine of his first ten starts, four of them on shutouts, en route to another (17-12, 2.81) ERA title. In his first forty-four innings, he allowed three walks and one earned run. Utterly baffling, he struck out 25 batters in his first five complete games, mostly on called third strikes. This in the year the American League had its worst ERA (5.04) ever. Yet the 1936 Red Sox, the only losing team Lefty Grove ever played for, finished sixth, with a 74-80 record.

With all that power and pitching, all those impressive newcomers? Baseball is a team game, a lesson finally learned and practiced so well by the 1998 Red Sox. The '36 Sox had no pitching depth (Marcum went 8-13), were last in stolen bases (55) and double plays (139), and almost certainly finished last in clubhouse harmony. On August 21, Wes Ferrell stormed off the mound, and Cronin fined him $1,000. Whereupon, Ferrell threatened to "slug that damned Irishman right on his lantern jaw." Cronin told New York *Times* columnist John Kieran, "If he wants to slug me, I'll be passing through the lobby at six o'clock on my way to dinner." Ferrell never showed. Of more concern, Cronin and some of the ex-A's could not stomach each other. The old Mack pitchers, Grove, Marcum, and Walberg, groused aloud that Cronin couldn't manage like Mack or play short as well as McNair.

Cronin, who in an injury-filled season made 23 errors in 86 games, fielded .930, and temporarily ceded the shortstop spot to McNair, had certainly lost confidence in the field and was beginning to go down on one knee to field grounders. "For Christ sake, Joe," Melillo said, "if you're going to miss 'em, you might as well stand up and miss 'em like a big leaguer."

Melillo stood up to Grove in one famous incident. With the Senators hitting him freely, Grove lost his temper after a teammate made a bad throw to Melillo at second. The two men went at it eyeball-to-eyeball, then Grove blinked and left the mound. What had Grove said to him, travelling secretary Phil Troy asked Melillo. "He's never been to Pittsburgh," Melillo said. "He only asked me if I knew where you could get a cold beer there, and I told him."

In an even more legendary episode, a scoreless game in the ninth, Cronin knelt for a grounder and watched the ball deflect off his other leg while the winning run scored from second. Wouldn't you know the losing pitcher was Grove? Cronin raced through the dugout into his office and locked the door. Undaunted, Grove mounted a stool and screamed at Cronin through the wire transom separating the office from the player lockers.

Like so much else in the Lefty legend, the story is inaccurate. There is no record of Cronin costing Grove a 1-0 loss with a ninth-inning error. There is plenty of evidence, though, that Grove, with tacit support from Yawkey, freely blasted his manager. Cramer heard Grove tell Cronin he couldn't play short for a *high school* team.

In Grove's most infamous action of the year, he supposedly blasted the entire team. After losing to Chicago, 4-2, on June 16, he charged into the locker room bellowing, "Do you think Grove is going to throw his arm off for you hitless wonders?"

All his career Jimmie Foxx had been a standup guy, a friend to rookie and veteran alike. Now Foxx, Grove's old roommate and fellow Marylander, did his buddy a supreme favor. He stood up to him. "Mose, we're doing the best we can for you, like everybody else," he said. "Now you'd better shut up." Lefty did shut up. He also stayed away, walking back to the team's Michigan Avenue hotel rather than ride with his teammates from Comiskey Park. It was known as the "five-mile fury." The episode became part of the Grove legend, though third baseman Bill Werber insists it was out of character for both Grove and Foxx.

Grove lasted only 2-2/3 innings in his next start, a loss to St. Louis, and was 8-9 afterward. The lion in spring had become the lamb in summer.

This is not to say that Grove was the same grouchy fellow he had often been in Philadelphia. Foxx, for one, noted a significant change. He had seen Grove tutoring Cincinnati pitcher Johnny Vander Meer in the spring; shagging balls and feeding them to a young Red Sox pitcher; joking with Yawkey, Collins, and the women in the office. Being around Yawkey had changed Grove, except when he was pitching.

With the Red Sox, Grove advanced from "thrower" to "pitcher." His fastball gone, he developed a system he described as "curve and control."

Lefty Grove and Wes Ferrell were the hardest workers in Boston's 1937 spring training camp. Referring to them as "temperamental hurling aces" who cared more about individual stats than team wins, the *Transcript*'s Harold Kaese nonetheless concluded that they were "too egotistical to be cursory in their training."

Eventually, Ferrell's ego overwhelmed his training habits. Yawkey sent both Ferrell brothers—catcher Rick and pitcher Wes—to Washington, for righthander Bobo Newsom and speedy outfielder Ben Chapman, and traded Werber to the A's for Pinky Higgins. Ugh. When Cronin walked to the mound to advise Newsom, he was told, "Who's telling old Bobo how to pitch"? Chapman, a clubhouse lawyer, racist, and anti-Semite, was ordered to bunt, and instead grounded into a double play. "I don't bunt," he told Cronin. Higgins hit .302 but two decades later distinguished himself as one of the last, and perhaps the most recalcitrant Red Sox manager before the club finally integrated in 1959. Vintage Bosox.

Boston improved to fifth place with an 80-72 record. The Yawkey strategy, though, wasn't producing contenders. "He tried to do it quickly by buying a pennant," says Sam Scimone, who sold peanuts in both Boston ballparks, "and it didn't turn out."

None too soon, Yawkey began planning for the future. Noticing the success of the Cardinal and Yankee farm systems, he purchased minor-league teams and sent scouting director Billy Evans to the West Coast, where he eventually signed future Sox stars Bobby Doerr, Ted Williams, and Dom DiMaggio to minor-league contracts.

Meanwhile, Lefty was still a show. Trainer Doc Logan told Kaese that Grove's arm was "soft and limp as a piece of liver." Kaese enthused: "Grove's delivery is the poetry of pitching motion. He has complete relaxation, which not only is a factor in producing his fastball, but which is largely responsible for his excellent control."

His pitching in the 1937 opener—three runs, seven hits, four walks, three K's in a six-inning no-decision against the Yankees—didn't sound like much unless you were catching him. "Every pitch I called, I would move my glove a little bit—wherever I wanted him to throw it," said his new receiver, Gene Desautels. "And I could have caught the ball with my eyes closed. He was that good."

Grove carried so much respect that the team trundled all the way to Cumberland, Maryland, to play an exhibition during the town's sesquicentennial. He finished the season at 17-9, with a 3.02 ERA. The Yankees' Lefty Gomez, who had won the ERA title in 1934, did so again to bracket his Red Sox rival. If Grove had been obsessed with Walter Johnson early in his career, his attention was probably now shifted to the other Lefty G., a Yankee and a more quotable guy. Said El Goofy, who made the Hall of Fame on 189 wins for a New York team, an unmatched three victories in the All Star Game, a 6-0 record in the World Series, and considerable charm: "The secret of my success was clean living and a fast-moving outfield."

So what was it like when Ted Williams and Lefty Grove got together for the first time in spring training of 1938? The Kid, soon to be shipped out for one more season in the minors, thought Grove was a "funny-looking geezer" when he saw him in the lobby. Then he saw him pitch. Later, Williams told John B. Holway: "My first letter home after I saw Lefty Grove, I wrote, 'Boy, you ought to see Lefty Grove pitch! He's the smoothest and prettiest.' And Grove knew it, too. He really tried to make it look good. They said, 'You ought to have seen this guy pitch ten to fifteen years ago.'"

Incredibly, Grove improved in 1938. He won his first eight

decisions, then drew 83,533, a Yankee Stadium record, to watch him duel Red Ruffing on May 30. Six thousand fans were refused admission, while another 511 got refunds when they found no place to sit. Grove finally proved mortal, losing 10-3.

With Grove 11-1 by June 18, visiting newsmen acted as deferential as country priests in an audience with the Pope. "Grove is lean but hard as nails," Franklin W. Yeutter of Philadelphia's *Evening Bulletin* wrote. "He's not muscular, that is the muscles don't bulge all over him like a magazine advertisement of strong men. He has those long, rawhide muscles that feel like a bundle of wire cables when you grasp his arm. He's a different Grove these days, too. Not the grumpy, moody fellow he was. He's pleasant, talks willingly and volubly. Still smokes those atrocious cigars, however, and smiles that bashful, country boy grin."

You give a guy like this considerable slack. You tolerate his eccentricities, laugh off his vices. Bill (Lefty) Lefebvre joined the Red Sox right from the Holy Cross campus. His college coach, Connie Mack's old shortstop Jack Barry, advised him to stay away from Grove, who supposedly hated rookies. "We had to buy our own equipment, so I arrived with a new glove, spikes, sweatshirts, jockstrap and so on," says Lefebvre.

Things happened quickly for Lefebvre. While he was mopping up a 15-2 loss to Chicago, he homered on the first pitch ever thrown to him.

"One day in St. Louis I was shagging flies," says Lefebvre, "and Grove came up to me. 'Hi, kid,' he said.

" 'Hi, Mose.'

" 'New glove?'

" 'Yeah.'

" 'Let me see it.'

213

"I showed it to him, and he gave me his, a puddingbag, with the fingers bent back.

" 'Like it, kid?' he said.

" 'Yeah.'

" 'Sure?'

" 'Yeah.'

" 'Well, keep it.' And he walked off with my glove! I eventually sold his glove for $500. I think mine is in the Hall of Fame."

After experiencing Grove's rookie treatment, Lefebvre witnessed the Grovian temper. On June 14, Grove singled in the seventh, contributing to a three-run rally, and took a 3-1 lead over the Browns into the bottom of the inning. Lefty walked a man, got an out on a fly ball, then gave up a run-scoring double. The next batter singled, and there were runners on first and third. "Black Jack Wilson, who wasn't liked by Grove, was warming up," Lefebvre says. "Cronin told the umpire he wanted Wilson. On the first pitch, Wilson got the batter to ground out, but the tying run scored. The Red Sox rallied to win, 5-3, but Wilson got the victory. Lefty accidentally kicked an iron chair, then threw it through the window."

By Bastille Day, Grove was 13-3, with nearly one-third of the team's victories. Behind him the Sox had won eleven of their past fourteen games. Grove fielded a first-inning grounder by Charlie Gehringer, threw off-balance to Foxx at first and thought nothing of it. But after the first two batters in the fifth singled, Grove signaled to Cronin and told him he couldn't grip the ball with his suddenly lifeless fingers. He left the game (which he eventually won) and the team doctor was summoned.

Grove declared that he hurt his arm fielding Gehringer's grounder. Examining Lefty in the clubhouse, the doctor found no pain, but no pulse, either. Not in the wrist, not any-where else in the arm. X-rays revealed nothing, and he was said to be suffering from "intermittent claudification," or "a spasm of the blood vessels, pertaining to the circulatory system." So said Edward J. O'Brien, the attending physician at St. Elizabeth's Hospital in Boston. One doctor claimed there could be a recurrence resulting in possible gangrene and amputation.

"At last I've discovered what has made you a great pitch-er," Sox coach Tom Daly told Grove. "You haven't got any pulse. Why, hereafter, if I'm out scouting young pitchers, I'm not going to watch them throw. I'll just check their pulse. If they haven't any, why I'll sign them right on the spot."

The next day a slight pulse was found in the wrist, and Grove was ordered to rest the arm and enclose it for several hours a day in a "glass dome," the better to expand the arteries and promote circulation. He wanted nothing to do with anything but pitching. Doctors had to hide his pants, or he'd have left the hospital.

Grove returned August 5 to throw eighty-five pitches in a no-decision, but that was really it for the season. "I suppose this is my finish," he said after lasting just two innings on August 11. He called his arm "lifeless as a board." Far from the com-bative Grove of old, he greeted an old A's pitcher, Jack Coombs, who would be coaching Lefty's son Bobby at Duke, and said, "Maybe I'll be down to assist you next spring."

Three more two-inning performances scarcely gave him comfort. After taking his last loss on August 11—he finished the season 14-4, with a 3.08 ERA—Grove threw his glove into the dugout. "Boys, she is dead as a dog," he told writers in the clubhouse later. "Maybe she's all done, huh? There's just so many pitches in an arm. This is my nineteenth year throwin' 'em."

Even without Grove, though, the Red Sox had their best record since 1918, 88-61, and finished eleven games behind New York. Foxx nearly won another triple crown, leading the league with a .349 average and 175 RBI, plus his 50 taters, and the team hit .299. In an increasingly familiar pattern—the Sox finished second five more times in the next eleven years—Boston had just enough pitching to fall short. Both Foxx and Grove must have been reminded of the 1920's, when their very good teams trailed otherworldly Yankee clubs.

Now Grove was surely through. If injuries didn't do him in, advancing age would. But not without a fight. Back home, Lefty's Place was well stocked with athletic equipment—a punching bag, a rowing machine, an "exercise table"—in the basement. He would not go gentle into that good night.

Over the winter Grove worked out, and then some. He hunted. He fished. He added to his considerable gun collection. And on the top floor of his home he worked on his wood-turning machines to make miniature furniture and toys for kids. This was the Lefty Grove largely invisible to Bostonians: the small-town boy appreciative of his true friends. "Growing up in Lonaconing, he knew who was a friend and who was after him," says his niece, Betty Holshey. "He valued what a small town can give you: respect, friendship." And, plainly, he believed in giving something back.

Grove must have been happy when Chapman was traded, enabling Ted Williams to make the 1939 Red Sox. The team had previously hit, in Grove's words that must have applied to *clutch* hitting, "with one foot in the American Association." Well, now they had landed a real bat from the American Association. At twenty, Williams batted .327, with 31 homers and a league-leading 145 RBIs, helping the team

(89-62) repeat in second, 17 games behind another powerful (106-45) bunch of Yankees.

When doctors told Grove that nicotine reduced the circulation in his pitching arm, he gave up his daily regimen of seven cigars and a can of chewing tobacco. Lefty pitched three times for nine innings in spring training. Cronin decided to use him once a week. Almost instantly, Grove became known as "the Sunday pitcher," an endearing term for an old man. And, incredibly, the old wing twitched to life.

Once again, he was the best sentimental story in baseball. Despite suffering shin splints in spring training, a "surprisingly rejuvenated" Grove, according to the New York *Times*, pitched a strong eight innings but was done in by two Joe DiMaggio circus catches in a 2-0 loss to New York on April 20. Grove lasted six good innings nine days later against the A's, then won five straight against Detroit, Washington, Detroit, Washington, and Cleveland. Outdoing even himself on May 21, he homered in his home debut while beating the Tigers, 8-3. A Sunday crowd of twenty-four thousand filed out of Fenway Park in awe.

"Lefty Grove has attained such a sentimental stature in the hearts of baseball followers that everything he does touches them emotionally," Victor O. Jones wrote in the *Evening Globe* the following day.

As in 1931, every one of Grove's losses and a no-decision came with an explanation. On April 29, he was leading the A's 2-1 on three hits after six innings, when Cronin replaced him in the seventh. Grove was getting tired "and there isn't any use taking chances in April," Cronin explained. Grove's replacement, Wilson, gave up a hit scoring a run charged to Grove. Wilson got the win when Boston rallied in the ninth.

On June 11, Grove lost, 7-5, to Cleveland on Joe Kuhel's two-out, two-run, ninth-inning homer following an error by

*Supposedly washed up in '34, Grove (pictured four years later)
thumbed his nose at doubters and won four ERA titles in 1935-39.*

Cronin. Perhaps that was the day Grove stood at the partition
swearing at his manager. On August 31, Red Sox misplays
set up three Tigers runs in the first inning. Grove was
relieved after five, trailing 5-2, and Detroit went on to win,
11-4. And on September 6, Grove made two bad throws—firing a potential double-play ball wide of second and serving a
gopher ball to Joe DiMaggio—to lose at Yankee Stadium, 2-1.
John Drebinger's account in the *Times* began, "Lefty Bob
Grove, who has been defying time, tide and all the other natural elements these many years . . ."

In the Yankee clubhouse Bill Dickey, the old catcher, was
telling Tommy Henrich, the young outfielder, that Grove in
his prime threw faster than Cleveland's phenom Bobby

Feller. That was news to Henrich, who considered Grove purely a curveball pitcher. Feller, who had taken over as baseball's fastballer par excellence, says today, "He was pitching on smoke and mirrors, like Orel Hershiser late in his career." In twenty-three appearances, Grove went 4-0 against the pesky Senators, 15-4 overall and led the league with a 2.54 ERA. That's nine ERA titles in fifteen seasons. Holy Mose.[1]

No wonder the Sox treated him like a god. On days he pitched, Grove, clad in pants and cap, went to the trainer's room precisely forty-five minutes before game time and took a twenty-minute nap, while teammates tiptoed around him with their fingers to their lips. One time Bobo Newsom, then pitching for the Tigers, dared to invade Grove's sanctuary. "Where's that son-of-a-gun?" he roared, waking Lefty. "I'm going to beat your butt."

"Because you woke me up, you won't get a smell," Grove said. And he won easily. "You did it," an admiring Newsom told him afterward.

On Pullmans the superstitious Grove always slept in lower berth five, in hotels on the sixth floor if at all possible. He ordered without looking at menus—invariably choosing steak and baked potatoes—and his meal tabs were not to be challenged.

The height of the season was June 26, when Grove shut out the Senators, 3-0, and Williams went four-for-four. Or was it September 13, when Grove four-hit the Tigers, 1-0?

---

[1] Grove won four ERA titles between the ages of 35 and 39. Researcher Dixie Tourangeau compares Grove with the Yankees' Lefty Gomez (26-30) and Red Ruffing (31-35), the leagues other prime ERA contenders in 1935-1939:

	IP	Record	Team Record
Grove	1,143	83-41	409-350
Gomez	1,150	76-53	498-261
Ruffing	1,224	98-44	498-261

With runners on second and third and one out in the ninth, he elected to face Hank Greenberg and fanned him on what Gerry Moore described as a "backbreaking curve." Too bad only twenty-four hundred were on hand at the Fens.

Yes, Lefty had his peevish moments. "The batter before me hit a routine grounder, which the shortstop bobbled and threw away," says Wayne Ambler, who was playing short for the A's. "Lefty stormed around the mound and put his hands on his hips. Then he went to the mound and lobbed the ball in, as if the umpire had asked for it. I hit it for a single. Anyone else would have hit a homer."

Boston finished behind the Yanks despite winning eleven of nineteen games from them. But, oh, the personal stories. The Kid. The Old Man. Suddenly popular beyond his wildest dreams, Grove even consented to interviews. After a radio reporter babbled on, hogging air time, Lefty finally got to speak. "What do you think I am—just a pitcher?" he said.

Grove was his usual magisterial self in March, 1940. "I was a young kid in the clubhouse, and I was afraid to approach him," says Dom DiMaggio. "I had said hello to everyone else, but I hadn't spoken to him and he hadn't spoken to me. After two weeks, I was driving with a friend to visit someone in the hospital. "Lefty said you haven't said hello to him," my friend said. "Why not?"

" 'I'm just a young punk kid,' I said. 'It's not my place.'

"Well, my friend convinced me I ought to do something. We went back to the hotel, and I saw Lefty sitting on the hotel porch in one of those wrought-iron swinging chairs. I started to go in, then summoned up all my courage, and let the door go. 'Hello, Lefty,' I said.

"He jumped up, put his arm around me and told the clubhouse boy, 'Let Dom sit next to me.' We talked for a long time. After that we were very close.' "

Grove was nothing if not inspirational. Fourteen wins shy of 300, he opened the 1940 season with a two-hit, 1-0 shutout in Washington. Facing just twenty-nine batters, he pitched no-hit ball until the eighth inning, when he allowed two singles after a Ted Williams error. Grove won his own game with an RBI single, impressing President Franklin Delano Roosevelt and Postmaster General James A. Farley. "The President's pitching almost smashed a camera when he tossed out the first ball that officially opened the game and the season," an unnamed New York *Times* correspondent wrote. "By his own mound work, Grove made more secure his place in baseball history."

Grove didn't mind failing to throw a no-hitter. He said he was superstitious enough to believe it would have jinxed him. "They marvel that a man of forty retains enough stuff to pitch a two-hit game," he wrote in an as-told-to article with Boston scribe Joe Cashman.

"I see nothing particularly marvelous about it. I've been blessed with a stout arm, strong legs and excellent general health. Any pitcher so blessed should be a winner at forty, if he takes care of himself and trains properly.

"He can't, however, wait until he's passed his prime to become serious about the business of staying in shape. I've followed practically the same schedule during my sixteen years in the majors. I'm active on the ball field every day during the season. Except on the afternoon I'm pitching, I chase flies in the outfield before every game. And I throw on the sidelines every off day except the day I pitch a game.

"When I used to do relief work in addition to starting in turn, I never pitched batting practice, but since retiring as a 'fireman' I do my share of throwing in batting drills. The fly shagging keeps my legs in shape. The constant throwing helps me retain my control."

He nearly blew a six-run lead in his next start and quickly was struggling, however, with his weight up to 215 pounds and his energy down. When Daly told Grove he wasn't working hard enough, he began hustling like a rookie. Once again, the better to practice bending, Grove fed batting-practice balls to a young Sox pitcher, and once again, the better to lose weight, resumed smoking. Picking up the pace, with three wins in five starts when the warm weather arrived, Grove began moving inexorably toward the magic number.

At this time Grove was both a player you worshipped and a guy you could identify with. Modestino (Musty) Vitale, a semi-pro pitcher, used to study Grove in Fenway Park. "I was a righthanded pitcher with good control, a good curve, and a mediocre fastball," he says, "but what Lefty taught me was self-control. He was a frozen puss who never showed his emotion on the mound. I tried to be stone-faced. I had a temper, and if the other team saw it, they would eat you alive."

The aging Grove was extremely popular with Fenway fans. "All he had was guile," says Vitale, who later taught school and ran a public relations/advertising firm. "He could spot the ball. He had good stuff. What we call a changeup today was a Lefty Grove slowball then.

"He would always go into the sixth or seventh and then fall apart. The moment Joe Cronin moved from shortstop to the mound, the booing would start. If Cronin just wanted to talk to Grove, he would be cheered when he returned to shortstop." Grove was allowed to finish nine of his twenty-one starts.

Before a June 8, 1940, day in his honor, Grove visited the offices of "Red Sox Ramblings," the team's house organ, and rated his four greatest events in baseball:

"1. The day in 1931 when I threw 21 straight strikes against the Yankees in Philadelphia, mowing down Ruth,

Gehrig, Lazzeri, and Dickey among others.

"2. Striking out 12 Yanks in six innings that same year.

"3. Winning 31 games while losing only four in 1931.

"4. Being traded to Boston in 1933. I've certainly made many friends in this city."

The Yankees were on his mind, although his recall was less accurate than his pitching. In 1931 he struck out more than four Yankee batters only once, fanning eight in 5-1/3 innings on August 29. There was no report of striking out three batters on nine or ten pitches that year, or of 21 straight strikes, though he threw 15 straight against the Indians in 1928. He did strike out 12 Yankees—on July 5, 1926.

Grove's tribute actually began on June 7, with "Highlights in the Life of Lefty Grove," a dramatized radio program, playing over the Colonial Network. On June 8, there was a pregame presentation before a Fenway game with the Tigers. American League president Will Harridge and Boston mayor Maurice J. Tobin were there. So was Grove's son Bobby, eighteen, a star pitcher for the Duke freshmen, and and daughter Ethel Doris, sixteen, a high school student. Lefty's parents stayed home, because his mother was ill. Jimmy Coughlin's 101st Veterans Band played musical selections.

Following the game against the Tigers that Lefty didn't play in, there was a dinner in his honor at the Copley Plaza Hotel. "The menu itself demonstrated how far Lefty had strayed from simple Lonaconing," old friend Ruth Bear Levy reported in the summer, 1988, issue of *Maryland Historical Magazine*. "The potatoes were 'Delmonico,' the peas 'au beurre,' and the soup 'aux Souffles'; for dessert there were 'fresh strawberry bombe' and 'Friandises.' "

Grove's wars with the press seemed a distant memory. Both the *Christian Science Monitor* and the *Globe* were in

Grove and Boston manager Joe Cronin in 1938.
Talk about poses: Grove loathed and rode Cronin.

attendance along with at least four hundred well-wishers. On the menu program, shaped like a baseball, were signatures from Foxx, Williams, DiMaggio, and—in the center—Grove, "The Living Legend of Lonaconing."

Inside the cover a tribute began:

> It's not so much an epic we're honoring this evening; not altogether a man who learned how to throw a baseball, but altogether a man who learned to live a life. Here's Americana at its truest and best, the small town boy who grew to national fame, but who still calls the little town "home," and the chums of his boyhood, the friends of his maturity.

But a man can only mellow so much. With Grove trailing the Senators, 1-0, on August 11, Washington's George Case opened the eighth inning by singling to Cronin and taking second on his wild throw. The next batter, Cecil Travis, singled him home. Grove could have lived with a 2-0 loss, but he must have been infuriated when the Red Sox scored one run in the ninth to lose, 2-1. Do you suppose *this* was the day he mounted the transom and yelled at Cronin? Pitcher Charlie Wagner remembers that Grove took out his anger on the clubhouse, because "every chair was loosened up."

After a chipped bone in his left ankle sidelined Grove for three weeks, he lost a September 2 heartbreaker to the Senators, 1-0, in thirteen innings. "I was dressing next to him," says DiMaggio. "After the game we both sat a long time without saying anything. 'That was a hell of a game you pitched,' I finally said. 'You deserved to win.' "

"Lefty suddenly spread out his shirt, and all the buttons popped. 'Dom, if they played as well as you did, we'd have won in nine,' " he said.

Grove was especially annoyed at Williams, who went on to reporters about a triple he'd hit. "Nothing in thirteen innings and he's talking about 'wham, wham, did ya see me hit that one?' " Grove muttered.

Lefty wasn't through venting his anger. Remember, the otherwise hot-hitting Red Sox had been beaten in his last two starts, 2-1, and 1-0, and had just stranded ten runners. He seemed to be going out as he had come in, losing to the Senators. Lefty was fed up. He had had it. He was ready for the ultimate gesture. After the 1-0 loss, there was another game to be played the same afternoon. Grove undoubtedly smoldered during the second game of the doubleheader, smoldered during the train ride back to Boston on the *Federal Express*, and smoldered when he reported to Fenway Park for a workout attended only by him and Foxx. Where there's smoldering, there may be fire. At some point in his extended fury, Lefty burned the Red Sox bats! At least, this is what team veterans told Ted Lepcio, a Red Sox infielder in the 1950's. "I don't think Lefty had the authority to do that," says outfielder Tony Lupien, who finished the 1940 season with the Red Sox. But Wagner says, "It could have happened. I used to hesitate about going into the clubhouse after a loss. But it was all forgotten afterward."

On September 10, hobbling when his bad ankle froze in football weather, Grove went another thirteen innings to beat the Tigers at Briggs Stadium, 6-5. In what the *Globe*'s Gerry Moore called "one of the most courageous performances of his entire career," Grove scored a twelfth inning run by singling, refusing a pinch runner, hobbling to second on a base hit, hobbling to third on a bunt single, and hobbling home on a sacrifice fly. He struck out Rudy York with two runners on to end the game.

Before a 1939 old-timers game in Fenway Park, Grove visited with a gallery of greats: Yale coach Smoky Joe Wood (34-5 with the 1912 Red Sox), Cy Young, and Grove's idol Walter Johnson.

At season's end, though, Grove was only 7-6, with a 3.99 ERA. With a serious problem of pitching depth—yeah, they led the league in hitting—the 82-72 Sox finished fourth in a close pennant race won by the Tigers. Plainly, though, Grove wasn't through. He had won 293 games, and no one doubted he would remain focused and fierce enough to win 300.

As Grove approaches his final season, it seems appropriate to take a seventh-inning stretch and examine his relationship with his teammates. The legend is that everyone backed him, defended him, and put up with his tantrums. The reality is not so simple. When third baseman Jim Tabor made an error, Grove walked over to berate him. Tabor immediately challenged Grove. "You're hired to pitch," he said. "I'm hired to play third base. Get out there and pitch." Grove backed down.

Some teammates, like second baseman Melillo, were afraid to have balls hit at them in the ninth inning when Grove was pitching. "That Lefty was a terror," Melillo told the Cleveland *News*' Ed McAuley years later. "He was sore because we always seemed to be winning the 10-8 games for Wes Ferrell and losing the 1-0 games for Grove.

"Before he'd go out to warm up, Lefty would stamp up and down the dugout, sticking that long arm of his in our faces.

" 'Do you see this arm?' he'd ask. 'Do you know what it's going to do today? I'll tell you. I'm going to pitch a shutout against these bums. But are we going to win? We are like h—. One of you no-good so-and-sos is going to boot an easy chance in the ninth inning and we'll be licked, 1-0.'

"So there we'd be in the ninth, and so scared of that wild man you could hear our knees knocking. I'd say to myself, 'I hope this guys hits it to Joe Cronin;' and I knew Cronin was hoping he'd hit it to Jimmie Foxx and Foxx was hoping he'd hit it to Bill Werber."

Melillo, for one, didn't keep his fears to himself. "I hope to Christ they don't hit it to me," he told Lefty Lefebvre. There is no record of anyone suggesting to Grove that his tactics might have been, you know, counterproductive?

"Bobby Doerr had a very clear memory of Grove's temper," David Halberstam wrote in *Summer of '49*. "Early in Doerr's career, Grove was pitching batting practice, and Doerr, in his last swing, hit the ball hard toward the pitcher's mound. He thought nothing of it and left the batting cage to pick up his glove, which was lying near first base. As he bent over to pick it up, a baseball whistled by about two inches from his head. Doerr looked up, and there was Lefty Grove screaming at him, 'Don't you ever hit it at me again, you little son of a bitch.' Unfortunately, such antics were more about preserving the dignity of Grove than they were about making Boston a better team, Doerr realized."

And yet, living teammates go out of their way to praise Grove, even at the risk of being disbelieved. Asked to elaborate on his feelings about Lefty's selfishness, Doerr said, "It was just a spontaneous thing. He later treated me well." To Wagner, Grove was "a great guy. And a great pitcher. You always put him up front in the first game of a series." Says Bill Werber: "[his teammates] understood his frustration and were in sympathy with it. The guy was a winner. He gave the maximum effort every time out and so did the players on his team. They were not afraid of him nor afraid to try hard for him. His 'rages' were never directed toward the players but toward himself. He was a competitor. He was respected and liked. I surely liked him."

Grove's behavior was scarcely unprecedented. "I'm not basically a hothead. I'm a perfectionist, and I can't stand mediocrity in myself or anyone else." That wasn't Grove speaking. It was Rick Barry, the basketball star, talking to George Plimpton.

If anything, Grove's actions were routine, if somewhat exaggerated, among starting pitchers. Writing a story about Jim Palmer, Frank Deford once compared the pitching rotation to a woman's menstrual cycle. The words were evidently too racy for the editors of *Sports Illustrated*, because they never appeared in print. But Deford had a point: starting pitchers are cyclical. Working every fourth or fifth day, they torture their arms with that unnatural overhead or three-quarters motion, then fret constantly that they may have thrown for the last time. No wonder they are baseball's prima donnas, men who focus on their own play while in action, their last or next start while resting. In *Tim McCarver's Baseball for Brain Surgeons and Other Fans*, broadcaster McCarver, the former catcher, could name only three starters, Jim Lonborg, Jim Kaat and Hershiser, he'd seen taking an active interest in the team on their off-days.

In fairness, there was more to like than dislike about Grove. Unlike many dissolutes so common in baseball at the time, he stayed in shape. "Grove's faults are of temperament rather than character," F.C. Lane wrote. Grove didn't throw at batters' heads—just their back pockets. He didn't get kicked out of games and never got into fights. Grove was not above passing on the wisdom of his own experiences. "Kid, when you kick a water bucket, never kick it with your toes," he is said to have told rookies. "Always use the side of your foot." Sometimes, he impulsively bought ties or hats for players, coaches, even Yawkey. In all, Grove was gentle in a big guy kind of way. (If big guys behaved like little guys, there wouldn't be any little guys.)

Teammates didn't care if he stiffed the sportswriters; they'd have liked to themselves. Of more importance, Grove was a winner, and winning is a great equalizer in baseball. Early in the season, before his family arrived and the Groves moved into a house, he had a short walk from the Hotel Kenmore to the ballpark. "Eddie Collins told me that he was certain that if you told Grove that if he were to walk over to Commonwealth Avenue and then down Beacon Street, and then went to the park, a four- or five-mile walk, he would win an extra game, he'd walk it every day," newsman Cashman said. "Collins said, 'For one game, he'd do that.'

"No one hated to lose more than he did. Nobody."

Grove understood the sporting adage, "The more you lose, the easier it gets." Because he never let losing become easy, he never did much of it. "Did I get mad at my teammates?" Grove once said. "Did I yell at Joe Cronin? Yes, sir. Guess I did. I was out there to win. That's the only way to play the game. Yes, sir." There was no levity and no compromise in Grove's approach. Asked to describe some humorous events he'd seen or experienced, Grove told a reporter, "I never saw anything funny about the game."

The theme repeats itself in conversations with other teammates. "He had to have been a great player, because he hated to lose," says Dom DiMaggio. "That determination and drive—it all goes together." Grove hated to lose at anything. Doerr recalled a familiar sight on road trips. When a teammate passed Grove the queen of spades in a hearts game, he'd throw his cards down the aisle.

"He was a nice fellow and generous," says pitcher Wagner. "He did things for people—little things you didn't hear about. 'Here's $100,' he'd say. He'd help you out of a jam." Grove hated talking about himself and certainly didn't broadcast his wealth. "One year he was paid by check and he didn't cash them," says Wagner. "He kept them in his locker. The club had to speak to him. He was screwing up their accounting."

Grove was more egotistical about his pitching and appearance. He well understood the effect his full head of hair had on the opposite sex. On Ladies Days he would warm up hatless before the Red Sox dugout. "The ladies would say 'Ooh!' " Wagner remembers.

Teammates liked Grove's country touches. "One night I was in his Boston home eating dinner, and corn on the cob was served," says Werber. "Lefty took a slice of white bread, spread butter on it thoroughly and wrapped it around his corn on the cob to butter it. Very effective."

And there were simply touching touches, too. Grove was the only player on the team allowed liquor in his locker. "What the devil," Cronin told Wagner, excusing the boozing. Listen to Wes Ferrell telling Donald Honig what Grove did with it:

> Grove was pitching [on July 21, 1935] and he was getting beat by one run [actually two] going into the last of the ninth. Now, you know Lefty: he was a great competitor and a hard loser. A very hard loser. He's sure he's lost his ball game and is madder'n hell over it. He goes into the clubhouse. We get a man on base [actually two], and Cronin sends me up to hit. Tommy Bridges is the pitcher. Well, I hit the first pitch I see and knock it over the left field fence, and we win the ball game.
>
> So we all rush into the clubhouse, laughing and hollering, the way you do after a game like that. And here's Lefty, sitting there, still thinking he's lost his game. When he saw all the carrying-on, I tell you, the smoke started coming out of his ears.
>
> "I don't see what's so funny," he says. "A man loses a ball game, and you're carrying on."
>
> Then somebody says, "Hell, Lefty, we won it. Wes hit a home run for you."
>
> Well, I was sitting across the clubhouse from him, pulling my uniform off, and I notice he's staring at me, with just a trace of a smile at the corners of his mouth. Just staring at me. He doesn't say anything. I give him a big grin and

pull the sweat shirt up over my head. Then I hear him say, "Hey, Wes." I look over and he's rolling a bottle of wine across to me—he'd keep a bottle of one thing or another stashed up in his locker. So here it comes, rolling and bumping along the clubhouse floor. I picked it up and thanked him and put it in my locker. At the end of the season I brought it back to Carolina with me and let it sit up on the mantel. It sat up there for years and years. Every time I looked at it I thought of Old Left. He rolled it over to me.

"He treated me like he treated everybody: bad," says out-fielder Lupien. "He liked to humble rookies. But you regarded him as a god."

300 AND OUT

"The time has come.
The time is now.
Just go. Go. GO!
I don't care how."

–*Marvin K. Mooney, Will You Please Go Now?*,
a Dr. Seuss book (1972)

efore the 1941 season, perhaps the most remarkable ever, all eyes weren't on Ted Williams or Joe DiMaggio. They were on Robert Moses Grove and his 293 wins. "He has been a great ball player," said his old teammate and rival, Wes Ferrell, "I only wish I had a right to carry his glove."

"I want my 300," Grove said.

In a scene Boston newsman Harold Kaese later fleshed out in *The Saturday Evening Post*, Grove actually signed a blank contract:

> He had been on his annual hunting spree at Yawkey's island estate in South Carolina, and was

anxious to start for home. His car was loaded with deer, turkey, preserves, pine trees, chickens and eggs, and he had his foot on the starter when Yawkey suddenly shouted, "Hey Mose, what about the contract? We forgot—"

"Damn the contract," answered Grove. "Where is it anyhow?"

Yawkey hurriedly got a blank contract, and Grove, grabbing it from him, scrawled his signature, then stepped on the gas, as Yawkey roared, "But what about the money? How much?"

"Put in anything," came back Grove's words faintly as he sped away in a cloud of dust.

Yawkey's millionaires? The Red Sox owner had plainly been paying Grove less than the supposed Philadelphia skinflint, Connie Mack. Grove was sent and willingly signed a contract for $10,000, all of $3,500 more than he made as a rookie. Of course, Grove was capable of acting like a rookie himself. On March 17, he cut the palm on his pitching hand when he and some teammates tried to attach a firecracker under the hood of Ted Williams's new Buick while he was eating. The hood handle broke and Lefty needed one stitch, limiting him to a single three-inning outing before opening day.

Williams and Grove were at once the strangest and most natural of bedfellows. True, they were at opposite ends of their careers, but in 1941 a budding star and an old veteran were married as never quite before in baseball history. It had taken them awhile to become friends. Self-involved men have trouble reaching out. Williams admired Grove's pitching, and Grove certainly admired Williams's swing. The tough part was getting together.

Once Williams got over his awe of Grove and Grove

stopped complaining about Williams's fielding and talking, they found they had much in common. One about to become the game's greatest hitter, the other having been the game's greatest pitcher, they would lie in the outfield grass at Fenway, talking and shooting pigeons with shotguns before games. Sometimes Yawkey would do some shooting himself. By the time the animal police put a stop to the practice—the authorities complained to the Red Sox after a newsman spotted Williams and Yawkey with their guns in the outfield—Ted and Lefty had more than their share of pleasant conversations. About what? When you talk with Ted Williams, you talk about hitting. With a home-run stroke of his own—15 downtowners is no small feat for a pitcher—Lefty warmed to the subject. Their hitting philosophies, differed, oh, ever so slightly. Williams was one of the most selective hitters in baseball history. Grove's philosophy was, "Keep swinging and you might hit something."

"He was a moody guy, a tantrum thrower like me," says Williams. "But when he punched a locker or something else, he always did it with his right hand. He was a careful tantrum thrower."

Grove began the 1941 season as everyone's irascible uncle, difficult but lovable. Even the New York *Times* called him "Old Mose." The twenty-two-year-old Williams, on the other hand, was still groping for maturity and acceptance. Despite fine freshman and sophomore seasons, he hadn't won a batting title and was still considered an incomplete hitter. His tendency to practice his swing in the outfield and head for the dugout rather than run out weak grounders or popups didn't speed acceptance. Nor was he the ruggedly handsome and commanding John Wayne character he would become in later years. Talkative and ingenuous, he sometimes stumbled into unfortunate headlines. Midway through the 1940 season, feeling constant pressure in Boston, he blurted out to a syndicated reporter, "Nuts to this. I'd rather be a fireman." In March 1941 he arrived late in camp, smiling and shaking everyone's hand, then suffered a broken ankle that sidelined him nineteen days.

If Williams was floundering, he was also victimized by a cutthroat press that had dubbed him, unkindly, "the Kid." Williams was a loner, which is no crime. In notable contrast to Grove, he didn't trash clubhouses, teammates, or bats. He just went off alone. If there's one thing sportswriters can't abide, it's inaccessibility. Boston columnist Bill Cunningham wrote that Williams took "as brutal and as cruel a cuffing from some elements of the sports press as a kid was ever called upon to suffer. Maybe from one way of looking at it he asked for it . . .[but] whether he asked for it or not, he got it and there was never anything in modern times exactly like it."

Grove opened the season with a two-hitter. Unfortunately, one of those hits was a two-run homer by Sam Chapman, and he left after seven innings trailing his old A's, 2-1. Bobby Doerr's ninth-inning homer won it for reliever Herb Hash.

Lefty didn't pitch again for eleven days, then was knocked out by Detroit after three disastrous innings He got on track against the Browns on May 4, winning, 11-4, with Williams contributing three singles and a stolen base. Grove had 294 wins and counting. Alas, the world was watching another front. Dedicating the birthplace of Woodrow Wilson, in the historic Shenandoah Valley's Staunton, Virginia, President Franklin Delano Roosevelt declared that "we are ever ready to fight again."

Eight days later—Hitler deputy Rudolf Hess had just bailed out over Scotland—Grove completely outpitched Lefty Gomez at Fenway Park and beat the Yankees, 8-4, for number 295 and his 20th consecutive home victory. He threw seven innings in a no-decision against the Tigers, then returned on May 25 to the scene of so much heartache and triumph, Yankee Stadium.

Before 36,461 fans, Grove beat the Yankees, 10-3, for number 296, while Williams had three hits to go over .400 and finally take the lead in the batting race. With the memory of the 1924 brushback incident faded, there was nothing but respect for Grove. "We mostly admired how great he was," outfielder Tommy Henrich says. "We didn't talk about a player's character. He had to be a nasty person for that."

Moving to Chicago on June 8, Grove outdueled his old rival, Ted Lyons[1], and the White Sox, 5-3, on Dom DiMaggio's single in the tenth, for number 297. Though he had taken an oh-fer in the day's doubleheader, ending a twenty-three-game hitting streak, Williams was thrilled. "Say, you should have seen Grove and Lyons fight it out for ten innings," he told Dan Daniel of the New York *World-Telegram*. "It was the greatest exhibition of pitching I ever hope to see. Certainly Feller is tops. But you should have watched those two old-timers maneuvering, outwitting hitters, making their heads do for them what their arms used to do. It was beautiful. I became so engrossed watching the game, I guess I just forgot to hit." The 36,859 in attendance saw one for the ages.

In his next starts Grove was kayoed by the White Sox and Browns—the latter loss ending his home victory streak—but on June 25, amid news of the U.S. waiving its neutrality in favor of the Soviets, he beat the Indians' Jim Bagby, Jr.[2], 7-2, for number 298. Williams again said he was thrilled to watch the the great man in action.

---

[1] Grove and Lyons were the only pitchers involved in both Babe Ruth's 60 homers and Joe DiMaggio's 56-game hitting streak.

[2] Grove was constantly linking up with historic figures, or at least their relatives: Bagby's father, Jim Sr., had been the last pitcher before Grove to win 30 games, when he went 31-12 in 1920.

Nonetheless, Lefty's quest for 300 wasn't supplying the drama. As far as everyone was concerned, it was just a matter of time before he got there. Here was the real race: The same day Grove reached 298, Joe DiMaggio homered during New York's 7-5 win over St. Louis and ran his hitting streak to thirty-seven games, four short of George Sisler's 1922 record and seven back of Wee Willie Keeler's less revered (at the time) nineteenth-century record.

Because of his salary holdouts, DiMaggio had not been an especially popular figure in Yankee Stadium. Even as he began hitting every day, there was initially more attention paid to the Yankees' record-breaking consecutive-game homer streak, which passed 20 in late June. Things changed on June 26, when DiMaggio was nearly shut out. With the Yankees leading in the last half of the eighth, there were three batters ahead of a hitless DiMag. Fortunately, Red Rolfe walked, and the next batter, Tommy Henrich, got manager Joe McCarthy's permission to bunt rather than risk swinging away and hitting into a double play. Henrich sacrificed successfully. Then DiMaggio singled on the first pitch, and the spectacular save caught baseball's attention. When he reached Washington for a June 29 doubleheader, starting the day one short of Sisler, reporters and cameramen from everywhere were on hand. DiMaggio didn't disappoint them, doubling off Dutch Leonard in the sixth inning of the opener, then singling off Red Anderson in the seventh inning of the nightcap with a borrowed bat after a spectator stole his favorite. Good copy, great drama. On July 1, DiMaggio hit in both ends of a doubleheader, tying Keeler, while the Yankees routed the Red Sox—no one was eyeballing Williams's .408 average at the time—7-2, 9-2. New York's homer streak ended at twenty-five in the first game. Suddenly, DiMaggio had no competition whatsoever.

Now that people were hanging on the streak, his silences had morphed into dignity. In the public mind, DiMaggio was "class." He had become as famous and recognizable and popular as Muhammad Ali would be later. In his fine chronicle of the season, *Baseball in '41*, Robert W. Creamer wrote of his old *Sports Illustrated* running mate, "Andy Crichton told me that he and his brother Bob and two high school friends drove across the country that summer in an old jalopy. In Montana they stopped for coffee at a dusty cafe in a dusty town. Farm hands and ranch hands came into the cafe for breakfast. This was before television, remember, and radio news was sketchy before we got into the war, particularly in the smaller towns. You found out what was happening from newspapers. Almost every man who came into the cafe, Crichton said, would glance toward a newspaper lying on the counter and ask the proprietor, 'He get one yesterday?' He didn't have to explain who 'he' was, even though this was two thousand miles from New York and a thousand miles west of the westernmost major league city, which in those days was St. Louis. Every day, all over the country, people asked, 'Did he get one yesterday?' "

On July 2, DiMaggio homered over Williams's head into the left-field bleachers at Yankee Stadium to break Keeler's record. The next day, in Philadelphia, Grove beat the A's, 5-2, for his 299th victory, yielding 10 hits and no walks, striking out two, and enjoying Jim Tabor's three-run double and Williams's two-run homer. A Ladies Day crowd of seven thousand—disappointing, but fifty-five hundred ahead of the previous day—cheered lustily when Grove left the mound at game's end. He was 6-2. Not bad for a forty-one-year-old man pitching once a week. "Just so long as any club will give me the chance, I'll keep on pitching," he told Boston sportswriter Joe Cashman. "You see, I wouldn't know what to do with myself if I didn't have a baseball job."

His eye doubtless on a legacy, Grove was making a special effort to court reporters. The line Frank Graham wrote about Bob Meusel, the taciturn Yankee outfielder who turned friendly in his last season with the club, seems appropriate: "He's learning to say hello when it's time to say good-bye."

Baseball events were dizzying: DiMaggio, Williams, Grove, the pennant races. Baseball had never needed a midseason break so much. On July 8, Williams, who was batting .405 at the break, hit a two-out, three-run, ninth-inning homer off the upper right-field parapet in Detroit's Briggs Stadium to win the All Star Game, 7-5. As dramatic a moment as any in the midsummer classic—right up there with Babe Ruth's homer in 1933 and Carl Hubbell's five consecutive strike-outs in 1934—it was "the most thrilling hit of my life," Williams said later. The Kid became a man that day.

Grove went back to work. The 300-win mark was tantalizingly close yet elusive, that brass ring just out of reach. On July 11—when President Roosevelt appointed Wild Bill Donovan (not to be confused the the Tigers pitcher) to head a new intelligence agency (later called the CIA) and an American destroyer saved survivors of a sunken British vessel—Grove pitched a complete-game five-hitter but lost to one of his old patsies, the Tigers, and Bobo Newsom, 2-0. Going into the game, Grove had a 59-18 record against Detroit[3] and considered a victory against them as his birthright, but he had failed to beat them in three '41 starts. "Go out and get me 10 runs, you fellas, and maybe I'll hit my 300 mark," a disgusted Grove told his teammates afterward. Even Williams had gone zero-for-four, his average dropping under .400 for the first time since May. The same day Joe

---

[3] Grove's career record against other teams: Boston (35-8), Chicago (41-18), Cleveland (45-22), New York (34-27), Philadelphia (13-5), St. Louis (42-17), Washington (31-25).

DiMaggio had three singles and a homer, extending his con-secutive-game hitting streak to fifty.

On July 18, the day after DiMaggio's streak was halted at 56, Grove again tried for number 300, but lost, 4-3, in Chicago, in ten innings when rightfielder Lou Finney dropped a fly ball. With 54,674 fans looking on, Grove walked back to the clubhouse, his composure apparently intact, then ripped open his shirt, buttons flying, and snarled at Jimmie Foxx, whose error early in the game led to another run. Boston *Globe* columnist Jerry Nason called Grove "a seething volcano of frustrated ambition."

On July 25, 1941, the Nazis were stalled two hundred and thirty miles west of Moscow. In Boston it was ninety degrees outside, and sixteen thousand Fenway fans—including six thousand freebies on Ladies Day—sweltered while Grove faced the Indians. The *Globe*'s Fred Barry pronounced the day fit for a record. "Lefty, being a family man and all that, will not be lacking for vociferous (and screeching) support." This was the same writer who referred to the contingent from Lake Erie as "the visitors from the banks of the Ohio."

"Pop, this is a nine-inning game," Cronin told Grove. "I'm not coming out to get you." The Indians scored once in the second and had five straight hits in a three-run third, prompting "Take him out!" calls from the Fenway not-so-faithful. No fool, Cronin left Grove in. In a rock-'em, sock-'em game, the wildest of the year as everyone on hand agreed, the Red Sox scored twice in the fourth to drive out Cleveland starter Joe Krakauskas; Ted Williams tied the score with a two-run homer in the fifth, and a Lou Boudreau homer put the Tribe up, 6-4, in the seventh. Listening to the game at the family cottage on Pine Island Lake in Westhampton, Massachusetts, thirteen-year-old Stan Finn wondered aloud, "He's getting pounded. Why don't they take him out?"

Plainly, Cronin's strategy had not been communicated to the public. In the bottom half of the inning Jim Tabor re-tied the score with a round-tripper. When Bobby Doerr struck out and Johnny Peacock singled, the Indians replaced pitcher Mel Harder with Al Milnar. During Milnar's walk from the bullpen, next-batter Grove sat down in the dugout, prompting some fans to assume he'd been pinch-hit for.

No such chance. The Red Sox were determined to let Grove pitch until he got the big win. As Boston *Globe* columnist Ray Fitzgerald wrote years later, "That shiny 300 apple was still on the tree, and Grove was reaching for it." Indeed, Grove almost won his own game with a single to left-center that got by centerfielder Larry Rosenthal and was bobbled by leftfielder Gee Walker, sending Johnny Peacock scurrying for home. Alas, he was nailed by Boudreau's relay. "He arose covered with dust and the show went on," the *Globe*'s Gerry Moore wrote.

With the score still 6-6, Dom DiMaggio walked to open the Red Sox eighth and was sacrificed to second by Finney. Cronin was intentionally walked, and Williams, who wanted nothing more than to help his buddy enter the record books, came to the plate with two walks, a single, and a homer under his belt. Try to appreciate the drama he brought to every at bat, not just this one. He was six-foot-three and slim, but with a long, powerful neck and heavily muscled forearms. Thinking hard, he tapped dirt from his spikes, slowly and deliberately. Tossing his head back and forth like a colt, he dug a deep hole in the back of the batter's box, gripping his bat as firmly as a farmer wringing the neck of a chicken. When the pitcher wound up, Williams relaxed and lashed at the ball with his classic uppercut swing. Even his misses, which left him spinning around like a corkscrew, brought oohs and aahs from the crowd.

Perhaps trying too hard this time, Williams popped up to third baseman Ken Keltner and threw his bat high in the air. Well, maybe it was better that Foxx, Lefty's best friend in baseball and teammate for fifteen seasons, should come to the plate with two out, the game tied, and a man in scoring position. With a patented swing and a patented result—deep and majestic—Foxx lashed a triple off the distant center-field fence, driving home two runs and scoring a third after Ray Mack's relay got away from Keltner. When Foxx returned to the dugout, Grove uncharacteristically hugged and kissed him. Tabor immediately homered again to make it 10-6.

Too exhausted to back up third, his curve gone, Grove got through the last two innings on fastballs, three forkballs, and adrenaline. While losing eight and one-half pounds in "the toughest game I ever sweated through," he somehow retired the side in the ninth. He had won his 300th game, 10-6, on a nifty 12-hitter. DiMaggio, who caught a fly ball on Grove's one hundred and twentieth pitch for the last out, headed toward a crowd that surrounded Grove, hugging him, patting him on the back. Half a dozen cops got Grove to the dugout, where he was mobbed by more fans. "The thrill of a lifetime?" said Grove, when DiMaggio finally handed him the ball. "This is it."

Grove bought beer for his teammates and a bottle of brandy for himself. "Quit now?" he almost yelled at a questioner. "They'll have to cut the uniform off me. I'm going out for another 300. They couldn't be any harder to get than the first 300."

"I didn't have a thing out there," he told another reporter.

"That isn't so, Mose," said his catcher, Peacock. "You may not have had good stuff, but you had control." Indeed, he only walked one batter and threw just 38 balls, while striking out six. It was no pathetic last gasp, as reported.

"That Jimmie," Grove said, grandly crediting the supporting cast, "he's hit some mighty important baseballs for me over the years. But never one as important as that one today. I had a hunch Jimmie would hit one for old Mose."

Williams, who had raised his average to precisely .400, wasn't seen in the postgame celebratory picture. Accused of sulking because Foxx, not he, drove in the winning run, Williams said he was upset with an error he'd made. "I drove in two and let in three that day," he said later, "and that's why I was so mad at myself. And I'm mad now that I'm not in the picture with my arm around Lefty Grove. That's a picture I really wish I had."

After the game, Grove threw a champagne dinner party at the Myles Standish Hotel. Seventy-four-year-old coach Hugh Duffy, who hit .440 for the 1894 Boston Beaneaters, was there. Lefty's chief guest was press room attendant Tom Kenny, whose son and Lefty's son Bobby were best buddies. Williams neglected to get the time and place of the party. He missed some good-natured roasting and some serious moments of pure tribute. "Lefty was the main man," says a surviving teammate, pitcher Charlie Wagner. "We were all behind him."

The twelfth player to win 300 games, the fifth since 1900, and only the third in a quarter-century—Walter Johnson in 1920 and Pete Alexander in 1924 had most recently preceded him—Grove became the first modern lefthander and first 300-game winner whose career was virtually all in the lively-ball era.

There was still a season to finish. In the National League the Dodgers, once Bums, now America's sweethearts, were winning a wire-to-wire chase over the Cardinals. Many a war film would have a dumb but lovable Brooklynite in it. In the American League there was nothing left but Williams,

*On July 18, 1941, a dejected, 215-pound Grove left the field at
Comiskey Park, a teammate's tenth-inning error having cost him his 300th
win. A week later Grove beat the Indians in Boston for his final victory.*

although he didn't catch the public fancy until a big September series in New York. DiMaggio's 56-game hitting streak had been halted. The Yankees were winging to another pennant, finishing seventeen games ahead of the runner-up Red Sox. And Lefty Grove was heading straight downhill. After running his record to 7-4 with the big win, he lost his last three decisions. "I'm throwing the ball as fast as ever," he said. "It's just not getting there as fast." He probably didn't have quite the will to win, or at least the urgency, he had before number 300. When he pulled a rib-cage muscle pitching to Tigers' leadoff hitter Tuck Stainback on August 27, Grove was sidelined for a month.

Boston writers told him to quit. "A nice lesson in irony these days is to see reporters, photographers and feature writers stumbling over the feet of such fading stars as Foxx, Cronin and Lefty Grove in their haste to get at Ted Williams," Kaese wrote on September 13.

When he realized Boston no longer wanted him, Grove supposedly stood in the clubhouse and made a fiery speech, concluding, "And if the Red Sox don't want me, Connie will give me a job." Or so it was said. "I don't remember any of that," says Wagner. "Lefty was sort of quiet, except when he lost. And [general manager] Eddie Collins wouldn't have released him. He loved him. When Cocky was coaching at Philadelphia, Lefty used to grab him and lock him in his locker. In those days you could play tricks on coaches."

Yawkey suffered with Grove, perhaps his all-time favorite player until Carl Yazstremski arrived. When the owner asked to speak with Lefty about his future, he said, "Not now. I'll see you down at the island in the winter. I want to do some thinking."

Grove's last day in the city of Boston was typically stormy. Kaese wrote in his September 24 column: "Lefty Grove was so hurt by the thought that his big league pitching career was finished that he sneaked into the Red Sox clubhouse early Sunday morning for his personal belongings and left for Lonaconing, Md., without saying good-by to anyone except Johnny Orlando, clubhouse custodian."

Grove returned to Philadelphia for the season-ending series, but on Sunday, September 28, everyone was focused on Ted Williams. Going into the first game of a doubleheader, he was batting .39955, which rounds off to .400, and Cronin had given him the option of sitting out the whole afternoon. Ted said no, he would play. Hitting .400 wouldn't be easy. He not only had the record to think about, but poor visibility in Philadelphia's Shibe Park "crater," buried in shadow by its high stands. Location, location, location.

"I hope I can hit .400," Williams said nervously, turning the discussion to a barnstorming tour he had planned with Foxx. He was in no mood for extended drama. In the second inning, he grounded through the right side for a single. Three innings later he homered 440 feet over the right-center fence. His teammates were yelling and screaming for Williams, no longer an unpopular figure in the clubhouse. When he singled again an inning later, Williams ended all speculation. He finished the game four-for-five, although a Sox pitcher, Wagner, had the winning RBI in a 12-11 marathon.

Between games, in a ceremony honoring Grove, his old coach Ira Thomas, then an A's scout, presented him with a silver chest. An unnamed Athletic, musing about the old Lefty, said, "Well, he's a better guy now. All he used to have was a fastball and a mean disposition."

Connie Mack agreed. "I took more from Grove than I would from any man living," he said. "He said things and did things—but he's changed. I've seen it year by year. He's got to be a great fellow."

Grove started the second game, lasted just one inning, gave up four hits and three runs, and took the loss. "That pathetic figure," the Boston *Herald*'s Burt Whitman called him. It was his last appearance, and back where he started his career. He had 300 wins and 298 complete games, numbers obscured by the number of the moment: .406.

"It was bitingly sad," Kaese wrote, "because while the greatest pitcher of his generation stumbled toward oblivion, cheers were ringing for the new idol, for a Ted Williams who was making six hits in eight times at bat that sunny Sunday afternoon, to be the first American Leaguer in eighteen years to hit over .400. The contrast was painfully perfect."

When he had just five singles in the 1946 World Series, Williams was somehow stamped as a poor clutch hitter. How fast his critics forgot the events of 1941. What could be more pressure-laden than batting with two outs in the ninth inning of the All Star Game, with two men on and your club two runs down? How about passing up the chance to bat .400 on the bench, knowing that by playing you would have to hit safely several times in a doubleheader? And then going six-for-eight. Talk about class. Talk about dignity. Talk about clutch.

In early December, Grove and Yawkey were walking through Yawkey's hunting preserve in South Carolina, rifles under their arms. "It's tough to take your shoes off like that," Grove said.

"It sure is," said Yawkey. "But what's the use of going on. Why keep on? Who cares if you win seven or eight more games? Why force yourself to get in condition just to win a couple of games in the spring and fall?

"That's why I'm quitting, Tom," said Grove. "I've been thinking it over. It's hard work getting in shape, and pitching in the summer is just about too much for me. I guess I'm through."

His words didn't sink in for a day. The next morning at dawn, Grove and island superintendent Jim Gibson were walking through the preserve. Suddenly, Grove yelled, "Well, I'm through! There's nothing left for me now except spend my summers fishing—fishing!"

Lefty's retirement, announced December 9, was obscured by bigger events at the baseball winter meetings, the news of Pearl Harbor on December 7, and the declaration of war the next day. He left baseball without the catchy quotes or endearing anecdotes to generate a lasting legend. Grove's career had been Shakespearean, if not exactly tragic. The ravaged clubhouse in St. Louis lived after him; the quiet acts of goodness were interred with his moans.

Nonetheless, Grove did not slink off to a retirement of unfulfillment and muttered regrets. Instead, in complete defiance of the athletic stereotype, he moved smoothly to the next stage of his life.

LEFTY AT REST

★ ★ ★ ★

"If I had it to do all over again, I would. If they said, 'Come on, here's a steak dinner,' and I had the chance to go out and play a game of ball, I'd go out there and play the game and let the steak sit there. I would."

–Grove in retirement

fter hearing of Pearl Harbor, Lefty took out the big righthander's glove with the rising sun/stars and stripes logo that the Japanese had given him during the 1931 tour. There was only one thing a good patriot could do, as far as he was concerned. He cut out the rising sun.

Although Grove had retired, he volunteered to replace one of the three lefthanders the Red Sox lost to the service. They politely declined. Hoping to keep him with the club, owner Tom Yawkey offered Grove a job as pitching coach for $12,000, evidently upping the ante, be, because figure was fully $2,000 more than he'd made in his last year as a player. Now it was Grove's turn to politely decline. He felt he'd have to remain in shape to demonstrate pitches, an ordeal worthwhile only if he stayed in the rotation.

So Lefty retired to Lonaconing. Next spring the *Globe*'s Harold Kaese visited him on assignment for his paper and *The Saturday Evening Post*. When he arrived, Grove was planting potatoes in a garden filled with tomatoes, corn, peas, and grapes. He was down fifteen pounds from his last playing weight of 215, and proud that wading through water in hip boots had strengthened his legs.

"I'm sure happy being home," Grove said. "I've done more fishing already than in all the time I played baseball. You should see the trout."

Asked if he missed baseball, Grove admitted he missed "the games, the traveling, the crowds—but most of all I miss being with the fellows."

Nonetheless, he was staying away deliberately. "I haven't seen a ballgame all spring, not even a high-school game.[1] Bob, my boy, hasn't lost a game for Washington College [in Chestertown, Maryland where he had transferred from Duke], but I haven't gone to see him pitch. I haven't thrown a ball, haven't even had one in my hand."

"Why?" Kaese asked.

"It would only make me want to go back and play again."

If he was worried about his life after baseball, Lefty didn't show it. Lefty's Place, with its candy-stuffed counter, bowling alleys, and pool table, not to mention 247 of Lefty's game balls, was still in operation. In his spare time, Grove hunted with his dogs, Jif Alfonso and King Alfred, fished, and worked out on his rowing machine. He lost any interest in returning to the majors. "I'd seen enough trains and hotels," he said. "And cities. I never did like cities. I just went fishing."

---

[1] Actually, he attended the Red Sox opener in Washington. "He was very warm, shook my hand wished me well," says Johnny Pesky, who had been promoted from Portland to play shortstop. "He told me, 'At least you'll never have to have a hand down [on one knee, *á la* Joe Cronin] to field the ball.'"

Many ballplayers suffer a painful transition to the real world. Missing the competition, the money, and the camaraderie, lacking another skill, they let their bodies go, drift into alcoholism, depression, and poverty, and die well before their time. By making a clean break from baseball and finding other activities to interest him, Grove retired happy.

Lefty certainly fared better in the long run than the other Hall of Famers on the A's championship teams. In 1934, Mickey Cochrane took over a fifth-place Detroit team and led it to a pennant. Cochrane played 129 games despite being so exhausted he had to sleep during the World Series at a hospital near Tiger Stadium. The Cardinals won the Series, but in 1935 Cochrane led the Tigers to a repeat pennant and scored the Series-clinching run against the Cubs. "It was my happiest day in baseball," he said.

And one of his last as a player. The pressures of managing the Tigers, and then assuming the general manager's job as well when owner Frank Navin died after the '35 Series, caused Cochrane to suffer a nervous breakdown during the '36 season. On his way to recovery in May of 1937, Cochrane homered off the Yankees' Bump Hadley and in his next at bat took a fastball to the temple on an errant 3-1 pitch. Hospitalized in New York for ten days, unconscious and critical for forty-eight hours, he never played again. In 1938, when Detroit's stadium was expanded and renamed from Navin Field to Briggs Stadium, Tigers owner Walter Briggs unceremoniously fired Cochrane as manager. His average record, projected over 162 games, was 94-68, tops among Tigers managers. "Mickey did more for baseball in four years here than Briggs can do in a lifetime," said Grove, in town one 1938 day with the Red Sox. "Just look at the stadium—that's the stadium that Mickey Cochrane built."

Cochrane lost his son Gordon Jr. in World War II, when he

*Behind his home in Charlestown. An enthusiastic hunter,
Grove collected guns and shot just about everything, including,
on one unfortunate occasion, a fellow hunter.*

himself ran the Navy's fitness program and the baseball team at the Great Lakes Naval Training Station. He was elected to the Hall in 1947—the same year as Grove—served as an A's general manager under Mack, a scout for the Yankees and Tigers, and a Tiger vice president. Considered by some historians the greatest catcher in baseball history, Cochrane died of cancer at fifty-nine in 1962.

Al Simmons had eleven consecutive 100-RBI seasons in his first eleven seasons, 1924-34. A few years after Mack relented and gave Simmons a three-year contract in 1931, his play declined. "When I finally realized I had it made, I was never again the kind of ballplayer I was when I was hungry," he said. Simmons played for six other teams, plus two more stops with the A's, made the Hall in 1953, and died of a heart attack at fifty-four in 1956.

Jimmie Foxx was the saddest case. Baseball wasn't the Beast's problem. He had a record twelve consecutive 30-homer, 100-RBI seasons, and finished his career with 534 homers and a stunning .609 slugging percentage. "Next to Joe DiMaggio, Foxx was the greatest player I ever saw," Ted Williams once said. "I truly admired him. He was such a good-natured guy, a big farm boy from Maryland. He never bad mouthed anyone. What a disposition, always a giggle. He never made any bones about his love for scotch. He used to say he could drink fifteen of those little miniature bottles and not be affected."

No, baseball wasn't Foxx's problem. Life was. A bon vivant with a penchant for bad schemes, the immensely likable guy, as soft on the inside as he was hard-muscled on the outside, invested in two golf courses that failed. He fell into short-term jobs after the majors: managing the Fort Worth Daisies, a women's team; coaching the University of Miami nine; working as a broadcaster, salesman, and truck driver. "I earned $175,000 playing baseball," Foxx said in 1950, "and didn't have a dime to show for twenty years in the game. I don't feel badly for myself. The money I lost and blew was my own fault. I had to wonder if I wasn't born to be broke."

In 1967, he choked to death when a piece of meat lodged in his throat at his brother Sam's house. He was only fifty-nine. Double X's Bunyanesque feats of strength, however, deserved as much immortality as his election to Cooperstown in 1951. In 1997, a life-sized statue of baseball's Samson was unveiled in Sudlersville on Maryland's Eastern Shore.

A teammate of Grove's for fifteen seasons, Foxx was his

best friend in baseball. They hunted grouse and turkey in the Carolinas and headed to Lefty's cabin on the Potomac for fishing. Lefty even invited Double X into the mines (Foxx refused). Nonetheless, Lefty was somewhat uneasy with his buddy's silk shirts and chauffer-driven limousines. "Too high-living for me," Grove told old friend Jim Getty.

To Grove's delight, Connie Mack kept on ticking. After dismantling his second championship team, Mack settled mostly for losers—he did have one first-division team, in 1948—until his retirement in 1950[2]. Even so, he never lost his dignity. Allen Lewis, a retired baseball writer for the Philadelphia *Inquirer*, remembers feeling honored the night he met Mack at a banquet in 1946. "I am very happy to meet you, young man," said Mack, bowing slightly. "I shall remember you."

Alas, his mind was slipping. On August 21, 1949, the old man was honored by the Yankees at Old Timers' Day. Mack feebly sat in a dugout. Cochrane was nearby. Grove approached.

"Hello, Mr. Mack," he said.

Mack didn't flicker. "Your boy, Robert, Mr. Mack," Grove said. "I'm Lefty Grove."

"Ah, Groves," Mack said, mispronouncing his name again.

Mack died at ninety-three in 1956. He won 3,731 and lost 3,948 games, both records. He succeeded in both the dead- and lively-ball eras, judged talent on a par with the best managers, and may have had no peer in handling people.

"Well, I don't know about other 'systems,' but I do know that Connie Mack handles a team as individuals," Cochrane, just traded as player-manager to Detroit, told Boston columnist George C. Carens in 1934. "He talks to each man

---

2 The A's lead the American League with sixteen 100-loss seasons. The Phillies lead the National League with fourteen. No wonder Philadelphia fans are difficult.

calmly and peacefully. And he can 'lay it in' when he thinks it necessary. He's just as likely to hop on you when your [sic] going good. Thinks you can take it better, maybe."

"He hates a loafer," Cochrane continued. "Tries to make a man know what it means to do his best. Thinks a player can eat and sleep better when he makes baseball a game of play, of fun. He figures slumps come when a man loafs or sulks. That's how I would size up the Mack system which had given Eddie Collins to the Red Sox, [Jimmy] Dykes to Chicago, Cy Perkins and myself to Detroit."

Baseball lets go of its memories quickly. Crusty old players are eventually bathed in a glow of affection and nostalgia. Though Kaese's *Saturday Evening Post* profile was scarcely positive in 1942, other accounts soon began surfacing about Grove's philanthropy. "This fellow used to come up to the plant and buy baseballs in four- and five-dozen lots," a Phillies executive named Bill Phillips, who previously worked for a sporting-goods manufacturer, told Philadelphia *Bulletin* writer Ed Pollock in 1943. "I made the mistake of asking him what he did with them. He said he used them, period. There was no point in asking him for what purpose. It was apparent he didn't want to tell me.

"One morning he said he wanted to buy some uniforms. If he could have walked out with the uniforms he wanted, he wouldn't have told me anything about them."

Grove was reminded that uniform sizes were needed. "He told me I could get the measurements by sending someone to a sandlot in North Philadelphia where a gang of youngsters played ball," said Phillips. "He often stopped his car on his way to Shibe Park and watched the kids. I found out he had been giving them the baseballs he had been buying from us. He autographed them and gave them away as souvenirs. And he also saw that the boys had a good supply for their games.

He outfitted the whole team. That cost him a pretty penny. All the kids and those of us at the plant had to promise we wouldn't say anything about it."

Grove sent balls to kids in hospitals and orphanages, and refused to buy the cheaper brands. In Boston, a friend told Phillips, Grove put two youngsters through college and didn't talk about it. "I was one of the few who knew about his charities and I always look at that as the real Lefty Grove," said Phillips.

"He was kind and considerate," says Grove's old friend, Getty. Also the picture of contentment. "There was a picture of him with a setter, a shotgun and a pipe in his mouth," Getty says. "The Granger company gave him a hunting outfit, $750, and a lifetime supply of pipe tobacco."

Suter Kegg of the Cumberland *Evening Times* was assigned to interview Grove early in his retirement. "I had read about how difficult the guy was for newspapermen and being a young sports reporter at the time, I almost backed out of the assignment after the interview had been set up for me by the late Gene Gunning, our editor then," Kegg told Ruth Bear Levy.

"I was shaking in my shoes and my voice may even have been quivering when I walked into the Republican Club at Lonaconing along with Leo Leasure, then taking photos for our paper. To my delightful surprise, the great portsider was extremely cordial. He broke out a bottle of Canadian whiskey and asked us to join him in a drink."

Life was basic in Lonaconing. Virtually all the Protestants were Republicans, and virtually all the Catholics were Democrats. Methodist/Republican Grove attended the state Republican convention, his pockets lined with cigars, was elected Lonaconing police chief, and held the post for six years. One winter a coal company house caught on fire, the

In 1961 Grove, recently relocated to Norwalk, Ohio,
showed a photographer how he gripped his forkball.

plugs were frozen and firefighters had to break the ice on George's Creek. Grove showed up with a case of miniature scotch bottles. In a surreal scene, firemen came running out of the burning house in search of, well, firewater.

Lefty coached youth teams and kept interest high by awarding prizes for excellence. When he took an American Legion team to Forbes Field for a game, Philadelphia newsman Stan Baumgartner, a teammate of Grove's in 1925-26, was amazed by his friendly greeting. Grove gave his MVP trophy to Lonaconing's Central (later Valley) High School instead of the Hall of Fame. "He would work out with the varsity," said the late John Meyers, a legendary coach and athlete in the region. "He'd throw a curve and tell the catcher not to move his mitt. Hit it every time. He tried to teach the players a major-league curve. Only one got it."

Raymond B. O'Rourke of the Cumberland *Evening Times*, writing for the Baltimore *Sun* on August 25, 1946, described Lefty's Place:

> Inside, appropriately, the first thing the visitor sees is a baseball scoreboard, and directly above it, a huge autographed picture of Lefty's favorite manager, Connie Mack. Old-time showcases, cluttered with candy, peanuts, chewing tobacco, and assorted odds and ends, share the fore part of the storeroom with a single pool table; three bowling alleys stretch toward the rear of the building.
>
> The walls surrounding the pool table are covered with autographed pictures of Babe Ruth, Lou Gehrig and other baseball greats and many of them bear sentimental inscriptions: "To my old pal, Lefty, the greatest of them all," or "To my good friend, Lefty, the greatest southpaw ever."

The walk along the aisle beside the No. 1 alley is strung with Lefty's sporting trophies. There are a couple of fish, several squirrels, a pheasant, and the head of a Canadian ram, several deer and an elk.

In his "madroom," an old storeroom, Lefty was telling O'Rourke how excited he was about his local youth team, sponsored by the Republican Club next door, getting ready to open its season. Grove was asked if he used his contacts to get equipment.

"Have to," he said. "The way things are now we probably wouldn't be able to get enough equipment otherwise."

Going over to a case of new bats, he began drawing them out one by one.

"Louisville Sluggers," he said, "all autographed. Got them direct from Kentucky. Here's Babe Ruth's, Lou Gehrig's, Al Simmons'"—

Then he pulled out one and didn't say anything.

"Whose was that?" he was asked.

"Mine," he answered in an almost apologetic voice.

With the enthusiasm of a boy hero worshipper, he pointed to the quality of the new equipment: caps, $2.65 apiece; base bags, $5—"Got 'em from Boston"; balls, $19.80 a dozen—"Think prices haven't gone up? Last year a dozen only cost $18.

"Everything's big-league," he said. "The uniforms cost 25 bucks apiece and they're the real thing. They have an elephant sewed on the blouse." He grinned. "For GOP, that is."

Lefty also used the storeroom to play cards with his buddies Alvin Green, a civil engineer; Jim Getty's father, Gorman E. (Doc) Getty, a dentist; Tom Holmes, a clothier; and others. Grove left Lonaconing only when necessary, like the time he was honored as Yawkey's guest at the 1946 World Series. When a Philadelphia *Bulletin* reporter discovered Grove midway through the 1949 season, Lefty had a fishing cottage on the South Branch River and was a regular at the Cumberland Country Club.

"It's a great life as long as you can get away with it," he said, "and I'm getting away with it."

In 1969, Grove and Bob Feller were named the best living lefthanded and righthanded pitchers.

In the early '50s Grove would sit his one grandchild, his son Bobby's daughter Lynn (now Lynn Grove Horning), on the counter and fix her ice cream cones. "My little round girl," he'd call her affectionately, even when she was thin. "I can still smell the cigar smoke," she says.

"I can visualize him after he was selected baseball's best living lefthander in 1969 and went to Washington to be honored by President Nixon," says Getty. "He was sitting at the White House, with his legs spread out and white cotton socks rolled down over his shoes."

★   ★   ★   ★

And yet, there was much missing from his life. For one, a proper hometown legacy. Though he was known as the Lion of Lonaconing, Lefty wasn't universally lionized there. He has a plaque in Furnace Park, amid picnic tables, benches, and play equipment, but the Hall of Fame insignia was loosened by a would-be thief, removed for repairs by Mayor Joe Krumpach, and given to park neighbor John Meyers. The plaque has gone undiscovered among his possessions after his death. Though local Westmar High School has a Lefty Grove Award for the top student-athlete, he goes unmentioned on the welcome-to-Lonaconing sign, which carries a Big Vein Furnace insignia to honor the local landmark. As if Lefty didn't deserve landmark status. To the chagrin of his friends, neither the Little League field nor an elementary school built after his retirement was named after him.

"I don't think he got enough credit in this town," says Brian Kidwell. A nursing assistant, Brian is married to factory worker Susan Grove, whose grandfather was Lefty's brother Dewey. They live in the cramped but comfortable two-story home the great man himself inhabited at 89 Douglas

Avenue, a quarter-mile from downtown Lonaconing.

Why not enough credit? "It was a coal-mining town, and he was once the richest man," says Kidwell.

There was Lefty's not-always-winning manner, too. He had mellowed, but the old Grove temper would occasionally resurface. He was not above breaking a pool cue over his knee or firing a nonworking radio against a wall. "He was [pause] all [pause] right," says a waitress in Marshall's, a downtown restaurant Lefty frequented. Run by a Boston sports fan, the restaurant has walls covered with photos of Larry Bird, Bobby Orr, Carl Yastrzemski, Fred Lynn, Fenway Park, the old Boston Garden and, yes, quite a few of Lefty. It's the noon-to-one rush hour, and customers are eating Sloppy Joes, baked pollock, and chickenburgers, while quaffing vanilla Cokes.

No doubt the unfortunate divorce of Lefty and Ethel in the early 1950's, caused by his involvement with another woman, forced people to take sides. Immediately after Ethel threatened to divorce him, Lefty stopped seeing the woman. Unfortunately, both Lefty and Ethel were stubborn people and they never reconciled. "I think three of Ethel's friends put some ideas in her head," says Grove's niece, Betty Holshey. Another source said that Ethel later regretted the separation. Lefty and Ethel did take their granddaughter to the river cottage together, with Ethel sliding down in the back seat of the car so that tongues wouldn't wag, and Lefty visited his ex at the hospital when she was dying in 1960. "The divorce was his one main regret," says Lynn Grove Horning. "He never stopped loving her, and when she died, it nearly killed him."

There were financial problems, too. They came in direct contradiction to events across the country. The G.I. Bill of Rights had been passed during World War II, enabling veterans to attend college. The class system was starting to crumble. Levittown and other suburban developments enabled people to leave grim urban tenements for suburban houses, $100 down. Having saved money during the war, when there was little to buy, consumers embarked on an unprecedented spending spree. Alas, Lefty shared in none of the booty. He retired six years before baseball players received pensions, and his father retired unpensioned, too. Lefty took care of both parents and employed his wife's brother, one of his own brothers, and Betty Holshey's husband Pete, a wounded World War II veteran, at Lefty's Place. Though he lived cheaply in a room next to the Republican Club, at some point he needed financial assistance from major-league baseball and his son.

Betty Holshey sits in her house, like so many other Lonaconing homes built on a slope. "Come in," she says. "It's just home." It is a Lonaconing greeting—in effect, *"Mi casa es su casa."*

Gray-haired and bespectacled, still trim in her seventies, wearing shorts, T-shirt, and running shoes, Holshey motions a visitor to a hundred-year-old rocking chair and pulls out photos, scrapbooks, and a solid-coal ball with "A's" on it that Lefty gave her. "I have a daughter Dorothy," she says. "She was growing up as a southpaw. 'Don't you dare break her,' Uncle Bob told me.

"I remember a lot of happy times. There would be a family dinner. Uncle Bob always came in a suit, white shirt, and tie. He liked the liver and gizzard and would pull them out of a roast chicken and eat them. 'That's the best part, Bett—I can leave now,' he joked.

"Oh, there were a *lot* of happy times. Lefty, Grandpap, my father Dewey, and my husband Pete would sit and talk for hours about baseball, hunting, fishing, and things. I can still hear my grandma. 'Just listen to them,' she'd say, 'and he said he had to go home early. Just *listen* to them!' "

"He was just Uncle Bob to me," says Holshey's daughter Dorothy Thompson, who saw him frequently during the first ten years of her life. "He always had a cigar on him. He would talk loud, and he gave bear hugs. The Republican Club had a big glass window, and every time I passed by, he would bang on the glass with his World Series ring. He was constantly giving things away. Everyone in town has something of his. I have a desk lamp."

★　　　★　　　★　　　★

Ethel died in August, 1960, and on March 8, 1961, Lefty, now sixty-one, moved to Norwalk, Ohio, a town of fifteen thousand about ninety minutes from downtown Cleveland, to live with his son Bobby and his family. Lefty had always been close to Bobby, less so to his daughter Ethel Doris, now deceased, then a pianist and singer with a great voice who married a man named Monnett, moved to Funkstown, Maryland, and had no children. Back in his playing days, Lefty used to take Bobby to his games. A bit of a loner like his old man, Bobby would sit by himself in the second deck of the grandstand, with the full understanding that he'd have to find his own way home if Lefty lost. An excellent sprinter, a high-jumper, and a fairly good righthanded pitcher (some people called him Lefty) who had better control than his old man at the same age, Bobby went to Cheshire Academy in Connecticut, then Duke, where he performed well for the freshmen. But he didn't like school far from home and transferred to Washington College in Maryland.

Like so many young Americans, Bobby was changed forever by World War II. Receiving a dollar bill from home, he and two buddies divided it in three, vowing to reunite after the war and put the pieces together. There was no reunion. One friend was killed in action, the other moved back to Oklahoma.

On October 28, 1944, Bobby was wounded in Holland. After receiving the Bronze Star and the Purple Heart, he returned to college a more serious student and graduated with honors. But he was a war casualty, damaged by shrapnel in an arm and both legs. He would pitch a game, then be on crutches two days later. A sales rep for the Kelly-Springfield tire company and later an industrial engineer for Philco Ford, Bobby and his wife Jean separated in the mid-'60s. Lefty who had become comfortable in Norwalk, stayed there with Jean, an invalid, and his high school-age granddaughter Lynn. He visited Bobby, who was transferred to Sandusky, Ohio, and later Connersville, Indiana.

In 1972, Bobby died of the coronary thrombosis that had ravaged his mother's side of the family. "My father was a charming man," says his daughter. "He lived every day as if it were his last. I've never known anyone like him." Nor had Lefty, who was brokenhearted. And now he had to live out his life in double sorrow he usually kept inside: a marriage neither partner wanted to leave but did, and the horror of outliving his only son. "I know Dad missed Bobby a lot," says Jean, who refers to Lefty by the same name his kids did. "He'd say, 'Oh, Jean, my girl, I hope nothing happens to you while I'm alive. No one could take care of me like you do.' "

By then sporting a big mop of silver hair and thick, dark-framed glasses, Lefty sat in a rocking chair with two televisions and a radio on, following three baseball games at once. Grove attended plenty of old-timers' games. A tough old bird to the end, he probably dislodged more than a few dentures with his thundering claps to the back. At one old-timers' game he threw at Eddie Collins. At least, Joe Cronin swore he did. "I went to an old-timers' game with him in Houston," says granddaughter Lynn. "Monte Stratton, Lefty Gomez, and Dizzy Dean were there. Around 11 p.m., he sent me to the hotel room so they could have a bull session."

Sometimes Grove would fall into conversation with Bob Feller, a man he had much in common with. They were the unparalleled fastballers of their time, men who had lost wins to forces beyond their control—the absence of a major-league draft from the International League in Grove's case, World War II in Feller's—and could be gruff with strangers (Feller to this day). But these weren't two old-timers mooning for the past. Feller remained active in baseball. Grove thought modern players hustled as much as the old-timers, but that managers were too quick to change pitchers. Joking with his old friends Rick Ferrell and Tommy Thomas at the 1972 World Series, with the Boston *Globe*'s Harold Kaese taking notes, Grove said, "I won't be surprised if one of those hitters goes up to the plate tonight with a hair-dryer."

"I don't think Dad was very fond of Feller," says Jean Grove, although Lefty included Feller in his personal all-star team. "A perfect gentleman," Feller says of Grove.

Asked what memories from his career Lefty shared with his granddaughter, Lynn cited two: Al Simmons' absence the day in 1931 when Grove tried to win his seventeenth straight ("That was an annoyance that lasted his entire life.") and his 1-0 win over Mel Harder to open Cleveland's Municipal Stadium in 1932 ("He won—that's what it boiled down to for him."). He was not given to bragging, even about the Municipal Stadium triumph. "It was hard to see that day," Grove insisted to Hal Lebovitz of the *Cleveland Plain Dealer* in 1961. "The fans were sitting in the center-field bleachers. Wore white shirts. They hid the ball."

*After he retired, the grouchy Grove became
a patient supporter of youth baseball.*

Grove threw out the first ball of the 1970 World Series in
Baltimore. A few days later, sitting with his pipe in a
Cincinnati hotel, he held forth to AP newsfeatures editor
Frank Eck. "Mr. Mack was the greatest of all managers," he
said. "He was like a fifth infielder and a fourth outfielder,
using his scorecard to shift the players for certain hitters. He
knew exactly how to set the defense for certain situations.

"And Jack Dunn was a good one, too. I was with him
almost five years and I'm told that in seven pennant-winning
seasons he never had a team meeting."

Eventually, Grove tired of baseball functions. Perhaps he
was thinking of Satchel Paige's words: "The social ramble

ain't restful." One day, returning from an event, Lefty asked Jean, "Do you know what they had for the banquet?"

"Green beans?"

"Right."

"I never saw anyone less impressed with what he meant to baseball," says old friend Getty. "In 1975 he was again elected the best lefthanded pitcher in baseball history. I called him up to congratulate him. 'Yeah, that's pretty nice,' he said. 'Not bad.'

"The last time I saw Lefty was at a Dapper Dan charity dinner. He made a few comments and then said, 'Well, I'll tell you, you do the talking and I'll do the pitching.' "

"I saw him sitting at the Hall of Fame," says Bob Burns, an old A's fan. " 'See this picture?' he said. 'These are the three greatest men I know.' The three men were Cochrane, Mack, and Grove. His eyes were sparkling.

"He was aware of his importance. 'You know, you gotta be presentable,' he'd say. 'Let's smile, so we can get some autographs.' "

Some relatives remember Grove as a friendly man who with sense of humor who liked kids. Others found him stand-offish. "He was a real jerk in his old age," says Shawn Poe, a paramedic and Lefty's great-great-nephew. "He was a 'leave-me-alone, I-had-to-put up-with-this-stuff-when-I-was-young' kind of guy.' "

Well, it helped to understand the man. Suter Kegg, the Cumberland, Maryland, sportswriter, wouldn't press him when he was troubled, and Kegg was rewarded later by stories Grove told voluntarily. Kegg wasn't offended when Grove walked into his office, put his hand over the typewriter and said, "No more work today." That was just Lefty's sense of humor.

In defense of Grove, the respected old Baltimore sportswriter and editor John Steadman says, "Lefty was a kid with little opportunity for education or sophistication." Lynn Grove Horning elaborates. "I don't think people appreciate the odds he overcame. He was from a small mining town, one of eight children, with an eighth-grade education. I don't deny that he could be difficult. Tact was not his strong suit; he didn't sugarcoat anything. And he never learned how to handle success gracefully. He might grumble about giving an autograph, but the next day he could be gracious.

"I wish people could have seen his other side. He could be funny, caring, kind." Grove was certainly a favorite at George Schild's grocery store in Norwalk. Grove would drive over in his green Mustang and sit in the break room out back, drinking coffee, smoking cigars, and talking baseball with employees and truck drivers.

"He used a little profanity," says Schild. "He was pretty rough. But once you got to know him, he was a jolly good guy." After a few cups of coffee and a good cigar, he was ready to kick back and talk about the old days. "He said Babe Ruth was a drunk," Schild recalls. "Drank a pint of whiskey with his orange juice. Of course, Lefty drank some himself. One time he and Lefty Gomez got knocked out early in a game, and they went off and shared a pint of whiskey."

"He told one story about Ruth," says Schild's son David, who now runs the store with his wife. "Lefty threw the ball behind Ruth to shake him up. Ruth was glaring at him. 'O.K., Ruth, here's your coconut,' Lefty said. Then he threw one at his head. Ruth weakly missed the next three pitches."

Is this accurate? Grove had repeatedly told people he never threw at heads. Ah, well, in his old age a man is entitled to have it both ways.

"He told another one, about the day Red Ruffing was inducted in the Hall of Fame," David Schild says. "Lefty was

In 1972 Grove threw out the first ball at the World Series. The catcher is Baltimore's Andy Etchebarron. The Commissioner, partly obscured by Etchebarron's mask, is Bowie Kuhn.

on the platform with him, and while giving his speech, Ruffing turned and pointed at him. 'Just to prove to you what a great pitcher he was, we had a weekend series with him when I was playing with the Red Sox,' Ruffing said. 'He started and won the first game of a doubleheader, then relieved and won or saved the second. Then he relieved to win or save the third game and started and won the fourth.' "

Ruffing was not far off. On May 26, 1927, Grove started and won, then saved both games of a doubleheader on May 28. All told, he allowed one run in fourteen innings. Or maybe Ruffing conjured up the events of May 1-2, 1929, when Grove won a five-inning start, then pitched a complete-game victory the next day. Ruffing also could have been describing September 3, 4, and 6, 1930, when Grove won a six-inning start, pitched nine innings of relief to win again, and threw three innings of relief to win a third time.

The crowd gasped at the story about Grove, and gaped at him everywhere he was seen in Cooperstown. Tall and upright, his full head of white hair combed back, with a noble hawk nose and steely eyes, he had grown handsome over the years. "I remember walking into the Hall with Lefty," says David Schild. "Attendants and ushers came to attention. 'What can we do for you, Mr. Grove?' people said to him. He was like a god to them. He would grunt, hem and haw, but he loved the attention.

"When he saw other old players, like Joe Cronin, he would just haul off and sock them. If he considered you a friend, he would punch you in the stomach or slap you on the back. If he really liked you, he'd hit you both ways."

But woe to the person Grove despised. "There was a bar in the basement of the Otesaga Hotel," Schild says. "Mrs. Ruth came down there, and she always tried to talk to Lefty. He'd grunt. For whatever reason, he just didn't like her."

On May 22, 1975, Grove was perched in his rocking chair, with the television lighted up before him. He was in an especially good mood, even though his feet had swollen up the night before. He had spent the day like many, having his coffee at the grocery store, picking up some shirts, cashing a check for Jean. When he returned home, he stood at the entrance to her room, rubbing his back gently. "I think I'll go where it's cooler," he said, and headed downstairs to watch an afternoon soap opera, one of those doctor shows.

The housekeeper called down, "Mr. Grove, dinner is ready." The fan was on in the kitchen, and she figured he hadn't heard. When she came downstairs, she found the old man sitting still, arms on the chair.

"Jean, Mr. Grove is gone," the housekeeper said.

"What?"

"Mr. Grove is cold."

Jean called for an ambulance. Then her daughter phoned, something she rarely did at that time of day. "Oh, Lynn, get over here," she was told. "Dad's gone."

"I found him in his rocker with a cigar out, in his lap," says Lynn. "He looked very peaceful."

"He didn't suffer," the doctors told the women. "He just went to sleep." According to newsman Kegg, the B & O railroad pass he'd been given to go to Martinsburg in 1920 was still in his wallet.

Grove played too soon to make big money and died too soon to see his great-great-grandchildren Anthony Sidoti and Alexis Horning (he also had three great-granddaughters and two other great-great-grandchildren) play in a Norwalk Little League bearing his name. But he was properly mourned back home in Lonaconing. After some three hundred and fifty well-wishers viewed the body at Eichhorn Funeral Service, another crowd of close to one hundred, including Ken Smith, director of the Hall of Fame, attended the service in a small Presbyterian church on a knoll. Flowers arrived from Commissioner Bowie Kuhn, American League President Lee MacPhail, Oakland A's owner Charlie Finley, and Ted Williams. A wire service report said that Finley sent a bouquet three feet in diameter in the shape of a baseball. Getty and Kegg swear that Williams sent the baseball-shaped bouquet. The presiding minister, F. Blaine Rinker of the Midland United Methodist Church, drew from the letters of the Apostle Paul, who according to legend was a visitor to the ancient Olympics. Paul's Biblical writings compared life to races like those he had seen. "Life is like a race," Rinker said, "but occasionally an exceptional runner is born to the sons of man. We have been privileged to witness a legend, and now we remember 'Lefty' Grove, the greatest lefthand pitcher that ever lived.

"Today we share grief for him … but his accomplishments are much … much greater than our sorrow."

After the service, a chapel bell tolled, people gathered on the street, and a hearse carrying Grove's light-blue casket preceded a caravan of fifteen cars on the ten-mile trip to Frostburg Memorial Park.

Finally reconciled with his wife, Grove is buried next to Ethel and shares a headstone with her. His portion simply says, "Robert M. Grove 1900-1975." Also interred adjacent to Lefty is the dentist Doc Getty. A few feet away, catty-cornered to an intersection in the narrow road that runs through the cemetery, stands a $4,500 monument to Lefty paid for by private donations in a campaign organized by Suter Kegg. Vaguely resembling a fireplace, it consists of two rows of stones, with smaller stones in the shape of a cross and a stone angel blowing on a trumpet. There are two black vertical pipes for flowers and a carved replica—a very bad replica—of Lefty's face. Lefty's admirers were not impressed when it was unveiled. A brown bronzed plaque on the monument reads:

> One of baseball's greatest pitchers in 17 seasons (1925-41) as an American Leaguer. He compiled a record of 300 victories and 141 defeats for a .680 percentage.
>
> A native of Lonaconing, Lefty was voted into the Hall of Fame in 1947 and in baseball's centennial year (1969) he was honored as the greatest

lefthanded pitcher of all time.

He won 20 or more games on eight occasions, led the American League in earned-run percentage nine times, won 16 straight games in 1931 (a league record) and was the American League's Most Valuable Player in 1931 when he won 31 games and lost four.

There are tract houses in the distance and the sound of vehicles on Highway 68. Don Robertson, a retired B & O railroad worker, ambles over. "I grew up in Coney. I thought Lefty Grove was a real nice man," he says. "He would talk to us teenagers about baseball when we came to his pool hall. Bobby was a year ahead of me in school and Doris a year behind. Just regular kids."

Robertson scoffs when a visitor says it seems like a restful place for Lefty's body. "From here to West Virginia," he says, pointing to brown spots in the hills representing strip mines, "they got it tore to hell.

"Most of the miners died of black lung. I had two brothers who died in the mines and one who was killed on a picket line. They closed for good in 1950. It was all scabbing after that. You say you're from Massachusetts? That's a hell of a state. A poor person's got a chance there."

How are we to judge Lefty Grove? He was a frontier throwback: a don't-tread-on-me, rugged individualist. He hated cities[3]. He relished pitching on Independence Day, when he won five times and lost only the 14-2/3-inning classic to Herb Pennock in 1925. He liked pumpkin pie and "Little House on the Prairie." He hated British imports. He was adaptive. Rolling corn in buttered bread? Producing a rubber-stamp autograph? Friends, that is called Typical American Ingenuity. If Lefty Grove wasn't exactly Will Rogers, he could be funny and homespun, too. Remember his remark, "Let the teeth fall where they may?"

For such an antiquity, Grove certainly left his mark on the 20th century, arriving in 1900, making his major-league baseball debut in 1925, being named the game's outstanding lefthander for the first time in 1950, dying in 1975.

He was, of course, an athlete. As the sports columnist and social theorist Rick Telander has written, athletes are like kids: innocent, naive, egocentric, fiercely competitive. They have tunnel vision. Their success rises or falls on simple events: a ball thrown or struck, a base stolen. Little is expected of them but superhuman skills. Asked his ideal quality for a ballplayer, Merv Rettenmund, the San Diego hitting coach, said, "Selfishness."

The tunnel vision that makes the best of them spectacular performers may make them deficient in other life skills. Let's isolate baseball. We can only start with Babe Ruth. He was perfect for the Roaring Twenties. Were he in his prime today, he'd be admired by many as a countercultural hero, told to grow up by others. Ty Cobb, possibly the greatest all-around player ever, was a boor and a bigot. Pete Rose was one of the best baseball interviews ever, one of the saddest performers off the field. Lefty was as dedicated a competitor as any of them—all purpose, no manners on the field. Away from baseball, he was a better citizen than the other three.

In other respects, athletes are way ahead of their peers. At an early age, they learn to perform, to fail publicly, to compete furiously, to be part of something larger than themselves. They're taught discipline, self-reliance, concentration, loyalty, time management, work ethic. They experience joy and passion others miss. They get in shape; they're healthy.

[3] When a B&O train carrying Grove and Suter Kegg westward crossed the Allegany County line, Grove looked out the window and said, "Now we are in God's country."

There is no such thing as a dumb jock. His intelligence may not show up on SAT scores, but he cannot succeed without intelligence in his discipline: moving without the ball, learning a play book, studying opposing pitchers and hitters.

Sometimes a star signs enough autographs, smiles enough, gives enough pleasant interviews to seem heroic. Sometimes he is. Lou Gehrig and Jackie Robinson were not just baseball heroes, but American saints. If Lefty wasn't heroic, he was far from boorish. Some of Lefty's modern defenders compare him with Orioles pitcher Mike Mussina, another straight, unsophisticated small-town man.

When we think of Lefty Grove, we should think of more than a man at the top of a very rarefied calling. We should think of a man whose enjoyment of that calling was far more heightened than anything most of us experience in our humdrum lives.

"The best of it all was the feeling in you after the game went right and you came back in the locker room and got undressed," Grove told James H. Bready of the Baltimore *Sun* in 1957. "I used to take my shower and swallow an ounce of whiskey slow and get a rubdown, and I'd go off to sleep right there on the table. It was very damn good."

THE BEST PITCHER EVER: GROVE? JOHNSON? KOUFAX?

★　　★　　★　　★

"They were sweet to hit. They were just cousins. Walter Johnson and Grove were just as fast as a rifle shot."

–Babe Ruth

In a 1997 poll conducted by the Baseball Writers' Association of America, Walter Johnson was named the game's outstanding righthanded pitcher and Sandy Koufax the best lefthander. Historian and statistician Bill James responded that Lefty Grove (who was named the best left-hander in several earlier polls) pitched significantly better than Koufax. Was Grove also, as James has claimed, better than Johnson? Was he the best pitcher ever?

Let's be clear on one thing before we start. You cannot compare pitchers by matching their numbers. Koufax and Johnson played in pitchers' eras, Grove in the century's hitting paradise (hence, his relative obscurity). Of course Koufax and Johnson have more impressive pure numbers.

That doesn't make them better or worse than Grove, just different. The only objective criterion for judging a pitcher is to compare him with his contemporaries and decide whether he was more or less dominant than pitchers in other eras.

The two most popular standards for judging ballplayers are the Jamesian criteria of career value and peak value.

Career value—This measure applies to sustained careers. Since Koufax pitched only twelve seasons and dominated the National League for five, we'll save him for peak value.

Grove and Johnson deserve not just pairing, but poetry. They were the dominant fastball pitchers of their time. They threw almost nothing but heat in their prime. Being forced to swing at them was a crime.

Wins—Johnson won 417 games in 1907-27, Grove 300 in 1925-41. Johnson missed at least half a season with ailments modern medicine could have cured immediately. Grove missed many starts because he pitched four and one-half seasons (1920-24) in a no-draft era for the greatest minor-league team ever, the Baltimore Orioles. He won 108 games before owner Jack Dunn sold him to Connie Mack's Athletics. Grove joined the A's in 1925 at age twenty-five. Johnson was a nineteen-year-old rookie in 1907.

Was Grove ready for the majors at twenty? We'll never know. According to one account, the Orioles bought him from the Martinsburg, West Virginia, team of the Blue Ridge League two hours before a telegram arrived from the Giants. According to another story, he was sold four hours before a Dodger offer arrived. If we optimistically prorated his wins over another four and one-half seasons, Grove would move into third place at 379, passing Warren Spahn (363), Christy Mathewson, and Pete Alexander (373 each).

In Johnson's era, before the home run was an important offensive weapon, pitchers could pace themselves through games and start often. In Grove's lively-ball era, pitchers had to bear down for most of the game and started less frequently. Johnson averaged thirty-two starts a year, Grove twenty-seven. The Big Train had more wins, but he also had more opportunities to win.

From 1903 through 1919, there were fifteen 30-win seasons. Between 1920, the start of the hitting era, and today there have been four 30-win seasons[1]. In 1941, Grove became the first 300-game winner since Alexander in 1924, and the last until Warren Spahn won his 300th in 1961. Lefty was the only 300-game winner to pitch most of his career during the lively-ball period between the two world wars.

Grove claimed an unmatched five winning-percentage titles and completed his career with a lifetime percentage of .680, the best among 300-game winners and the fourth highest ever[2]. Johnson led the league in winning percentage twice and finished at .599. On the other hand, Grove pitched on only one losing team to Johnson's[3] eleven. Grove's teams averaged 89 wins, Johnson's 74. Certainly, some of Grove's percentage owes to his excellent teams, although plenty of Hall of Famers on better teams (Mathewson, McGinnity, Plank, Coveleski, Haines, Ford, Gomez, Dean, Marichal) had fewer winning percentage titles. It is also reasonable to assume that both Grove and Johnson would have been big winners for any team. Within the confines of their eras, Grove and Johnson won about as many games as anyone

---

[1] Jim Bagby (31-12 in '20), Grove (31-4 in '31), Dizzy Dean (30-7 in '34), Denny McLain (31-6 in '68)

[2] Ahead of Grove: Dave Foutz (.690), Whitey Ford (.690), and Bob Caruthers (.688).

[3] How did Grove rate against his contemporaries? A telling comparison jumps out at us: Grove pitched for the A's and Red Sox in 1925-41, and Carl Hubbell pitched for the Giants in 1928-43. The A's and Red Sox averaged 89 wins in the 17 years Grove was pitching for them. The Giants averaged 83 wins in the Hubbell years. The difference in their pitching, however, was far more pronounced: Grove was 300-141, Hubbell 253-154 (.622).

could expect of them. You pick the better pitcher.

ERA—According to *Total Baseball*, Grove's lifetime ERA of 3.06, when adjusted for league average and parks, tops all others with 148 points. Grove's ERA was 46 percent better than the league average, the greatest difference in baseball history. Johnson (2.17) finishes second in points with 147[4]. Grove won nine ERA titles, the most ever, in seventeen seasons. Think about it. More than half the years he pitched, Grove allowed fewer earned runs per nine innings than anyone in his league. Johnson won five ERA crowns in twenty-one seasons. Grove led the league in ERA and winning percentage four different seasons—twice as often as Johnson or anyone else.

In terms of adjusted ERA, it's virtually a dead heat. In terms of dominance, no one in baseball history matches Grove.

Performance under pressure—*Total Baseball* places Grove 29th in its "clutch pitching index." Johnson, perhaps unfairly, doesn't make the chart. In the 1929-31 World Series, Grove had a 4-2 record and two saves, a 1.75 earned-run average, six walks and 36 strikeouts in 51-1/3 innings. He won the opening game of the 1930 World Series with a broken blister on his pitching hand. In the 1924 and 1925 Series, Johnson was 3-3, with a 2.16 ERA, 15 walks, and 35 strikeouts in fifty innings. Pitching in relief, Johnson won the seventh game in the 1924 Series.

Of course, it is impossible to precisely measure performance under pressure. So much is left to chance. How many opportunities did the pitcher have? At what point in his career did these opportunities arise? Grove got his chances at his peak. Johnson didn't get his until the twilight of his career. Who would you want on the mound if your life depended on it? A case could be made for either man.

---

[4] Carl Hubbell had a lifetime ERA of 2.98 (130 points).

Versatility—Happy to relieve, Grove pitched eight times in ten games over eleven days early in 1933, winning four, saving four. It has been claimed that Johnson was less likely to relieve in his era, when pitchers finished more games. In the lively-ball era, the argument goes, pitchers finished fewer games and therefore were more likely to relieve.

This position doesn't hold up. "Mr. Groves, this ball is yours," A's manager Connie Mack, who always got Lefty's name wrong, told him on the days of his starts. "Pop, this is for nine," Red Sox manager Joe Cronin told an elderly Lefty. In other words, Grove was expected to finish games, lively ball or not. In both 1931 and 1932, he completed twenty-seven of thirty starts. Yet he still had the stamina to pitch out of the bullpen. Grove relieved 159 times, Johnson 136. Grove had fifty-five saves[5] to thirty-four for Johnson.

Pitching strictly in relief during the 1929 Series, Grove had two saves, a 0.00 ERA and 10 K's in 6-1/3 innings.

Grove's relief pitching is worth a longer look. There were virtually no full-time relievers in his day, and the best starters usually went both ways. Grove had more saves than any Hall of Fame starter this century. Indeed, he may have been a better reliever than starter:

GROVE AS STARTER

G	CG/SV	IP	H	H/9	W-L	ERA	BB	BB/9	K	K/9
457	298	3563	3509	8.9	268-119	3.08	1034	2.61	2023	5.1

GROVE AS RELIEVER

G	SV	IP	H	H/9	W-L	ERA	BB	BB/9	K	K/9
159	55	377.2	340	8.1	32-22	2.84	153	3.65	243	5.8

---

[5] The save rule was adopted in 1969 to cover any reliever who finished a game his team won. The rule has since been changed, but pre-1969 saves are calculated using the original rule.

Comparing starting and relieving numbers is baseball's ultimate apples-and-oranges game. Wins and losses are terrible stats for relievers, because they're not supposed to get either. (Most top relievers have won-lost relief records around .500.) ERA is equally bad for two reasons. First, relievers rarely continue pitching when they're tired; hence, their ERAs stay down. Second, inherited runners who score don't count against a reliever's ERA. Yet keeping them on base is a prime responsibility.

The area where apples can be compared successfully to oranges is ratio: hits, walks, and strikeouts to innings. Grove had better hit and strikeout ratios as a reliever, and a better walk ratio as a starter. Pitching so late in the day from the bullpen, he was undoubtedly so blinding that hitters took more pitches—hence, more strikeouts and walks. Lefty was as effective out of the bullpen as out of the dugout.

To whom shall we compare him? An obvious match is Dennis Eckersley, who spanned two relief eras: the old one in which pitchers could go for long stretches, and today, when they're rarely expected to pitch more than one and one-third innings. Their relief numbers:

GROVE

G	SV	IP	H	H/9	W-L	ERA	BB	BB/9	K	K/9
159	55	377.2	340	8.1	32-22	2.84	153	3.65	243	5.8

ECKERSLEY

G	SV	IP	H	H/9	W-L	ERA	BB	BB/9	K	K/9
710	390	807.1	680	7.6	48-41	2.85	126	1.40	792	8.8

No question: None finer than Eck. A better parallel, though, is Rollie Fingers. Like Grove, he was a traditional reliever who might go three innings one day, two more the next.

GROVE

G	SV	IP	H	H/9	W-L	ERA	BB	BB/9	K	K/9
159	55	377.2	340	8.1	32-22	2.84	153	3.65	243	5.8

FINGERS

G	SV	IP	H	H/9	W-L	ERA	BB	BB/9	K	K/9
907	341	1505.1	1275	7.6	107-101	2.72	428	2.56	1184	7.1

One era's full-time relief ace edges another era's part-timer. In his day, Fingers was incomparable. So was Grove in his.

Durability. Since both Grove and Johnson were asked to pitch complete games, innings per start is a fine measure. Johnson averaged 8.3 innings (and led the league in innings pitched five times), Grove 7.8. Both are extraordinary feats in any era. To place these numbers in perspective, let's sneak in a Koufax mention. In 1961-66, he averaged 7.64 innings per start.

Control. Johnson averaged 2.1 walks per game, Grove 2.7. Neither was in the top fifteen for his era.

Strikeouts. Johnson had 3,509 strikeouts in twenty-one seasons to Grove's 2,266 in seventeen (pro-rated to 2,866). Johnson led the league a record twelve times to Lefty's runner-up seven.

Shutouts and complete games. Johnson (110 total) won 7 shutout titles, Grove (thirty-five) three. Johnson (531) led the league in complete games six times, Grove (298) thrice.

Fielding and hitting. Johnson was an exceptional fielder; Grove wasn't. Johnson (.235, 24 homers) was a fine hitting pitcher. Grove was a good bunter and had power (15 homers), but struck out a pitchers'-record 593 times and hit only .148.

James cites Grove's nine ERA and five winning-percentage titles as proof of Grove's superior career value. Lefty's relief work helps his case further. Johnson was better in other significant categories and pitched four more seasons.

Peak performance—This statistic isolates the time in a player's career when he was at the peak of his powers. Now we can compare all three men.

Single-game dominance? Koufax's four no-hitters begin and end the debate. Johnson threw a sore-armed no-hitter in 1920 and won 1-0 games in 15 (1913) and 20 (1918) innings. Hitters could always anticipate Grove's fastball in his best years. Perhaps that explains the absence of glittery games. He did, however, end the Yankees' 308-game streak of no shutouts when he throttled Ruth & Co., 7-0, on August 3, 1933.

For single-season performance, Grove's 31-4 record in 1931 has the highest (.886) winning percentage. Grove's two-year (59-9) record in 1930-1931, three-year (79-15) record in 1929-31—when he, uniquely, led the majors in winning percentage, ERA and strikeouts three seasons running—four-year (104-25) record in 1929-32, and five-year (128-33) mark in both 1928-32 and 1929-33 are equally dominant. Indeed, his five-year percentage (.795) is the best of the century—better than Koufax in 1962-66 (.766), Three-Finger Brown in 1906-10 (.743), Christy Mathewson in 1904-08 (.724), Pete Alexander in 1913-17 (.711), Johnson in 1911-15 (.703), and Cy Young in 1900-04 (.680).

In a procedure that has gained much currency of late, researchers examine ERA as a percentage of the league average. Herewith a five-year accounting of Grove, Koufax, and Johnson at their best. It has been asserted time and again that no one was as dominating in his prime as Koufax. Judge for yourself:

GROVE				KOUFAX				JOHNSON			
YR	ERA	AL	%	YR.	ERA	NL	%	YR.	ERA	AL	%
1928	2.58	4.04	64	1962	**2.54**	3.94	64	1910	1.36	2.52	54
1929	**2.81**	4.24	66	1963	**1.88**	3.29	57	1911	1.90	3.34	57
1930	**2.54**	4.65	55	1964	**1.74**	3.54	49	1912	**1.39**	3.34	42
1931	**2.06**	4.38	47	1965	**2.04**	3.54	58	1913	**1.14**	2.93	39
1932	**2.84**	4.48	63	1966	**1.73**	3.61	48	1914	1.72	2.73	63

Boldface—Led league

Johnson (two ERA titles, 51 percent of league average during the span) and Koufax (five and 55 percent) match up well with Grove (four and 59 percent), don't they? But Grove and Johnson had two periods of peak performance to one for Koufax.

In Grove's second peak period he was playing for the Red Sox. After a sore-armed season in 1934, he became a control pitcher at age thirty-five and won four ERA titles in five years (1935-39). The last came after a temporarily dead arm—literally no pulse—shortened the 1938 season. Yes, a lefthander pitching home games in Fenway Park. This was more than a comeback. It is the greatest resurrection in baseball history.

I'm arbitrarily dividing Johnson's ten-year run of greatness into two five-year periods. He was a less effective pitcher in the second half, but those five years would pique anyone's interest.

Johnson averaged 59 percent and Grove 60 percent of the league ERA. Grove had four ERA titles and five good percentages, Johnson two and four.

Johnson later staged a comeback that was positively Grovian. Halfway through the 1920 season he went home with an 8-10 record and a sore arm. He struggled (for him) through 1921-23 with records of 17-14, 15-16, and 17-12.

Then, as a thirty-six-year-old has-been in 1924, he went 23-7, leading the Senators to a pennant and the league in wins, winning percentage (.767), shutouts (6), strikeouts (158), ERA (2.72), and other categories. In 1925, Johnson was 20-7, and the Senators repeated. This two-year curtain call qualifies as a third, albeit shortened, peak period for the great man.

GROVE					JOHNSON			
YR.	ERA	AL	%		YR.	ERA	AL	%
1935	2.70	4.46	61		1915	1.55	2.93	53
1936	2.81	5.04	56		1916	1.90	2.82	67
1937	3.02	4.62	65		1917	2.21	2.66	83
1938	3.08	4.79	64		1918	1.27	2.77	46
1939	2.54	4.62	55		1919	1.49	3.22	46

What, finally, are we to conclude? To me, Grove's domination of ERA, winning percentage, and relief pitching in a starter's era trumps Johnson's longevity and last hurrah. Like all good things in baseball, it's debatable. Grove and Johnson, Johnson and Grove. Let's just link them together forever, the Ruth and Williams of pitching.

Lefty, Walter, Sandy, and the field
Records of major-league Hall of Fame starters who pitched primarily in the 20th century:

Pitcher/Yrs	WON	LOST	PCT	ERA	K	BB/G	SV
L. Grove/17	300 (4)	141	.680 (5)	3.06 (9)	2,266 (7)	2.7	55 (1)
W. Johnson/21	417 (6)	279	.599 (2)	2.17 (5)	3,509 (12)	2.1	34
S. Koufax/12	165 (3)	87	.655 (2)	2.76 (5)	2,396 (4)	3.2	9
P. Alexander/20	373 (6)	208	.642 (1)	2.56 (5)	2,198 (6)	1.6	32
C. Bender/16	212	127	.625(3)	2.46	1,711	2.1	34 (2)
M. Brown/14	239 (1)	130	.648	2.06 (1)	1,375	1.9	49 (4)
J. Bunning/17	224 (1)	184	.549	3.27	2,855 (3)	2.4 (1)	16
S. Carlton/24	329 (4)	244	.574 (1)	3.22 (1)	4,136 (5)	3.2	2
S. Coveleski/14	215	142	.602 (1)	2.89 (2)	981 (1)	2.3	21
J. Dean/12	150 (2)	83	.644 (1)	3.02	1,163 (4)	2.1 (1)	30(1)
D. Drysdale/14	209 (1)	166	.557	2.95	2,486 (3)	2.2	6
R. Faber/20	254	213	.544	3.15 (2)	1,471	2.7	28 (1)
B. Feller/18	266 (6)	162	.621 (1)	3.25 (1)	2,581 (7)	4.1	21
W. Ford/16	236 (3)	106	.690 (3)	2.75 (2)	1,956	3.1	10
B. Gibson/17	251 (1)	174	.591 (1)	2.91 (1)	3,117 (1)	3.1	6
L. Gomez/14	189 (2)	102	.649 (2)	3.34 (2)	1,468 (3)	3.9	9
B. Grimes/19	270 (2)	212	.560 (1)	3.53	1,512	2.8	18 (1)
J. Haines/19	210	158	.571	3.64	981	2.4	10

Pitcher/Yrs	WON	LOST	PCT	ERA	K	BB/G	SV
W. Hoyt/21	237 (1)	182	.566 (1)	3.59	1,206	2.4	52 (1)
C. Hubbell/16	253 (3)	154	.622 (2)	2.98 (3)	1,677 (1)	1.8	33 (1)
J. Hunter/15	224 (2)	166	.574 (2)	3.26 (1)	2,012	2.5	1
F. Jenkins/19	284 (2)	226	.557	3.34	3,192 (1)	2.0	7
A. Joss/9	160 (1)	97	.623	1.89 (2)	920	1.4 (2)	5
B. Lemon/13	207 (3)	128	.618	3.23	1,277 (1)	4.0	22
T. Lyons/21	260 (2)	230	.531	3.67 (1)	1,073	2.4 (4)	23
J. Marichal/16	243 (2)	142	.631 (1)	2.89 (1)	2,303	1.8 (4)	2
R. Marquard/18	201 (1)	177	.532 (1)	3.08	1,593 (1)	2.3	19
C. Mathewson/17	373 (4)	188	.665 (1)	2.13 (5)	2,502 (5)	1.6 (7)	28(1)
J. M'G'n'ty*/10	246 (5)	142	.634 (2)	2.66 (1)	1,068	2.1	24(3)
H. Newhouser/17	207 (4)	150	.580 (1)	3.06 (2)	1,796 (2)	3.8	26
P. Niekro/24	318 (2)	274	.537 (1)	3.35 (1)	3,342 (1)	3.0	29
J. Palmer/19	268 (3)	152	.638 (2)	2.86 (2)	2,212	3.0	4
H. Pennock/22	241	162	.598 (1)	3.60	1,227	2.3 (3)	33
G. Perry/22	314 (3)	265	.542 (1)	3.11	3,534	2.3 (1)	11
E. Plank/17	326	194	.627 (1)	2.35	2,246	2.1	23
E. Rixey/21	266 (1)	251	.515	3.15	1,350	2.2	14
R. Roberts/19	286 (4)	245	.539	3.41	2,357 (2)	1.7 (4)	25
R. Ruffing/22	273 (1)	225	.548 (1)	3.80	1,987 (1)	3.2	16
T. Seaver/20	311 (3)	205	.603 (3)	2.86 (3)	3,640 (5)	2.6	1
W. Spahn/21	363 (8)	245	.597 (1)	3.09 (3)	2,583 (4)	2.5	29

Pitcher/Yrs	WON	LOST	PCT	ERA	K	BB/G	SV
D. Sutton/23	324	256	.559	3.26 (1)	3,574	2.3	5
D. Vance/16	197 (2)	140	.585	3.24 (3)	2,045 (7)	2.5 (1)	11
R. Waddell/13	193 (1)	143	.574 (1)	2.16 (2)	2,316 (6)	2.4	5
E. Walsh/14	195 (1)	126	.607 (1)	1.82 (2)	1,736 (2)	1.9 (1)	34(5)
V. Willis**/13	249	205	.548	2.63	1,651 (1)	2.7	11
E. Wynn/23	300 (2)	244	.551	3.54 (1)	2,334 (2)	3.5	15
C. Young***/22	511 (5)	316	.618 (2)	2.63 (2)	2,803 (2)	1.5	17(2)

Numbers in parentheses = years led league

* Played one season before 1900.
** Played two seasons before 1900.
*** Played ten seasons before 1900.

Sources: Total Baseball, fourth and fifth editions.

ACKNOWLEDGMENTS

★　　★　　★　　★

This book was not only written for SABR, but by SABR. I had so much help from so many Society members I'll never quite spread the credit around.

Nonetheless, with apologies to those I miss, here goes. Marty Fleisher suggested this book, and Mark Alvarez, SABR's director of publications, masterfully shepherded it to completion, with help from A.D. Suehsdorf. John Bowman did a demon job of text analysis. Dixie Tourangeau gave the book a historical and factual gut check. Scot Mondore of the National Baseball Library at the Hall of Fame sent mountains of research. Baltimore baseball historian Jim Bready and minor-league historian Dave Howell were a fount of facts on the old Orioles. Steve Gietscher of *The Sporting News* ran down details of the 1920-24 Little World Series. Bob Broeg, the Hall of Fame St. Louis newsman, verified the details of Lefty's unfortunate day in Sportsman's Park. Allen Lewis's book, *Baseball's Greatest Streaks,* helped me nail down Lefty's. I travelled to Lefty's roots in Lonaconing, Maryland, with Norman Macht and Lois Nicholson, respectively a Philadelphia A's and Grove scholar par excellence. Macht's comments and corrections on A's history lent this volume credibility. When I advanced to Lefty's Boston years, Steve Adamson all but wrote a chapter by lending me his voluminous scrapbooks of the 1934 season, and Phil Bergen provided the kind of expertise only a Boston baseball historian could. Fellow Lefty scholar Eric White had reams of notes. Bill Deane, Gerry Beirne, Jack Kavanagh, and Len Levin were their typically helpful selves. With extra assistance from Bruce Kuklick, Ray Robinson, Bob Tiemann, Dick Thompson, Ernie Green, Rich Westcott, John Holway, Jim Riley, Dick Bresciani, John Korsgaard, and many others, the SABR roster was easily forty deep.

Among nonmembers, Donald Honig wrote the foreword and gave my copy a good reading, Jim Degnim provided expert copy-editing, and Glen Stout added his Bosox knowledge. Jeff Korman of the Enoch Pratt Free Library, Brenda Galloway-Wright of Temple University's Paley Library, and Elise Feeley of Forbes Library in Northampton, Massachusetts, put me in the Baltimore, Philadelphia, and Boston of another era. Robert W. Creamer knew something about baseball in '41. Brooks Robards added her keen writer/editor's touch and wifely forbearance. Greg Schwallenberg of the Babe Ruth Museum was a two-way threat for text and photos. The photos and memories of Grove's niece, Betty Holshey, and the clippings and artwork of Grove great nephew, Ernst Peterson, were invaluable.

Lefty's daughter-in-law Jean Grove and granddaughter Lynn Grove Horning, plus friends Jim Getty, Suter Kegg, Mary Meyers, and the late John Meyers, were always accessible. Former teammates, especially Bill Werber and Broadway Charlie Wagner, fielded my constant calls without complaint. Among the others who chipped in were Ira Berkow, Bill Acheson, Ernie Phillips, Milton Bates, Mary Beth Norton, and two redoubtable performers, Baltimore newsman John Steadman and Bob Rosen of the Elias Sports Bureau. My late mother, Felicia Lamport Kaplan, taught me more about writing than I could ever forget. Thanks finally to my agent Don Gastwirth, Judy Appelbaum, and Jack Handler of the National Writers Union for contract advice. Lefty could have used you.

Jim Kaplan
Northampton, Massachusetts
March 6, 1999

INDEX

★　　　★　　　★　　　★

INDEX

PHOTO CREDITS

★　　　★　　　★　　　★